THE COGNITIVE NEUROPSYCHOLOGY OF DÉJÀ VU

Déjà vu is one of the most complex and subjective of all memory phenomena. It is an infrequent and striking mental experience, where the feeling of familiarity is combined with the knowledge that this feeling is false. While until recently it was an aspect of memory largely overlooked by mainstream cognitive psychology, this book brings together the growing scientific literature on déjà vu, making the case for it as a metacognitive phenomenon.

The Cognitive Neuropsychology of Déjà Vu reviews clinical, experimental and neuroimaging methods, focusing on how memory disorders and neurological dysfunction relate to the experience. Examining déjà vu as a memory phenomenon, Chris Moulin explores how the experience of déjà vu in special populations, such as healthy aging or those with schizophrenia, provides new insights into understanding this phenomenon. He considers the extensive data on déjà vu in people with epilepsy, dementia and other neurological conditions, assessing neuropsychological theories of déjà vu formation.

Essential reading for all students and researchers interested in memory disorders, this valuable book presents the case for déjà vu as a 'healthy' phenomenon only experienced by people with sufficient cognitive resources to oppose and detect the false feeling of familiarity.

Chris Moulin is Professor of Cognitive Psychology and a senior member of the Institut Universitaire de France. After conducting his PhD on metacognition in Alzheimer's disease, supervised by Tim Hollins and Alan Baddeley, he held posts in Bristol, Reading, Bath and Leeds before moving to France in 2012.

ESSAYS IN COGNITIVE PSYCHOLOGY

Series Editors:
Henry L. Roediger, III, Rice University
James R. Pomerantz
Alan Baddeley, The University of York, UK
Jonathan Grainger, Université de Provence, France
Daniel Baker, University of York, UK

Essays in Cognitive Psychology is designed to meet the need for rapid publication of brief volumes in cognitive psychology. Primary topics will include perception, movement and action, attention, memory, mental representation, language and problem solving. Furthermore, the series seeks to define cognitive psychology in its broadest sense, encompassing all topics either informed by, or informing, the study of mental processes. As such, it covers a wide range of subjects including computational approaches to cognition, cognitive neuroscience, social cognition, and cognitive development, as well as areas more traditionally defined as cognitive psychology. Each volume in the series will make a conceptual contribution to the topic by reviewing and synthesizing the existing research literature, by advancing theory in the area, or by some combination of these missions. The principal aim is that authors will provide an overview of their own highly successful research program in an area. It is also expected that volumes will, to some extent, include an assessment of current knowledge and identification of possible future trends in research. Each book will be a self-contained unit supplying the advanced reader with a well-structured review of the work described and evaluated.

For updated information about published and forthcoming titles in the *Essays in Cognitive Psychology* series, please visit: www.routledge.com/Essays-in-Cognitive-Psychology/book-series/SE0548

THE COGNITIVE NEUROPSYCHOLOGY OF DÉJÀ VU

Chris Moulin

Routledge
Taylor & Francis Group

LONDON AND NEW YORK

First published 2018
by Routledge
2 Park Square, Milton Park, Abingdon, Oxon OX14 4RN

and by Routledge
711 Third Avenue, New York, NY 10017

Routledge is an imprint of the Taylor & Francis Group, an informa business

© 2018 Chris Moulin

The right of Chris Moulin to be identified as author of this work has been asserted by him in accordance with sections 77 and 78 of the Copyright, Designs and Patents Act 1988.

British Library Cataloguing in Publication Data
A catalogue record for this book is available from the British Library

Library of Congress Cataloging in Publication Data
Names: Moulin, Chris J. A., author.
Title: The cognitive neuropsychology of déjà vu / Chris Moulin.
Description: Milton Park, Abingdon ; New York, NY : Routledge, 2017. |
Series: Essays in cognitive psychology | Includes bibliographical references and index.
Identifiers: LCCN 2017013090 (print) | LCCN 2017034968 (ebook) |
ISBN 9781315524931 (Ebook) | ISBN 9781138696259 (hbk : alk. paper) |
ISBN 9781138696266 (pbk : alk. paper) | ISBN 9781315524931 (ebk)
Subjects: LCSH: Cognitive neuroscience.
Classification: LCC QP360.5 (ebook) | LCC QP360.5 .M68 2017 (print) |
DDC 612.8/233–dc23
LC record available at https://lccn.loc.gov/2017013090

ISBN: 978-1-138-69625-9 (hbk)
ISBN: 978-1-138-69626-6 (pbk)
ISBN: 978-1-315-52493-1 (ebk)

Typeset in Bembo
by Out of House Publishing

For Céline

CONTENTS

FIGURES

TABLES

1

AN INTRODUCTION TO THE COGNITIVE NEUROPSYCHOLOGY OF DÉJÀ VU

Felix, qui potuit rerum cognoscere causas

Virgil

What is déjà vu?

Déjà vu is the subjective experience of familiarity combined with the knowledge that this experience is false. It is a relatively striking but infrequent experience. In large-scale questionnaire studies it is estimated to be experienced by at least two-thirds of the population, and people generally report experiencing it less than ten times a year. For the person experiencing it, it is a somewhat mysterious and difficult-to-define feeling, although scientists are now beginning to offer some concrete suggestions about what causes the sensation and how it is produced in the human memory system. While it is experienced more in some conditions, such as certain forms of epilepsy, it is not thought to be particularly diagnostic of any type of cognitive problem or disorder. It is experienced by people with neurological and psychological disorders and healthy populations alike. Table 1.1 sets out a few descriptions of the experience and examples from those who experience it and those who study it.

These quotes set out the topography and the range of this book. They suggest there are a range of intense sensations and thoughts associated with déjà vu – ideas of premonitions or prescience, dreams and confusion about the present moment. They also centre on the idea that the experience is difficult to pinpoint for the experient and the scientist/clinician alike. Many people describe déjà vu as like being able to predict the future. For the patients and carers included above, déjà vu may be seen as a helpful or malignant force, but it is no less striking or strange for the healthy participants who experience it. One of the quotes mentions empirical

TABLE 1.1 Some descriptions of the déjà vu experience

Healthy research participants

"On the bus with my Uni friends and felt like I had been there before, had the same conversation and people had the same positions, although I don't remember seeing the faces before but when I was on the bus in that position the faces I saw fitted the vision perfectly."	Healthy research participant quoted in Moulin et al. (2014, p. 281)
"I had this one instance of it a couple weeks ago that really sticks out. I was at my school, in our dining hall for a meeting about a blood drive. And I was suddenly and all at once hit with the realization that the scene I was set in had been the subject of a dream at some point, every bit of it. The lighting was vaguely orange and dim on a muggy day, the table placement was how I knew it to be. I was standing and talking to my friend, which I also associated as having happened. And I felt tired that day, my eyes were droopy in a way that was compatible with the déjà vu snapshot I related it to. I don't remember ever directly dreaming about it, not at all, but I was hit with the idea that I had. I'm sure there's some truth to the matter of me having dreamt it, but the prominence of the déjà vu I felt was just … It was just such a vivid, intense thing."	Healthy participant from Fortier and Moulin (2015)
"Quite often I have experiences where I think I have seen something specific before, or have previously heard snippets from a conversation. When these experiences occur I usually feel like I am 'outside' of the scene looking in on it and I wait until I can no longer predict the next word/statement that someone makes. These experiences usually last no more than one minute, but are longer if my own statements are included in the experience (i.e. I remember/feel like I have previously experienced my own contribution to the conversation)."	Healthy research participant from Jersakova, Moulin, and O'Connor (2016)
"Déjà vu tends to happen to me a lot; one time my math teacher began saying something and I had a feeling that I had heard it before as if it were some dream. Everything she said, I knew she was going to say. Another experience was years before I began high school I had a dream about walking down a strange hallway, then years passed and the first day of high school came and there the déjà vu feeling was. (Of course maybe I never dreamt it, maybe it was just déjà vu that made me think I dreamt it.) One last experience I had was of a friend who	Healthy research participant from Jersakova et al. (2016)

TABLE 1.1 (*cont.*)

Healthy research participants

was telling me information and I knew exactly
what they were going to say next, it was a weird
déjà vu moment; as if I had been there before or
remembered them saying it before but it never
actually happened before. Déjà vu makes me feel
a little crazy because I tend to tell others that they
had told me once before or years ago I had a weird
feeling they would tell me that particular instance."

Clinical research participants

"It will start off with me hearing something e.g. someone talking or anything, actually. It will just be some information that I am taking in. I will briefly think that I have heard what is being said before. It almost feels like I am having a premonition. If it was just this then I could cope but it's what follows which is so disturbing and frightening to me. ... I suddenly feel like all the happiness in me has been sucked out. I explain this to people like the dementors in Harry Potter. Its simply as though I have no happiness or hope or future. All I can think about is what the déjà vu was about. Nothing else. Everything else in my life has vanished totally from my mind. If I am somewhere I like, I will hate it and feel uncomfortable to be there. It feels different to how it feels normally. It's like the way you see things in your dreams; you know them but they different in some ways and you feel disturbed by them. ... As for the déjà vu [experiences] themselves; it feels like I have either heard it before or more frequently it feels as though it has been in a dream. I don't think it has though. I sort of create a whole alternative world in my head for those few moments and nothing else in the world exists. I don't feel at all comfortable with it and I would do anything to get away."	Epileptic déjà vu experience described by young woman quoted from Moulin and Chauvel (2010, pp. 215–216)
"Another epileptic, an intelligent graduate school teacher, used to experience déjà vu sensations as a boy at school and these were often precipitated by the sound of the halting gait of a master with a club foot. Since this time he has experienced a similar sensation about once every three months, with a strange feeling in his stomach. He finds this experience pleasant and believes that he can cut it short if he wishes by concentrating his attention on other things."	Roth and Harper (1962) describing one of their research participants with temporal lobe epilepsy (pp. 139–140)

TABLE 1.1 (*cont.*)

Clinical research participants

"… I'm reliving something … but I can see you clearly … It's as if what is happening now has already happened to me, it's like an old memory that I am in the middle of living out."

Epileptic patient undergoing direct electrical stimulation of the temporal lobe, quoted from Vignal, Maillard, McGonigal, and Chauvel (2007, p. 92)

"In the last two years of her life (she died at 88) I would have to say that she essentially lived in almost a constant state of déjà vécu whenever she was removed from her narrowly defined daily routine (in an assisted living residence). Whenever she spent time with me, for example, there was continual reference to 'the trees have sure grown taller', total strangers on the road had 'gotten fat and, look, he has a new dog', and every stranger she met was assured that she knew them already. Newspapers had been read before, she had repairmen in to find out why the television kept showing programs she had seen before, newly published books had been read years before, etc."

Recollective confabulation patient as described by a carer, quoted in O'Connor, Lever and Moulin (2010a, p. 124)

"I recently went to take a test, I had been anxious about it as usual but for some reason when I sat down at the desk a calm began to come over me. When the test was handed to me a sensation as if I had already taken the test came over me, and somewhere in my head a voice, or thought came across with 'You know you will pass this, you've done it before'. I'm sure this will also sound strange, however it also felt as if there was someone watching over my shoulder as I took the test. I remember the feeling was so strong, that I stopped and slightly looked over my shoulder to see if someone was there. I have had several experiences like this while taking exams."

Respondent to an unpublished research survey, describing one of their 'less-severe dissociative episodes'

Déjà vu described by academics

"There is a curious experience which everyone seems to have had – the feeling that the present moment in its completeness has been experienced before – we were saying just this thing, in just this place, to just these people."

William James (1890) describing the experience (before the use of the phrase 'déjà vu' became common place) in his seminal textbook, *The Principles of Psychology* (p. 675)

TABLE 1.1 (*cont.*)

Déjà vu described by academics

"We set out to produce an illusion of memory of the sort described by Titchener (1928) and were successful in doing so. In Titchener's example, memory for a glance across a street was experienced as déjà vu when the street was later crossed. We produced a similar illusion of memory by presenting an unconsciously perceived word before presenting that word in a test of recognition memory."

Jacoby and Whitehouse (1989) describing their experiment which aimed to produce the memory illusion described by Titchener (1928) and which can be identified as being like déjà vu (p. 134)

"The déjà vu experience lacks any clearly identifiable eliciting stimulus or verifiable behavioural response, and these lacunae have presented impediments to systematic research efforts."

Alan Brown (2003) in his influential review of the déjà vu experience (p. 394)

---

evidence – Jacoby and Whitehouse claim to have produced something similar in the laboratory. Brown (2003) asserts that the experience has been difficult to study because of there being no identifiable trigger, and no measureable outcome other than subjective experience. The challenge, clearly, for a monograph on the déjà vu experience is to consider how the understanding of the experience might be advanced beyond the very subjective and mysterious reports of clinicians and experients.

How can déjà vu be studied?

The central thesis of this monograph is that déjà vu is – at its core – a memory error, and therefore it can be understood by drawing upon what is known about the memory system. This is not a new idea – Titchener (1919, p. 425) categorised the "'feeling that all this as happened before' which persists for a few seconds in spite of the knowledge that the experience is novel" as an 'illusion of recognition and memory'. This approach to studying memory more generally has been very successful – it is considered that some apparent faults of the memory are adaptive and expose the inner workings of this complex cognitive system (Schacter, 1999). Schacter (2001) in his 'Seven sins of memory' briefly considers déjà vu as a memory error, referring to Arnaud's article of 1896 (reviewed in Chapter 2). He concludes that déjà vu, whilst clearly a memory error – a 'misattribution', is not very well understood: "Déjà vu occurs relatively infrequently, and there is still no convincing explanation of precisely what features of a present experience would produce the kinds of mistaken judgements that Arnaud theorised about ... we know little more about déjà vu today than we did back in the days of Arnaud over a century ago" (Schacter, 2001, pp. 90–91). In fact, as this book will show, a great deal has been added to our knowledge in the last few years, and déjà vu can now seriously be thought of as one of the memory malfunctions which exposes the workings of the memory system.

Once déjà vu is seen as being the result of a memory error, it means that testable hypotheses can be made about what causes it, and ultimately it should be possible to experimentally induce the sensation. This is the ultimate goal of scientific research into déjà vu – to understand it to the extent that it can be recreated, or something analogous to it, in laboratory conditions. Once there is a reliable and theoretically driven means of generating false memories in undergraduate populations, we can then examine their relation to false memory in pathological groups, its association with false memory in the real world, how it is manifested in the brain, and so on. In Chapter 10 the existing research on the production of déjà vu in the laboratory is reviewed, and whereas there is a great deal of activity in this domain, it is possible that Schacter's claim still holds true in this regard: the field is still looking for a central paradigm to align itself with.

Déjà vu is not merely a false memory, because at the time we are experiencing it we know that it is false. It feels like we might be having a memory experience, but in fact, we are aware that we are not. It is this idea of awareness, of recognising the falseness of the situation, which leads many people to describe déjà vu as a meta-cognitive or metamemory illusion/error (e.g. Roediger, 1996; Moulin & Souchay, 2014; Kusumi, 2006).

Table 1.2 gives an overview of the methods of déjà vu research that are covered in this book. Aside of experimentation, déjà vu relies also on questionnaire research, which made up the bulk of all research before the publication of Brown's 2003 review of the experience. Questionnaires are useful for understanding experiences of déjà vu – and with such individual differences research the effect of certain factors such as age can be examined (see Chapter 6). For example, using our knowledge about the brains and memory function of older adults we can consider why people who are older or younger might experience more or less déjà vu. We can also consider descriptions and triggers and even the content and qualities of déjà vu in this manner, but clearly our ability to recall information about infrequent and difficult-to-describe subjective experiences severely limits the value of this approach. The final category of information which helps us better understand déjà vu comes from clinical cases, and the cognitive neuropsychology approach.

Why cognitive neuropsychology?

Cognitive neuropsychology is the study of cognition – thought processes – drawing upon experimental work on people with brain damage or disease, and the consideration of the brain in our understanding of psychological processes. One prominent method used by cognitive neuropsychologists has been to look for processes that are selectively damaged by brain injury or illness. In this fashion it should be possible to learn about déjà vu if we can compare groups of people with brain damage who do and do not have déjà vu. If there are systematic differences in the brains of these patients that coincide with the differences in the déjà vu experience, we

TABLE 1.2 Three main classes of research into déjà vu formation

Method	Description	Pros	Cons
Retrospective questionnaire studies	A large sample of participants answer questions about their experiences of déjà vu	Cheap Relatively simple	Forgetting Difficult to be certain participants are all referring to the same experience Difficult to pinpoint cognitive (memory) mechanisms at play in déjà vu formation
Clinical cases	Careful and close examination of people who, through disease, damage or distress, experience more déjà vu than others	Allows the study of déjà vu in people who experience it more frequently Possible to identify brain and psychological reasons for the déjà vu experience	Are clinical cases representative of healthy déjà vu?
Experimental work	Experiments are designed, with adequate controls, which aim to generate déjà vu–like experiences	Allows us to test hypotheses about what causes déjà vu in healthy people	Is experimentally induced déjà vu really the same as naturally occurring déjà vu? Do people report déjà vu just because they are asked to do so by the experimenter?

can triangulate on what is causing déjà vu. This rationale has been used in epilepsy (Chapter 7), dementia (Chapter 8) and psychiatric disorders, such as anxiety or schizophrenia (Chapter 9). It should be stressed, of course, that as well as 'using' such patients to understand the healthy mind, cognitive neuropsychological work also advances the care of such patients by better understanding and specifying their problems. Déjà vu is not always benign and infrequent but can be extremely distressing and nearly permanent where it occurs in clinical cases. Finally, it should be noted that déjà vu being as infrequent and unpredictable as it is, an approach which draws upon those people who experience it more frequently or for longer enables us to both speed up and focus our research efforts.

It is not appropriate to discard clinical cases of déjà vu as curiosities that cannot be incorporated into existing theory, or déjà vu as an anomalous, intangible experience. Cognitive neuropsychology has enabled researchers to draw upon different sources and methods to explore the human mind; it does not exist in isolation, but neuropsychological data can be used to test theories generated from elsewhere. Thus, a complete account of déjà vu should address many levels, requiring converging evidence from patient studies, experimental psychology carried out on healthy populations, the modelling of behaviour, and neuroimaging. An ultimate goal is to isolate the brain networks involved in déjà vu by imaging it – as it happens.

About this book

The aim of this book is to bring together the rapidly growing research into déjà vu into a coherent whole, considering both the neuropsychological and clinical cases of people with déjà vu and recent developments in generating déjà vu in the laboratory. The starting point is the idea that the familiarity inherent in déjà vu – and the evaluation of this familiarity which generates the conflict at the core of the sensation – are both processes which exist in the human memory system, and have been described elsewhere, but have not been related to déjà vu. This memory account of déjà vu can then be assessed and described accommodating many different sources of information, but for the first time offering a synthesis of the patient and experimental psychology literatures.

More specifically, déjà vu pertains to theories of recognition memory; which is the assessment of prior occurrence based on the evaluation of a stimulus in the environment. This is the theoretical entity which is closest to déjà vu – in some ways, déjà vu is somewhat like a momentary false recognition event: we experience something in the environment which we think we have encountered before. What makes déjà vu unlike false recognition is that we are metacognitively aware of the falseness of the sensation of déjà vu. It is not that we find something familiar when it should not be familiar (which would be a form of false memory), it is more that we find it is familiar but *know* ourselves that it should not be familiar.

One of the themes of this book is the classification of déjà vu types, and whether there may actually be different types of the experience (Chapter 4). Such taxonomic struggles are bound to arise when an experience is so subjective and difficult to classify, but also given what we know about recognition memory – that it can be described as having two processes, that of familiarity and recollection. It needs to be determined if these two separate theoretical entities are at play in déjà vu, whether they interact or give rise to separate forms of the déjà vu experience. Because such a debate focuses on theoretical advances in the understanding of recognition memory, a chapter (Chapter 3) is devoted to this theory and its relation to déjà vu, metacognition and epistemic feelings such as familiarity.

Why might the study of déjà vu be relevant for modern cognitive psychology? First, where people are in psychological distress due to the sensation, it would be beneficial to better understand the experience. Second, sometimes déjà vu is a clinical symptom that may be suggestive of neurological or even psychological dysfunction – and in these cases it is important to understand the symptom in detail and its causes in healthy and unhealthy groups. Third, déjà vu is an extremely complex subjective state. It is clear that if we can understand and explain this experience we will have come a long way in our understanding of the relationship between memory and consciousness. Rather than shying away from such subjective experiences, they should be at the centre of understanding how cognition works and how it is experienced. Because research into déjà vu needs to be understood in its context (that is, largely overlooked by memory researchers for 100 years), the book begins with a historical introduction to the topic, and the origins of the term.

Finally, it is always helpful to understand the coverage of a book, and so here are some comments on what is in the book, and possible lacunae. The adage of 'standing on the shoulders of giants' is apt here, as this monograph focuses more on what has been published subsequent to Brown (2004), and his book covers in more detail early questionnaire studies, parapsychological and psychodynamic works and definitional issues. Thus, the current book is stronger on recent work and patient studies, and especially those which postdate Brown's book. If there are gaps in the coverage of this book, it is most likely that it is because the scientific literature still needs to catch up with what might be commonly known about déjà vu in various clinical groups. There is, for instance, the idea that déjà vu might be experienced frequently as a signal of an upcoming migraine in people who experience migraine (e.g. Podoll, 2007), but this work is as yet unsupported by peer-reviewed articles in this area. To give an idea of what is as yet unknown or under-researched, the book finishes with a chapter on priorities for future research given the current state of the art in déjà vu research.

2

WHAT'S FRENCH FOR DÉJÀ VU?

A historical overview

> … "Supernature abhors a vacuum," and any vacuum in scientific psychology
> will inevitably be filled by parapsychology.
>
> *Walsh (2004, p. 284)*

Déjà vu has been described in art, literature and scientific works in a consistent and
steady fashion for about 200 years. What makes this historical perspective important is understanding the contribution of parapsychology and French neurologists
working in the late nineteenth century to the development of déjà vu as a scientific
concept. The early descriptions and arguments about déjà vu have undoubtedly
shaped contemporary research into the phenomenon. Most notably, the investigation of déjà vu as a key parapsychological experience is probably a reason why, in
comparison to other brief and infrequent mental events and perceptual illusions,
déjà vu has been overlooked by cognitive psychologists. A novel suggestion in this
chapter is that Boirac, widely cited as the originator of the phrase déjà vu, actually
preferred the term *paramnesia* for this experience. A better starting point for déjà vu
as a scientific concern, and the first concrete and well-reasoned use of the term, is
arguably Arnaud's article of 1896. This chapter considers the study of déjà vu in the
modern era from its origins in France through early work in epilepsy and electrical
stimulation of the cortex to contemporary developments including the measurement of subjective experience in memory and neuroimaging of cognition.

Terminological issues

Déjà vu is a French term and translates literally as 'already seen'. It is somewhat
contentious as to who first used the term, and as early as 1896, Arnaud was
debating what the scientific definition of the term should be and how it differed
from false memory and other strange memory sensations (Bertrand, Martinon,

Souchay, & Moulin, 2017). The term was probably in use in English in the latter half of the nineteenth century. The *Oxford English Dictionary* gives the first usage of the word in English as Myers' (1903) text, "Promnesia, the paradoxical sensation of recollecting a scene which is only now occurring for the first time; the sense of the déjà vu." In the scientific community, as Myers' quote demonstrates, it was mostly used for strange, false sensations of memory, as we tend to use it now, but it was also used to describe normal functioning memory processes (especially by French-speaking authors) to describe recognition memory more generally, such as in a famous case of Korsakoff's amnesia (Claperède, 1907 (translated by Nicolas, 1996, p. 1199): "The patient also shows a total loss of recognition memory. She won't recognise an etching that she saw only 15 seconds earlier. This lack of a sense of déjà vu, of being familiar with something, is very characteristic of the syndrome."

The Web of Science search engine returns 867 papers with déjà vu in the title (accessed December 2016). Fewer than one-tenth of these articles consider memory, psychology or the brain. Déjà vu has apparently become something of an in-joke for scientists. As an example, Rouse (2013) gives the title, "The misoprostol vaginal insert: déjà vu all over again", to an editorial discussing the value of a new means of inducing labour: the vaginal insert "seems like a new dog with all the old tricks" (p. 194). In fact, the term déjà vu does not appear in the body of the article itself.

For the popularisation of the term déjà vu, we probably have to thank the celebrated baseball player and manager turned-commentator, Yogi Berra,[1] whose famous tautology, 'it's like déjà vu all over again', is quoted ad nauseum. In fact, 238 articles use this phrase in the title, and *none* of them are about the phenomenon itself. This is no mere amusing observation – for those researching the topic, the 'witty' use of déjà vu in such contexts acts to clog up the literature and make scientific searches on the topic more difficult.

As the usage of the term increases, this has knock-on effects. Gallup and Newport (1991) reported that from 1978 to 1990 people who had experienced déjà vu increased from 30 per cent of the population to 55 per cent. This suggests that societal and media influences may alter the general public's understanding of the term, and as a result, more people say that they experience it. Whether this increase is for 'genuine' déjà vu is a point of contention, as there is also a sense in which any repetition, whether erroneous or not, leads to the usage of the term, such as the Pepsi advertising in 2006, "Déjà vu in every gulp" (see Figure 2.1). If the specificity of the term slips, more people will say that they experience it, but we will be less sure whether people are referring to a common experience. On the other hand, if people are not aware of the term, they will be unable to use it to describe their experiences. What is clear from an analysis of the use of the phrase (compared to the 'tip of the tongue' experience – see Chapter 3) is that there has been a clear increase in the use of the term. Figure 2.2 shows counts of the usage of déjà vu from the Google Books corpus (8 million books, or 6 per cent of all books ever published; Lin et al., 2012), as produced by Google Books Ngram viewer. The *y*-axis can be taken as the relative frequency of the word/phrase. There is some use

FIGURE 2.1 Pepsi advertising on a bus in Toronto (2006).

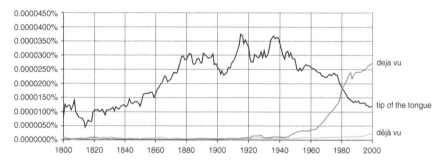

FIGURE 2.2 Counts of the usage of the term 'déjà vu' in the Google Books corpus. From Google Books Ngram Viewer, http://books.google.com/ngrams.

of déjà vu (with and without accents) throughout the nineteenth century, but with a clear growth occurring after the 1940s.

These issues of terminology are perhaps what are behind the change in the incidence of déjà vu over time (see Figure 2.3 – plotted from the review of incidence of déjà vu presented in Brown, 2003). There is presumably very little difference in the make-up of people's neurological systems in this short time period, so it might suggest there is a change in how the term is used – it has become less rare to describe a mental event using this phrase; more people can use the term to describe their experiences. These concerns about usage of the term are important when comparing people of different ages or cultures on their experience of déjà vu.

Lazerson (1994) reviews the use of déjà vu as a term in common parlance in American English, noting that the first dictionary definitions emphasise the scientific, illusory feeling, and that the term in this manner entered the lexicon (appearing in dictionary definitions) in 1903 (in agreement with the OED source, above). Lazerson argues that in the 1950s the term entered non-technical English, where its usage was largely pejorative and where it acquired the meaning 'tiresome familiarity' (p. 285), giving the example: "Two can lunch on dreary déjà vu for $47 in

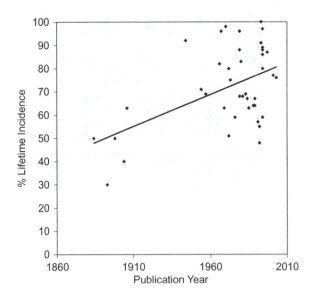

FIGURE 2.3 Relationship between lifetime incidence (percentage of people reporting having experienced déjà vu) and date of publication.
Adapted from Moulin et al. (2014).

our town's temples of serious French cooking" collected in 1975 in New York. But of course, the experience is not seen purely as negative: Pepsi would not suggest that their drink is tiresome or repetitive, nor would film-makers use the title déjà vu to market a blockbuster movie. The concern about how different groups of people understand the term déjà vu is considered in depth in Chapter 6, and the differences between lay use of the term and the scientific concept is considered in Chapter 10.

Déjà vu and nineteenth-century France

According to Brown (2004), the first scientific use of the term déjà vu is from Émile Boirac, who used it in a letter to the *Revue Philosophique* in 1876. Boirac was responding to an anonymous article in the previous edition describing a similar mental event. He describes an instance of an illusion of memory and uses the term déjà vu twice in the earlier passages (see Table 2.1). The first one is merely a literal use – 'I have already seen what I see'. The second, which is italicised in his original letter, is also accompanied with the term '*la sensation du*' (the sensation of). It is presumably this first usage of the term, even in its native French, which came to be used by English and French speakers.

Boirac was born in Algeria in 1851 and died in Dijon, 20 September 1917. At the time of the 1876 letter above, Boirac was affiliated to the Lycée at Poitiers. He was made president of the Université of Dijon in 1902, after a serving as president

TABLE 2.1 Original French text and translation into English of the key excerpt from Boirac's 1876 letter (original italics)

Il m'est arrivé, voyant pour la première fois un monument, un paysage, une personne, de porter tout à coup et malgré moi ce jugement: j'ai déjà vu ce que je vois. Impossible de dire en quel lieu ni en quel temps: la reconnaissance et comme la sensation du *déjà vu* n'en était pas moins très vive et très nette.	It has happened to me that when seeing a monument, a landscape, a person for the first time that suddenly, despite my better judgement, I have already seen what I am seeing. It is impossible to say in which place or time: the recognition, as with the sensation of *déjà vu*, was not very vivid, not very clear.

of the University of Grenoble from 1898. In France, he was mostly known as a proponent of Esperanto, and translated Moliere's *Don Juan* into Esperanto (1909), amongst other works. By the end of his career, Boirac's perspective was far from today's mainstream scientific psychology. His view was that psychology should be to psychic powers as astronomy is to astrology. He had a surgery in Dijon where he tested psychic powers, and published experiments on parapsychology.

Boirac was a prolific writer and researcher, and his early correspondence to the *Revue Philosophique* (its first issue was 1876, and Boirac's letter appeared in the second issue) was followed by a series of book reviews and observations. He wrote several books – two of which (on parapsychology) were translated into English. In 1913 Boirac was awarded the Fanny Emden prize by the *Académie des Sciences de Paris*, a sum of 2000 Francs. The award is peculiar because the citation from the awarding committee, which is published as a Preface to the second edition of *La Psychologie Inconnue* (*Our Hidden Forces*; Boirac, 1917), is negative about his experimentation: "Unfortunately, in that part of his work are the habits of thought of the professional philosopher, who is inclined to solve these problems by purely logical arguments rather than by experimental control" (p. xiv). It is also cautious about his theory: "However, although his theories are not free from confusion and other defects, his work remains *une ouvre magistrale*, a masterpiece, which coming generations engaged on similar lines will do well to consult" (Ibid.). In a letter published in *Science*, Jastrow (1914, p. 787) writes in critique of the prize and its winner: "Psychology receives so slight a recognition in scientific competitions that it seems unfortunate that its interests should be prejudiced by a recognition of a subject somewhat tangential to its main problems, and yet one upon which it has been forced to express itself in view of the widespread public concern." Of his aim to produce scientific experimentation on psychic powers, in its final summing up, the committee states: "Had M. Boirac succeeded in rendering such experiments incontestable to the most skeptical of scientists, he would have deserved much greater things than the prize itself, part of which we award him by way of encouragement."

Boirac is something of a champion for the 'scientific' study of psychic powers, and reprinted the above comments from the scientific committee in his own book as proof of the enthusiasm for his subject matter and his approach. In particular, he was excited about the resurrection of the topics of hypnotism and suggestion. Of these, he reported that the "… savants of the Eighteenth and Nineteenth Centuries believed they had irretrievably buried … conjointly with the 'fourth dimension' and 'perceptual motion'".

Bizarrely, whilst Boirac is credited with originating the term déjà vu, he did not seem to use it himself, preferring the term paramnesia (or *paramnesie*). In his book *Leçons de Psychologie Appliqué a L'Education* (1902, p. 106) he describes exactly the type of false recognition he described in his original letter: "Recognition is sometimes false – in spite of yourself, you immediately imagine having seen things before, even though you are certainly seeing them for the first time. This phenomenon, which more or less everybody has had in their youth, has received the name *paramnesie*."

This is little more than an interesting tangent in the history of déjà vu research, but it possibly explains how déjà vu became researched by the parapsychological community more than mainstream psychology. If it was Myers – himself an associate of Boirac and founding member of the London Society for Psychical Research in 1882 – who borrowed Boirac's term and in doing so aligned himself with the parapsychological research, it would explain why there was a strong bias to viewing déjà vu as a parapsychological entity. There is possibly more historical research to be done on this topic, but it would appear that the use of the term déjà vu may have signified allegiance to a certain view, whereas paramnesia was adopted for failures of recognition memory of a more mundane form. Boirac did not make much of a contribution to much else other than parapsychology, and although his description of déjà vu as an illusion or hallucination of memory is in line with current views, he is not cited as the originator of any of the various theories of déjà vu formation. Even in a history of metaphysics and psychology in France between 1880 and 1940 (Marmin, 2001) he warrants only a very brief mention.

The real pioneer of research into déjà vu is arguably Arnaud. In 1896, he presented Louis, a young man who had something like a permanent sense of déjà vu, not unlike the cases of recollective confabulation described in Chapter 8. What sets Arnaud apart is that he opens up a debate about the correct use of the term, and also presents a case study report to support his view of what déjà vu is. He writes:

> *Fausse mémoire* or paramnesia has been described as an illusion consisting of the belief that something is already known, *déjà connu* and as a consequence one *recognises* entirely novel events. The illusion can comprise the event itself, the details of the event, and the impressions associated to the event felt by the subject. The feelings associated with the recognition are so energetic that the false memory is confirmed as certain. I believe that the terms fausse mémoire and paramnesia should be abandoned as they have the double inconvenience of being vague and imprecise – because it is not certain that these are memory phenomena. In order to maintain clear expression, not implicating any theory, the term *illusion de déjà vu* is used. … Most of the authors think that this illusion is frequent in healthy populations to the point to which

every cultured person should have experienced it. In contrast, it is rare in people institutionalised with disorders of mental health. It appears to me that the frequency of the *illusion de déjà vu* has been exaggerated because it has been confounded with other similar errors: obscured memories, vague and distant reminiscences, etc. Specifically, the complete *illusion de déjà vu* presents two fundamental characteristics that differentiate it: First, the intensity of the illusory feeling, which leads to the sensation of certainty. Second and most importantly, there is a subjective state associated with the supposed repeated situation. These two characteristics will help one to identify this very specific illusion and distinguish it from other phenomena.

Arnaud, 1896, p. 455–456; translated in Bertrand et al. (2017)

As Arnaud was only 18 at the time of publication of Boirac's letter, Biéder (2005) claims that Arnaud's use of the term déjà vu was independent from Boirac's. Arnaud also asserts in his paper that no French author has tackled the subject of déjà vu. He was also the first to consider that there may be different forms of the experience (see Chapter 4). As will be seen, these ideas have been borne out in subsequent scientific works, and in essence, the first page of Arnaud's article could in fact sketch out the contents and concerns of contemporary research programmes into déjà vu.

Even if adopting Boirac's letter as representing the start of scientific thinking about déjà vu is inappropriate, the fact that we have a French term for the illusion is apt. Berrios (1995) provides a conceptual history of the debate about déjà vu and false memory and it is clear that the very earliest work on this topic was carried out in France, and had a clear neurological slant.

Déjà vu and literature

Despite being given credit for the phrase, it is clear that Boirac was not the first to describe the experience.[2] Here, the idea that déjà vu was described in literature before it was articulated well in scientific works will be developed. In fact, in the nineteenth century, scientific authors appeared to draw upon literary works in making their arguments. For instance, in a debate printed in the *Revue Philosophique* in the 1890s (see Berrios, 1995), Ludovic Dugas claimed that the phenomenon had been described by Verlaine in the poem *Kaléidoscope*:

> Dans une rue, au cœur d'une ville de rêve,
> Ce sera comme quand on a déjà vécu:
> Un instant à la fois très vague et très aigu …
> Ô ce soleil parmi la brume qui se lève!

Verlaine, Kaléidoscope (1884)

Thus, before there was one clear name for déjà vu there were literary descriptions of the experience. These are often clearest in creative works, where a large number of quotes from the nineteenth century describe the experience. For instance,

Dickens describes it particularly clearly in a passage in *David Copperfield* (published in 1850) – a quote that has been cited repeatedly in scientific works. Before that, Tennyson wrote in *The Two Voices*:

> Much more, if first I floated free,
> As naked essence, must I be
> Incompetent of memory:
>
> For memory dealing but with time,
> And he with matter, could she climb
> Beyond her own material prime?
>
> Moreover, something is or seems,
> That touches me with mystic gleams,
> Like glimpses of forgotten dreams –
>
> Of something felt, like something here;
> Of something done, I know not where;
> Such as no language may declare.

Tennyson (1842)

Such passages have appeared in numerous scientific articles in order to explain better the phenomenon in question (e.g. James, 1902; Crichton-Browne, 1895; Funkhouser, 1995). Crichton-Browne in his 1895 Cavendish lecture on the dreamy states (see below) gives quotes and examples from Thomas Hardy (p. 6), "Everybody is familiar with those strange sensations we sometimes have, that our life for the moment exists in duplicate, that we have lived through that moment before or shall again" (taken from *A Pair of Blue Eyes*, 1873); but also Wordsworth and Coleridge: "Oft o'er my brain does that strange fancy roll, Which makes the present, while the flash doth last, Seem a mere semblance of some unknown past" (from *A Sonnet Composed on a Journey Homeward*, written in 1796). Crichton-Browne also name-checks Rossetti and Sir Walter Scott.

Crichton-Browne's essay had the aim of describing 'dreamy mental states' which he suggested had not "yet received in this country [Great Britain] the amount of attention they deserve" (1895, p. 4). Of these dreamy mental states, he cites the most simple, "a sense of reminiscence it has been called by some, a sense of prescience by others" (1895, p. 4), which resonates with the description of déjà vu (but he does not use that term). Crichton-Browne's view was that these dreamy states were relatively common in epilepsy, and he even suggests that Tennyson was aware of the relationship between epilepsy and such disturbances of consciousness. In short, it is clear that before it was a topic of scientific consideration, writers were seeking to describe déjà vu and use it as a literary tool. Their ability to articulate this strange experience before the scientific community converged on the term déjà vu meant that their works were often drawn upon by those investigating mental phenomena, but in particular those researching epilepsy.

Epilepsy and déjà vu: a brief history

The history of déjà vu owes much to the study of epilepsy. Contemporary research into epilepsy is reviewed in Chapter 7. The term *epilepsy* comes from the Greek, to seize or to grasp, and its core feature is seizures, which can vary in magnitude and form. Crucially, one of the common features of epilepsy, in varying forms, is of a disturbance of consciousness (historically referred to as 'dreamy states'), and the prevalence of alternative experiential or behavioural states, with a paroxysmal (sudden, unexpected) occurrence. Epilepsy was long thought of as a sacred disease, giving the sufferer unique insights into the spiritual and mystic aspects of life (Saver & Rabin, 1997).

The modern history of epilepsy is dominated by Hughlings Jackson, a British neurologist working in the latter half of the nineteenth century (for an account of his contribution see Meares, 1999). Hughlings Jackson used the phrase 'dreamy state' to refer to the 'vague and yet exceeding elaborate mental states' that characterise certain seizures – he also was amongst the first to suggest that there were alterations in consciousness between and before seizures, and not merely seizures with overt, physical manifestations. Dreamy states include nebulous sensations and feelings, notably retrieval of scenes and experiences from the past, like flashbacks – these would nowadays be thought of as memory experiences. Hughlings Jackson (1888) reported a 37-year-old man who as part of his seizures detected strange smells, then began (uncontrollably) to think of 'things from boyhood's days'. Hughlings Jackson's contribution was to begin to understand that the workings of the epileptic mind, far from being an inexplicable or spiritual anomaly, were a window into the healthy function of the brain and mind. His exploration of dreamy states opened up the neurological examination of consciousness, and he was able to make links between the brain and its function – physiology and subjective experience. Hughlings Jackson did not use the phrase déjà vu in his writing, but it is clear that he is describing this experience as part of a broader set of alterations of consciousness and physiological symptoms.

Hughlings Jackson (1888) pinpointed these dreamy states to people with epilepsy in the temporal lobe, mostly due to the investigation of the dreamy state and the intellectual aura from the careful consideration of one case, Dr Z (see Taylor & Marsh, 1980). Dr Z, a medic, was actually Hughlings Jackson's neighbour and described his own symptoms in an article published in 1870, under the name *Quaerens*. He too made reference to the passages by Dickens and Coleridge in describing his own mental state. Dr Z had petit mal seizures which resulted in absences and forgotten passages – including clinical decisions he had made. Of déjà vu, he describes one of his seizures as starting thus:

> In October 1887 I was travelling along the Metropolitan Railway, meaning to get out at the fourth station and walk to a house a mile off. I remember reaching the second station, and then I recollect indistinctly the onset of

an 'aura', in which the conversation of two strangers in the same carriage appeared to be a repetition of something I had previously known – a recollection, in fact.

Dr Z cited in Hughlings Jackson, 1888 and Taylor and Marsh (1980, p. 759)

Hughlings Jackson noted that each case's intellectual aura usually took a consistent form. This was because each person's focus of epilepsy remained constant in the brain, and this part of the brain was consistently responsible for the same function. This was pioneering work – the official start date of psychology is usually given as 1879, with Wundt studying subjects' introspections of the contents of consciousness. People were trained how to report their subjective experience in order to illuminate the theories of psychologists. This method resonates with Hughlings Jackson's concept of 'self', which was similarly subjective, arising from the 'introspection of consciousness' (cited in Meares, 1999). Therefore, right at the birth of psychology, Hughlings Jackson was using parallel methods and theories to explore the subjective experience of people with epilepsy.

In terms of déjà vu research, Hughlings Jackson is well known for his early theories of consciousness (for review see Hogan & Kaiboriboon, 2003). A major starting point for his understanding of the brain–behaviour relationship was his view of "particular symptoms as pointing to a 'discharging lesion' of this or that particular part of cortex". His first description of the dreamy state came from 1876, which he variously described as a double consciousness, an 'all-knowing' or 'familiar' feeling.

For modern epilepsy and déjà vu research, one must acknowledge the work of Wilder Penfield. Penfield, a neurosurgeon, was one of the pioneers of the use of direct electrical stimulation of the cortex: if a neurosurgeon wishes to remove part of the brain responsible for seizures in order to treat the epilepsy, it is important that they locate the focus of the epilepsy. This procedure occurs whilst the patient is conscious – they are able to report the sensations of what happens whilst the electrodes are applied to the brain. Penfield and Perot (1963, p. 597) describe their results thus:

> … gentle electrical stimulation of temporal lobe cortex also produced sudden "feelings" – sometimes the feeling of familiarity that clinicians had been in the habit of calling déjà vu, sometimes an alteration in the apparent meaning of things seen or heard. … These are signals of altered interpretation of present experience. When they occur during a seizure they come as illusions of interpretation.

Penfield's *interpretative illusions* thus include feelings of déjà vu. Such interpretative illusions are postulated to arise when erroneous processing or brain dysfunction (however momentary or benign) produces feelings that are removed from current experience. Penfield and Perot (1963) report directly stimulating the cortex of 1,132 patients, 520 of whom received stimulation of the temporal lobe. Of these,

7 per cent experienced experiential *responses* (feelings) and 10 per cent of the 520 had spontaneous experiential *hallucinations* (images/sounds) following stimulation. As an example, Case 30 produces the following accounts of her experiences, each line being a response following brief stimulation (p. 642):

> "Sounded like I was singing a song."
>
> "I seemed to hear a song, sort of familiar, like on the radio."
>
> "Yes, I felt just terrified for an instant." Stimulation was continued. She was asked if she still felt terrified and she said, "No." She explained it was the kind of terror she has with her attacks.
>
> Patient said, "No." Then she said, "It reminded me of a song but I do not know what song it was."

The patient also reports a sensation of overwhelming familiarity, and one can imagine it is the sort of sensation that we sometimes feel when information is on the 'tip of our tongue' (e.g. Schwartz & Metcalfe, 2011). But note that no material is retrieved; it is a feeling that is divorced from normal processes.

Penfield believed that the temporal lobe memory system stored a 'stream of consciousness', a view of memory which does not tally with more modern, reconstructive views of memory. Penfield's belief was that he was – through electrical stimulation – allowing previously encoded memories to flow again in a verbatim fashion. The implication was that each and every experience was laid down in a near-sensory representation and stored in a permanent fashion. As such, Penfield's theories about memory and consciousness have been discredited (e.g. Loftus & Loftus, 1980) and dubbed a 'video-recorder model' of memory. Key figures in the cognitive revolution, Loftus and Loftus (1980) and Neisser (1967) both offer reconstructive accounts of Penfield's data. Neisser's account was possibly the boldest, comparing the activations in memory to the contents of dreams, concluding: "Penfield's work tells us nothing new about memory" (p. 169).

And yet they may tell us something about déjà vu. Penfield's methods were so diligent, and his reports so full and detailed, that through evoking current theory his case reports and observations continue to yield insights that can be incorporated into contemporary ideas. Moreover, researchers still continue to use stimulation in order to gain insights about the memory system, and, in particular, retrieval of memory (e.g. Jacobs et al., 2012) and déjà vu (e.g. Bartolomei et al., 2004). As such, contemporary research continues to refine the definitions of various aspects of the dreamy state, including déjà vu, still relying on first-person accounts of experience whilst receiving stimulation.

It has long been known that there was an association between epileptic activity in the temporal lobe and illusions and experiences such as déjà vu. For contemporary mainstream memory research, there are two main contributions of this approach. First, the network of regions activated in these patients, either spontaneously or in stimulation studies, converges on a network of temporal regions incorporating the hippocampus and extending to the amygdala that are known to be important for memory function. Second, these studies demonstrate that, however artificial, it is possible to have sensations associated with memory function (such as feelings of remembering and familiarity) which are devoid of content – and usually these feelings are described as déjà vu. Unlike Hughlings Jackson, these experiences are now considered as memory phenomena rather than being about consciousness or selfhood more directly. Where a distinction between Penfield's theories and contemporary memory theory must be drawn is in the consideration of the veracity of the memories generated in stimulation. It is now less critical to consider whether the material generated is complete/incomplete or veridical/false, but rather to assert that the 'memories' generated are experienced as being memories and not other forms of mental content: stimulation of the temporal lobe can make you think you are having a memory experience.

Psychoanalysis and parapsychology

Common to the paranormal, psychodynamic and religious views of déjà vu is that it 'means' something,[3] either metaphysical (such as being proof for reincarnation) or personal (such as being about repressed memories). Freud suggested that déjà vu was caused by re-experiencing issues and events that had at one point been repressed. The idea that déjà vu is psychologically meaningful or related to paranormal events has been a prominent theme since Boirac.

William James (1902) refers to déjà vu as a variety of religious experience, which he defines as: "a kind of insight into which I cannot help ascribing some metaphysical significance". His pioneering work is cited by philosophers of religion as well as by cognitive psychologists, and James thought that by studying mystical and nebulous experiences such as déjà vu, we might better understand people. An emerging topic in neuroscience and cognitive psychology is the understanding of religious experience and belief in general – for example, work on the 'Folk psychology of souls' (Bering, 2006), and the research into déjà vu is underdeveloped in this regard. Although James undoubtedly made a positive contribution to our understanding of feelings such as déjà vu, the rejection of functionalist ideas with the advent of behaviourism, and the overlap between his descriptions of déjà vu and 'psychic powers', probably helped put the topic out of bounds for mainstream psychology for a considerable period.

The parapsychological angle, perhaps emanating from Boirac himself, has proved difficult to shift, and we are left with a number of pseudoscientific researchers working in the domain. For instance, Vernon Neppe, a psychiatrist based in Seattle, claims that at least some types of déjà vu are anomalous experiences in that they cannot "easily be explained using our conventional laws of science" (Neppe, 2014). Neppe is cautious as to the causes of déjà vu, careful to outline that temporal lobe epilepsy can cause déjà vu, and that it can be experienced in anxiety. He also uses questionnaires as support for his ideas. Neppe's consideration of déjà vu is presented in the context of other anomalous experiences and parapsychology more generally, and he is a member of the parapsychological society, where he is reportedly "regarded as the world's leading authority on the déjà vu phenomenon" (Parapsychological Association, 2014). On the same site he presents his paradigm model:

> Dr Neppe's magnum opus is an ongoing project. With Dr Ed Close, he has developed a new "theory of everything", a paradigm called the Triadic Dimensional-Distinction Vortical Paradigm: The *N*-Dimensionometric CST Matrix Entropic–extropic Mathematicologic LFAF Model: An integrated space, time and "consciousness" matrix reflecting event-horizon, warping-*N*-dimensional extrapolation, extent–content–intent distinctional-C-matrix open–closed, holistic-unified, finite–infinite biopsychophysical reality (TDVP). This has been a labor of a quarter of a century and was privately released for peer-review in February 2011, and two scientific books are in process at present.
>
> *Parapsychological Association (2014)*

Neppe's ideas have gained a great deal of traction in the field of déjà vu. His work is scholarly, and his definition of déjà vu and his historical notes have been widely cited. In particular, Neppe's 1983 book, *The Psychology of Déjà Vu*, has been cited 89 times – mainly for its definition of déjà vu "any subjectively inappropriate impression of familiarity of a present experience with an undefined past" (Neppe, 1983, p. 3 – citation count from Google Scholar, August 2016), which as Brown (2003) has pointed out, has become the accepted definition of déjà vu in cognitive psychology.

Another writer with a parapsychological interest in déjà vu is Anthony Peake, who has written, amongst other works *Is There Life After Death?: The Extraordinary Science of What Happens When We Die* (2006). In this book, he draws upon experiences of déjà vu (it is the topic of his first chapter) and very carefully and enthusiastically gathers information about it from many different scientific and literary sources. The central thesis of his book is that some form of our consciousness persists after death, which continues in a personal or parallel universe ('the Daemon') rather than the physical plane of life before death. He supports his argument through citing research on near-death experiences and déjà vu (amongst others). He repeats the psychoanalytic idea that déjà vu might reflect a wish to correct something in the past, and suggests that déjà vu may exist to signal the separation of time. He concludes, "whatever happens to temporal lobe epileptics, it seems that they are tuning into a different version of reality than the rest of us, possibly the reality of the Daemon itself", echoing the notion of epilepsy as a sacred disease bestowing spiritual powers, an idea held since antiquity but which was opposed as long ago as by Hippocrates (Magiorkinis, Sidiropoulou, & Diamantis, 2010).

In the contemporary study of déjà vu, Arthur Funkhouser is the most prominent researcher working from a psychoanalytic perspective. He has received a great deal of attention for his work on déjà vu. Funkhouser is a Jungian psychoanalyst, and has researched the relationship between déjà vu and dreaming, producing empirical work (e.g. Funkhouser & Schredl, 2010). Funkhouser's (1995) fractionation of déjà vu into three separate experiences (déjà vécu, déjà senti and déjà visité) has been influential (see Chapter 5).

The danger of such parapsychological and psychodynamic interpretations is the idea that déjà vu may be a 'gift', or that temporal lobe epilepsy may have spiritual or metaphysical benefits, and this may influence treatment and care of potentially very serious conditions for certain people. It is likely that due to its peculiar phenomenology and infrequence, déjà vu will continue to be exploited by parapsychologists, even when a cognitive neuropsychological account for the phenomenon exists: it does not make the experience much less eerie, awe-inspiring or terrifying if the experient knows how it is produced (although there may well be anxiety around déjà vu in undiagnosed epilepsy which could be 'explained away'). Furthermore, the intensely subjective nature of the experience means that people will possibly hold to their own views about the experience even in the face of scientific evidence about its nature, as has been captured in responses to research questionnaires on this topic such as this somewhat typical response received in a comments box in an unpublished online questionnaire study:

> I'm an experienced and functioning continual déjà vécu'er … living longer with my 'peculiar' perception of time than Chris Moulin's been alive. You might want to factor 'precognition' into your studies, as well as the temporal research being done by physicists. Time itself is not solely linear. Our brains can, under certain conditions, serve as interfaces with 'higher dimensions' (Read 'Flatland'. Read Plato's 'Allegory of the Cave'.) Expand the horizons of your work, and you will benefit humanity. Continue to portray to the media that continual déjà vécu is merely an illness, and you will destroy many people who otherwise would survive. You choose. The glaciers are melting.

Subjective experience in the cognitive era

After the early work examining consciousness and introspection, the history of psychology is dominated by behaviourism, which had its origins in Pavlov's consideration of stimulus–response links. Skinner, a prominent behaviourist, suggested that memory actions, like other forms of 'mentalising', are in fact just agglomerations of very complex associations: "We say that a person recalls or remembers what he has seen or heard, but all we see is that the present occasion evokes a response, possibly in weakened or altered form, acquired on another occasion. We say that a person associates one word with another, but all we observe is that one verbal stimulus evokes the response previously made to another" (Skinner, 1971, p. 189). Skinner suggests that words referring to mental states (like 'recalls' or 'remembers') imply a kind of autonomy of the individual that is more apparent than real. With this being the prominent paradigm in psychology, déjà vu, which has no behavioural signal that can be externally verified, fell from prominence in mainstream experimental psychology.

Cognitive psychology considers thought as information processing and the idea that we can scientifically explore mental representations. The cognitive approach permits the study of consciousness and subjective experience, and it has become critical for research into memory. In an influential work, Tulving (1989) suggested that memory systems could be classified according to their availability to consciousness. Subjective report became an important variable in experimental psychology. Whereas behaviourism had considered the quantity of information retrieved by humans, within the cognitive approach it became legitimate to examine both the quantity of information and the quality of the information retrieved – or the subjective experience at retrieval. Within such a framework, it became easier to study déjà vu again, and other 'illusions' of memory.

Summary: history repeating itself

A number of themes have been drawn out in this chapter that need to be taken into consideration throughout this book. Notably, we have seen that the usage of the term déjà vu is prone to change, and that several different definitions of the term exist, and perhaps through an increase in popularity as a term, its meaning may have changed for the lay population. This can make it difficult when assessing the frequency and incidence of déjà vu, or when asking people if they have experienced it in the laboratory. Another issue was raised first by Arnaud (1896), who indicated that déjà vu was possibly confused with other mental states. Thus, we need to be a little cautious in how people use the term, and how it may mean different things to different people.

A second challenge, beyond that of terminology, is the parapsychological context in which déjà vu has been researched, which clearly is historical, but also probably derives from the characteristics of the experience itself: its strangeness, intensity, rareness, and so on. This means that déjà vu has seldom been seen as a serious scientific concern, and this difficulty has been added to by the work of Penfield, also, who, at least in the domain of memory research, has largely been discredited for his views on the permanence of memory. In this regard, it is interesting to note that whereas many theories of perception have been developed through the scientific study of visual illusions (notably Richard Gregory; e.g. Gregory, 1968), the field of memory has been slower to use illusions in empirical work. This is notable because many visual illusions are often, by definition, purely subjective, but give rise to distinct patterns of brain activation according to subjective experience (e.g. Rubin's vase; Andrews, Schluppeck, Homfray, Matthews, & Blakemore, 2002; see Figure 2.4). This means that, as with visual illusions, déjà vu could be a useful phenomenon in our theorising about complex, multi-factorial behaviours like recognition memory decision making. It also suggests that if we can 'see' different patterns of activation in the brain according to subjective experiences such as seeing a vase or two faces, we could also attempt to find the neural signature of déjà vu in the brain.

The history of déjà vu research includes a period when it was much less studied by mainstream experimental psychologists, and it rarely appears (even now) in

FIGURE 2.4 The Rubin's vase illusion: participants either see two (in this case, angry) faces looking at each other, or a vase. This illusion, like déjà vu, is subjective, and has no behavioural corollary – an external observer cannot judge whether someone else is perceiving the figure as a vase or two faces.

undergraduate textbooks. However, within the domain of epilepsy, the topic of déjà vu has remained a core topic of interest because it is clinically relevant and has been less seen as a random, difficult-to-explain event. It is interesting to note how, due to the unpopularity of déjà vu as a topic of scientific study in mainstream psychology for a certain period, several key articles have been overlooked which now can be reappraised in the light of current theory and data.

Notes

1 Lawrence Peter "Yogi" Berra (born 12 May 1925) is a former American baseball player, manager and member of Major League Baseball's Hall of Fame. As a baseball commentator, he is famous for allegedly using the phrase, "It's déjà vu all over again." According to Wikipedia, Berra claims that this quote originated when he witnessed Mickey Mantle and Roger Maris repeatedly hit back-to-back home runs in the early 1960s. However, Berra also admits that he didn't actually say many of the things people attribute to him. These range from malapropisms such as the déjà vu quote to more circular, clever maxims, such as "Never reply to an anonymous letter."

2 He wasn't even the first to describe it in the second volume of the 1876 issue of *Revue Philosophique* where the term was coined. The very paragraph before is an account of the sensation, by Horwicz, citing the popular idea that '*un cas de double conscience*' is produced by a disruption of processing between the two hemispheres of the brain.

3 Of course, for many people, déjà vu does 'mean' something. For people with temporal lobe epilepsy, the feeling of déjà vu may signal an upcoming seizure, so for such people the experience may be less of a curiosity and of more concern. Even in the quote in Chapter 1 about dissociation, the experient makes a personal explanation of her déjà vu as about success in her exam, drawing on the familiarity to help make meaning of her current situation. On an individual level, this 'meaning-making' of déjà vu is common place, even in healthy populations, and must be seen as a reasonable response to having encountered such an intense and unpredictable experience.

3

THE HUMAN RECOGNITION MEMORY SYSTEM

My memory is extensive, yet hazy: it suffices to make me cautious by vaguely telling me that I have observed or read something as opposed to the conclusion which I am drawing, or on the other hand in favour of it; and after a time I can generally recollect where to search for my authority.

Charles Darwin (1887)

The central thesis of this book is that the phenomenon of déjà vu can be considered within existing theories of human recognition memory. Recognition is the memory system that is responsible for detecting prior occurrences of stimuli in the environment. In short, déjà vu presumably arises because of a temporary glitch or misinterpretation of the recognition memory system, a system that is usually responsible for responding appropriately to familiar and novel environments, ideas and people. In this chapter, an overview of the recognition memory system is presented, focusing in particular on two key concepts: recollection and familiarity. The purpose is to give a neuropsychological account of how déjà vu may be considered in terms of the healthy function of the memory system. The chapter has two parts. The first gives an overview of recollection and familiarity. The second introduces the concept of epistemic feelings that are thought to govern memory function.

Dual processes theories of recognition memory

Recognition memory rests on a decision-making process. When we detect something as having been encountered before we make a comparison between what is represented in the cognitive system and what is currently perceived. When encountering a stimulus (such as a newly learned word, for example) for a second time, a number of processes and sources of information are brought to bear on your processing of the word: how fluently you can process it, the distinctiveness of its perceptual trace, the feelings generated when encountering it a second time, the effort involved in retrieving its meaning, and whether you can recall the specifics of your first encounter with the word: who used it and in what context. These complex sources of information can be used to retrieve the meaning of the word, or to gauge the certainty with which you have encountered the word before, and so on. Ultimately, they can all be used to make a decision about whether we have encountered the word before or not.

Recent theories of human decision making suggest that complex tasks requiring problem solving and judgement rely on two different types of thinking (Evans, 2008; Kahneman, 2011). Such dual-process accounts consider that people make decisions based on two separable streams of information: a fast, intuitive feeling and a slower, more deliberative evaluation. These separable processes in cognition are arguably also at play in memory decision making (e.g. Arango-Muñoz, 2010; Hintzman & Curran, 1994; Koriat & Levy-Sadot, 2001) and map neatly onto the concepts of familiarity (which is relatively fast and automatic) and recollection (which is slower and more deliberative) (Mandler, 2008). Human recognition memory decision making can be thought of as the combination of information drawn from two different processes: recollection and familiarity.

The idea of dual processes in memory and cognition is not new, and was probably inspired by the anatomy of the brain. Many early scholars posited that the two hemispheres of the brain represented a 'double organ' (e.g. Holland, 1840). Wigan's influential text (1844), *The Duality of the Brain*, was an extreme position. He argued that there were literally two separate brains that could work in synchrony or not. This early view of the 'dual' brain influenced Ribot's early conceptions of human memory and its disorders (Taylor & Shuttleworth, 1998). One prominent view of déjà vu is that it arises from a mismatch between two separate streams of consciousness (often blamed upon two hemispheres working out of synchronisation), something that Wigan discussed as early as 1844.

The contemporary view of recognition memory is that it is based on neurally distinct mechanisms of recollection and familiarity. Yonelinas (2002) describes familiarity as a direct evaluation of the memory trace, something that can be subjectively reported by the participant. In contrast, recollection refers to the retrieval of specific contextual information from the time of study, and is often characterised as 'mental time travel' or as having the first-person experience of 'remembering'. Recollection has been characterised as the ability to recall or report 'something more' at the time of making a recognition decision (Moulin, Souchay, & Morris, 2013). This can be captured by asking participants to justify their responses – "SUSHI – I know I've seen this word before because I remember thinking about my cat while it was presented earlier." Equally, it can be measured by a source-memory task (what colour ink a word was presented in, whether it was a male or female voice that spoke it, etc.).

The dual-process view of recognition memory is contentious, and more parsimonious single-process theories exist (see Diana, Reder, Arndt, & Park, 2006; Donaldson,

1996; Dunn, 2004; Squire, Wixted, & Clark, 2007; and Wixted & Stretch, 2004). Those who argue that remembering and familiarity lie on a continuum and reflect just one memory system suggest that the two differ along one dimension, the strength of the trace in memory. In experimentation, this is usually captured empirically as subjective confidence. Participants report higher levels of confidence for events that are 'remembered' than for those which merely feel familiar (Dunn, 2004). Recently, Berry, Shanks, Speekenbrink and Henson (2012) have argued that even implicit and explicit memory phenomena lie along the same continuum. In a series of experiments, they show that the rate at which someone can identify a very briefly presented word (typically seen as an implicit memory test) is related to the subjective report of whether the word has previously been seen. Critical for their argument, a mathematical model with one 'process' reproduces their data. In short, the same underlying trace strength is supposed to support not only familiarity and recollection decisions, but even implicit and explicit memory phenomena – priming and recognition memory.

The temporal lobe memory system

Neuroscientific and anatomical data can help resolve the single/dual-process argument, and the neural basis of recollection and familiarity is currently under debate. Aggleton and Brown (1999) put forward a widely cited neuroscientific model, focusing on the hippocampus as critical for recollection, and the adjacent parahippocampal gyrus as responsible for familiarity. Their proposal is briefly summarised in Figure 3.1. Aggleton and Brown further suggested that due to the network connecting the hippocampus to the fornix, mamillary bodies and anterior thalamic nuclei, these structures are also engaged during the encoding and retrieval stages of recollection. Moreover, they suggested that familiarity is supported specifically by the most anterior portion of the parahippocampal region (the perirhinal cortex, PRc).

This model predicts that hippocampal damage should affect recollection but not familiarity, and parahippocampal damage should lead to impairments in familiarity, not recollection. In support, patients with damage restricted to the hippocampus have displayed isolated impairments in recollection measured through a number of paradigms (e.g. Bowles et al., 2010). Later models have elaborated on the specific roles of the PRc, entorhinal (ERc) and parahippocampal cortices (PHc) due to the emergence of findings that extrahippocampal structures may be able to support some forms of associative memory. Such a departure, as Montaldi and Mayes (2010) describe, begins to view recollection and familiarity as 'kinds' of memory, because "each is a complex function, likely to depend on several different processes that are probably mediated by different structures that are functionally connected in a system" (p. 1294).

A meta analysis of event-related functional magnetic resonance imaging (fMRI) studies on healthy participants by Diana, Yonelinas and Ranganath (2007) found that recollection was associated with relatively more activation in the hippocampus than the perirhinal cortex, whereas familiarity was associated with relatively more

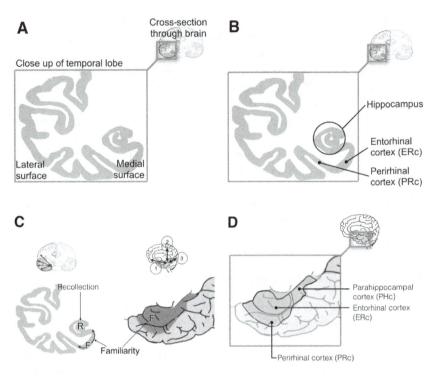

FIGURE 3.1 Anatomical schematic of recollection and familiarity. (A) Overview. (B) Coronal view. (C) Crude depiction of Recollection and Familiarity. (D) Sagittal view.

activation in the perirhinal cortex than the hippocampus. However, they also argue that "there is no simple mapping between MTL regions and recollection and familiarity, but rather that the involvement of MTL regions in these processes depends on the specific demands of the task and the type of information involved" (p. 379).

Just as cognitive single-trace accounts contest the assumptions of dual-process theories, there is also opposition to the above neuroanatomical models. Squire and colleagues (e.g. Squire et al., 2007; Wixted & Squire, 2011) argue that all structures within the medial temporal lobe (MTL) mediate recollection and familiarity equally. Their MTL Unitary Trace Strength (MUST) account suggests that functional heterogeneity exists within the MTL, but not for recollection and familiarity. Wixted argues (e.g. Wixted, 2007; Wixted & Squire, 2011) that recollection is a continuous process just like familiarity. In a source-memory experiment using fMRI, Wais, Squire and Wixted (2010) measured hippocampal activity at retrieval after equating memory strength of recognition decisions on item-correct plus source-correct or item-correct plus source-incorrect trials. Their analysis focused only on recognition trials where participants assigned high confidence ratings, regardless of whether the correct source was retrieved. They found that hippocampal activity was similarly elevated for both correct and incorrect source judgements, suggesting it is involved in both recollection and familiarity.

It is crude to think of the hippocampus and parahippocampus as the only areas of the brain responsible for recognition memory, even though disease and damage of these areas impairs memory function. fMRI investigations of episodic memory reveal that brain regions associated with attention and decision making are more reliably activated during memory tasks than would be expected compared to findings from patients with brain damage. In particular, the parietal and prefrontal cortices are reliably activated during episodic memory tasks. The parietal lobe is often thought of as integrating sensory information. In healthy groups, parietal lobe activation has been attributed to the support of episodic recollection at retrieval (as with the robust EEG finding of a P600 neural signature for recollection) and is involved in hippocampo-cortical memory and fronto-parietal 'resting state' networks (for a review of parietal lobe involvement in memory, see Wagner, Shannon, Kahn, & Buckner, 2005). That is, a large network including the parietal and frontal regions possibly determines memory activity and coordinates the whole memory network.

Frontal structures have long been thought of as responsible for controlling and monitoring the cognitive system (e.g. Stuss & Levine, 2002). They are seen as coordinating, reflecting upon and controlling the temporal lobe memory system (Moscovitch, 1994). The idea of the 'controlling' function of the frontal lobes is manifest in the neuropsychological deficits following frontal lobe damage, most notably confabulation (e.g. Burgess & Shallice, 1996). Fletcher and Henson (2001) reviewed the role of the frontal lobes in human memory as shown in neuroimaging studies. They subdivide the frontal lobes into three critical zones: the lateral surfaces of the ventrolateral, dorsolateral and anterior frontal cortex. They propose that these respective regions are responsible for updating/maintenance of information; selection/manipulation/monitoring of information; and the selection of processes/subgoals. Fletcher and Henson point out that whereas frontal lobe damage is very disruptive to working memory, it has a more restricted effect upon long-term memory. Patients with frontal lobe damage fail to suppress interference (e.g. della Rocchetta & Milner, 1993) and cannot reproduce temporal order (Shimamura, Janowsky, & Squire, 1990). Stuss and Levine (2002) also emphasise that frontal lobe damage leads to difficulties in organising material during retrieval and effectively generating cues to reproduce information. Frontal lobe damage contributes to, but does not in itself cause, a global amnesia.

Neuroimaging studies point to the activation of a 'retrieval mode' in the frontal lobe. In a recognition task where participants had to either respond 'yes' to all words they had seen previously, or to only reply 'yes' to words seen in a particular context, Henson, Rugg, Shallice, Josephs and Dolan (1999) found activation bilaterally in the dorsolateral frontal cortex, which is interpreted as reflecting source monitoring of the retrieved words (see also Mitchell & Johnson, 2009, for similar findings). Fletcher and Henson conclude that retrieval from episodic memory includes two main stages of frontal lobe involvement: the generation of search parameters, and the verification of the material generated in a memory search – and they propose these processes map onto ventrolateral and dorsolateral cortices, respectively.

Perhaps most critically for the study of déjà vu, patients with damage to the frontal lobes have been known to develop problems with false recognition. Schacter, Curran, Galluccio, Milberg, and Bates (1996) describe patient BG, who following an infarction of the right frontal lobe had abnormally high levels of false recognition accompanying the subjective experience of remembering (see also Curran, Schacter, Norman, & Galluccio, 1997). BG not only incorrectly recognised items (words, pictures and sounds) he had not previously studied, but he also reported 'remembering' these items, rather than just finding them familiar. BG did not show this pattern when required to learn a categorised list. Schacter et al. (1996) concluded that BG was only aware, when tested on uncategorised lists, that he had previously studied a list consisting of some words, pictures or sounds. When presented with a recognition test containing old and new items, he over-extended his 'recognition' to new items, perhaps on the inference that as these were similar to the previously studied items they were likely to be old. However, if more structure was present in the encoding environment, for instance from semantic categories, then he was able to use this structure to discriminate old from new items. Such cases of frontal impairment support the idea that the frontal lobes are involved in the coordination and monitoring of memory processes.

In sum, whereas there is consensus that recollection and familiarity are distinguishable psychological concepts, their status as neurological and/or cognitively separate entities is in question. Given that the two responsible brain regions – the hippocampus and the parahippocampus are both tiny and boast many complex interconnections between themselves and other brain areas, it is likely that a more nuanced view of these zones is required. Moreover, one needs to consider that these regions are imbedded into a large network of regions all implicated in memory function.

What is familiarity?

Familiarity is the central subjective experience in déjà vu. Assuming that this form of familiarity is that which is found in recognition memory, it is important to describe in detail how this experience is generated in the memory system. One problem with discussing familiarity is that – just as with déjà vu – there exist alternative definitions of this technical term. One of the most influential theories of familiarity comes from Bruce Whittlesea (e.g. Whittlesea, 1997). He pointed out that there are three common uses for the term familiarity that contribute to some confusion in the area:

1. "… a person has actually encountered a stimulus (or even one like it) previously. This sense pertains to the historical fact that a person has previous experience with an object, whether or not that experience influences current behavior and whether or not the person can report that experience."

2. "… the person has knowledge about a stimulus that permits them to perform appropriately toward an object, without necessarily having an

accompanying feeling of having experienced that stimulus previously. For example, in watching Hamlet for the 15th time, I know what to expect is coming next, but I have no pressing feeling of having seen it before."

3. "… the subjective feeling of having encountered a stimulus on some previous occasion, whether one actually has or not."

Whittlesea & Williams (1998, pp. 141–142)

Whereas cognitive psychologists may use familiarity in all these senses, for our purposes we are clearly interested in *subjective* familiarity, which is emphasised in the third definition. This definition captures the idea of subjectivity critical to the feeling of déjà vu – it is also, importantly, suggested in this definition that this form of familiarity can actually be false, which is both critical for our definition of déjà vu as being false, and as will be developed below, is also important for experimentation in human memory and inducing familiarity.

The butcher on the bus phenomenon

Subjective familiarity is perhaps most strongly felt when we are unable to know why we feel it so strongly, as Mandler discussed in 1980:

> Consider seeing a man on a bus whom you are sure that you have seen before; you "know" him in that sense. Such a recognition is usually followed by a search process asking, in effect, Where could I know him from? Who is he? The search process generates likely contexts (Do I know him from work; is he a movie star, a TV commentator, the milkman?). Eventually the search may end with the insight, That's the butcher from the supermarket!
>
> *Mandler (1980, pp. 252–253)*

This is the 'butcher on the bus' phenomenon. It describes the frustrating experience that occurs when we are unable to pinpoint the source of the familiarity. It shows that familiarity can be felt especially strongly in the absence of certain knowledge of how the person is familiar. Familiarity or 'just knowing' is the simple judgement of prior occurrence, and at its simplest, familiarity is easy to define, because it is a judgement of prior occurrence that is devoid of the retrieval of contextual specifics. Note that this sense of familiarity, although intensely subjective, is not the same as déjà vu. Somehow in the butcher on the bus phenomenon, we are sure that we are searching for a reason why the feeling is true – a search for why the person feels familiar. In comparison, in the déjà vu experience we know – immediately or soon after – that the strong sense of familiarity is false.

This does little to answer what familiarity *is*. Yonelinas (e.g. Yonelinas, 2002) sees familiarity as a 'signal-detection process'. A signal-detection process account suggests that at high levels of familiarity the trace strength of the memory is high, and we are able to read off the strength of the memory signal in order to report, 'I have seen this face before'. For weaker activations, familiarity is not sufficient to make a conscious report of prior occurrence, but it might be sufficient to influence our preferences, or 'gut' feelings. Thus, familiarity is a graded process with the strength of familiarity for a stimulus influencing behaviour. An item can be familiar, but below the level of conscious report.

Whittlesea's view is that the memory system is continuously trying to make sense of its inputs, so that it can interpret any signals arising from low-level processing of the environment. In this way, familiarity is a subjective feeling arising from the fluent processing of a stimulus. It is not an inherent feature of anything you have seen before. Familiarity is an attribution we can make to explain why we come to know something quickly, or why we can fluently process a word or a face. His theory is summarised in the title of one of his papers: 'Why do strangers feel familiar, but friends don't?' (Whittlesea & Williams, 1998). We do not feel overwhelming familiarity when we come home and see our husbands: we were expecting to see them there in the house at that time. His explanation of the butcher on the bus is that it is the fact that we cannot retrieve who the person is that gives rise to the feeling of familiarity. This theory is supported by various illusions of familiarity: where we use the fluency of processing to wrongly judge that we have seen something before.

Goldinger and Hansen (2005) report an experiment for which they built a chair that administered subliminal buzzes through the seat. They were interested in the way in which these subliminal buzzes influence recognition memory decision making. Participants sat on the chair and then conducted an episodic recognition memory test, where they reported 'old' or 'new' for a set of words, and also reported the confidence in their answer. The results showed that the subliminal buzz influenced the recognition decision (particularly for the most difficult items on the test). The effect was to increase the rate of responding 'old' to the items on the test, both the targets and the distracters in the recognition test. It also increased the confidence made to the false alarms, but reduced it for the hits. On his website, Goldinger describes his results thus:

> When you truly have no memory, the buzz gives you a tingle of confidence, but when you have a memory, the buzz gives you a tingle of doubt. These findings were in line with the predictions of a model called SCAPE, as the same signal created a different memorial interpretation, based on context (Whittlesea & Williams, 2001).
>
> *Goldinger (2017)*

These results suggest that low-level feelings are used when making explicit decisions about memory – it suggests an interchange between feelings and thoughts, and non-conscious feelings and explicit decisions. Whittlesea's SCAPE (Selective Construction and Preservation of Experience) model (Whittlesea & Williams, 2001) describes the interaction of attributions of memory and processing fluency. The current context generates a top–down expectation of processing fluency. When an expectation of fluency is violated, it triggers a search for why that has arisen. This is the search triggered in the case of the butcher on the bus. In the case of the buzz chair, the buzz contributes to the decision (note that if the buzz is not subliminal, the same effect does not occur): the attribution of the buzz is that it must 'mean' something for the ongoing memory task.

These experimental results converge on the idea that familiarity is a feeling that is generated from the processing of a stimulus – if a stimulus is processed very fluently, our attribution is that we have encountered it before. For a philosophical account of this possible 'attributionalist' nature of episodic memory, see Perrin and Rousset (2014). The fact that we can alter subjective familiarity and recognition memory decision making by altering the fluency with which items are processed suggests that we use familiarity signals in making attributions about whether we have encountered information before. As we shall see in Chapters 5 and 10, this means that generating false feelings of familiarity should be sufficient for generating déjà vu in the laboratory.

Neuroscientifically, familiarity can be seen as a low-level, quick-acting form of memory which works on perceptual inputs. Similarly, this system tries to match, as quickly and effortlessly as possible, the contents of mental representations stored in memory with the current contents of perception. Viewed like this, familiarity decision making is the last stage in perception – once we have composed and identified a scene or environment, we can 'read off' whether we have encountered it before. This is consistent with a neuroanatomical view of the temporal lobe memory system being the last point in the ventral visual stream (e.g. Suzuki & Amaral, 1994).

The remember/know paradigm

The dual-process debate is most pronounced when comparing the subjective experiences accompanying recognition memory in the remember/know paradigm, which has been used throughout the literature to examine episodic recognition memory (e.g. Tulving, 1985). The remember/know paradigm asks participants to distinguish between sensations of 'remembering' and 'knowing' (and/or finding familiar, e.g. Conway, Gardiner, Perfect, Anderson, & Cohen, 1997). Common definitions of these concepts are presented in Table 3.1. The paradigm is a straightforward means of estimating the relative contributions of the two separate processes in recognition memory. There are other means of assessing recollection and familiarity, as will be shown in later chapters, but these other methods tend to converge on the same construct (Eichenbaum, Yonelinas, & Ranganath, 2007).

The critical issue with the remember/know paradigm is the evidence for separable streams of familiarity and recollection in recognition memory. Importantly, Perfect, Mayes, Downes and Van Eijk (1996) tested both subjective report of remembering and the recall of contextual (or source) information: familiar responses rarely yielded reports of contextual information (e.g. where on the screen the item was presented) that were above chance. When participants *remembered* items at test, they were more reliably able to report source details from the study phase, suggesting

TABLE 3.1 Definitions of remembering and knowing. Selected quotations detailing subjective experiences were described to participants in various studies (adapted from Williams & Moulin, 2015, p. 983)

Authors	Response options in experiment	Representative quote and/or definitions provided to participants
Gardiner and Java (1990)	Remember Know	"Often, when *remembering* a previous event or occurrence, we consciously recollect and become aware of aspects of the previous experience. At other times, we simply *know* that something has occurred before, but without being able consciously to recollect anything about its occurrence or what we experienced at the time" (p. 25, emphasis in original)
Bastin and Van der Linden (2003)	Remember Know Guess	"… classify a 'yes' response … as 'Know' if you do not remember any information associated with the face. You are *sure* that you have seen it because you have a *strong feeling of familiarity*, but you do not remember any information encoded with the face" (p. 24, emphasis added)
Gardiner, Java, and Richardson-Klavehn (1996)	Remember Know Guess	"The subjects were told that a know response meant that they *knew for a fact* that the word occurred in the study list, because the word was *familiar* in the experimental context, but they did not recollect its occurrence" (p. 116, emphasis added)
Kelley and Jacoby (1998)	Remember Know	"A Know response is defined as the inability to recollect any details of the study presentation in combination with a *feeling of familiarity or certainty* that the word was studied" (p. 134, emphasis added)
Dewhurst and Anderson (1999)	Remember Know Guess	"A know response is one in which you recognize the item because it *feels familiar* in this context, but you cannot recall its actual occurrence in the earlier phase of the experiment. You recognize the item *purely on the basis of a feeling of familiarity*" (p. 667, emphasis added)

that the subjective feeling of remembering is indeed related to the recall of source information.

Moreover, remembering and familiarity are affected differently by experimental factors (reviewed by Yonelinas, 2002). In short, there are a number of neuropsychological dissociations that are important (such as in healthy aging, autism, Alzheimer's disease). There are also a number of manipulations at study and at test that can alter either familiarity or recollection, suggesting that they are separable processes. For instance, during encoding, a deep level of processing compared to a shallow level of processing leads to a greater change in recollection than familiarity.

Epistemic feelings and metacognition

Up to this point, a family of illusions and phenomena have been presented that give an idea of how familiarity works in the recognition memory system and how we can use feelings of familiarity and fluency to make inferences about prior occurrence. At some level these acts of attribution and making meaning of processing are metacognitive (i.e. thinking about thinking) because they involve reflections about our own performance. The remember/know paradigm can be loosely described as metacognitive, because it considers the first-person report of experiences and feelings that are involved in a recognition memory decision. A parallel literature considers such guiding metacognitive phenomena as 'epistemic feelings', which are central to cognitive processes. As such, the feeling of familiarity can be described as an epistemic feeling in that it is a sensation that guides our cognitive behaviours (Moulin & Souchay, 2014). Interestingly, as with human recognition memory, the discussion of epistemic feelings is often in the context of discussing dual-process theories, with epistemic feelings such as familiarity acting as fast, intuitive cues which guide cognitive processing.

Koriat (2007) described the low-level subjective states in memory processing as *experience-based metacognition*. Based on Koriat's view, Arango–Muñoz (2011) suggests that metacognition can be split into two levels, one that is metarepresentational, and can be described as 'thinking about thinking'. This includes making predictions of future performance based on the parameters of the memory task, the characteristics of the to-be-remembered stimuli, and our general dispositional characteristics, such as *I can never remember street names*. This basically concerns humans turning their ability to predict other people's intentions and behaviours on themselves (e.g. Flavell, 2004). Arango–Muñoz discusses a second level of *epistemic feelings* which is a quick-acting intuitive process, based on how things *feel* rather than an assessment based on stored representations and problem-solving heuristics. These include feelings of certainty, pastness, insight, fluency and mental effort (de Sousa, 2009). Again, these two levels of metacognition map nicely onto relatively recent developments in dual-process accounts of reasoning and judgement; distinguishing between cognitive processes that are fast and automatic, and those that are slower and deliberative.

Epistemic feelings are proposed to give a sense of 'truth' to a belief, or ascribe some meaning to our cognitive processing. As with emotions more generally, it is crude to think of these feelings as 'right' or 'wrong' – there are times when we cannot (*and should not*) objectively say whether someone is 'correct' to feel angry, for instance. However, we can consider, as with emotion, what the experient considers the feeling is 'about': people can report how the feeling is being interpreted – it is this face, or that word, which feels familiar, for example. For a philosophical debate about the nature of these epistemic feelings, see Proust (2007). Arguably, they are fast-acting, reflective and guide-processing in the same way that emotional feelings are, but much like an emotion, they do not deliver any content – they are just a signal.

There are a number of different feelings and states that can be experienced when trying to retrieve information, ranging from fast, automatic 'ecphoric' retrieval of facts to a complete failure to recognise a person or place, such as with the butcher on the bus. In many instances, memory retrieval will be strategic, and information and feelings generated during failed recall will be useful for the experient and guide-processing. We do not need to search memory in order to make a recognition decision on any one item – in this way there is a difference between failing to retrieve something and knowing that we don't know it. For instance, you can very quickly answer questions like "Did you ever eat in *DZ'envies* in Dijon, France?" without setting up an exhaustive search of French cities and their restaurants (see Kolers & Palef, 1976). There is very little research on how we 'know not', but presumably the capacity to quickly know that something is novel or unknown is one way we can generate the conflict in déjà vu: *this feels familiar but even without questioning my memory I know I've never been here before.*

Thus, an understanding of these feelings and their interpretation is central to the study of déjà vu, and in fact, déjà vu is often used by philosophers as an example of an epistemic feeling: when there is a sensation of memory without the content of memory. Philosophical material relating to déjà vu is beyond the scope of this book, but for some philosophical debates about déjà vu and recollective confabulation (Chapter 8) see de Sousa (2009), Brun, Doğuoğlu and Kuenzle (2009), Arango-Muñoz (2014), Bortolotti (2010) and Gerrans (2014). Moreover, understanding the metacognitive contributions to memory is critical. Roediger (1996) asserts that déjà vu is an "illusion of metacognition" (p. 95). Brown (2004) describes déjà vu as a "'pure' metamemory experience unconnected with the empirical world" (p. 5).

The literature on epistemic feelings in memory is rather underdeveloped, but the concept neatly maps onto a set of metacognitive phenomena and paradigms that are rather better researched and understood (such as the feeling of knowing, or FOK; e.g. Wojcik, Moulin, & Souchay, 2013). Epistemic feelings are possibly easiest to describe in instances where there is a mismatch or dissociation between the processing and the contents of cognition, such as in déjà vu, but also in the tip-of-the-tongue (TOT) state. A TOT occurs when there is a feeling that a piece of information is known, but it is not available for conscious report. In TOT and déjà vu there is evidence for the existence of epistemic feelings in that a feeling about cognitive processing has become divorced from the material being processed. Normally, when epistemic feelings are in concert with the goals of processing, we are not so aware of them, just as with Whittlesea's observation about friends not feeling familiar.

Summary: familiarity and recollection in episodic memory

Human recognition memory processes rely on processing in the medial temporal lobe and recognition memory decision making is subserved by two neurologically distinct but adjoining regions which are responsible for recollection and familiarity. In addition, frontal areas of the brain act in a network with the temporal lobes and most likely play a role in interpreting the activations in the temporal lobe. Crudely speaking, it can already be seen that an anomaly in activation in parahippocampal circuits may generate a feeling of false familiarity that is possibly divorced from the usual activation, which sees familiarity triggered as the last part of the ventral visual stream. The exact mechanics of déjà vu still need elucidation, but the temporal lobe is clearly the brain region most likely to be responsible for this experience, both in terms of early attempts at understanding the dreamy state and epilepsy and direct stimulation of the temporal lobe (see previous chapter), but this is also in agreement with contemporary theory about human memory.

In short, déjà vu can be seen as a false feeling of familiarity, which is opposed by top-down contextual information which points to this epistemic feeling being false. Clearly, a central proposal for this thesis is that familiarity can be viewed as a low-level memory 'experience' based on a (intuitive and fast) metacognitive evaluation of the memory system. Souchay and Moulin (2009) and Moulin et al. (2013) have summarised the above theories into a schematic representation about the relationship between familiarity and recollection in recognition memory. This model has been used to explain the search for information given the recognition of a stimulus in the environment, and pertains most clearly to the feeling of knowing (FOK; Hart, 1965). The FOK is a situation where one has the feeling or belief that they will later be able to recognise a currently inaccessible piece of information. Figure 3.2 shows a characterisation of the relationship between familiarity and recollection. This model proposes that the relationship between familiarity and recollection is metacognitive: familiarity is a signal which means something in the human memory system – that is we can act on our feeling of familiarity in order to guide memory search.

In this model, familiarity is proposed to be a trigger for the search for contextual information and occurs before the recollection of specifics (cf. Hintzman & Curran, 1994; Koriat & Levy-Sadot, 2001). An initial feeling of familiarity with a cue triggers the attempted retrieval of episodic detail about the cue and any associated information. In the absence of any contextual information, we can make accurate predictions of our future recognition (as is measured in the episodic FOK paradigm, e.g. Souchay, Moulin, Clarys, Taconnat, & Isingrini, 2007) based on the strength

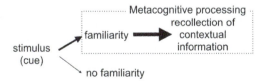

FIGURE 3.2 A sequential model of familiarity and recollection based on an initial feeling of familiarity and a subsequent search of memory. The relationship between familiarity and recollection in this model is metacognitive.

of familiarity for the cue, and also based on what other 'partial information' about the cue or searched-for-target comes to mind. This model is metacognitive because, judging our capacity to correctly gauge correct recognition of a currently unrecallable stimulus, it appears that we can use the familiarity of a cue in memory to make evaluations of the state of a target in memory. That is, familiarity can be acted upon metacognitively to investigate why – as in the case of the butcher on the bus – we find a stimulus familiar. This situation is analogous to searching for a target word when given a cue word. The model is a little simple, but it predicts, for instance, that we cannot recollect information for something that does not feel familiar to us. It does, however, suggest that, as in the déjà vu experience, people can find something familiar, but not be able to retrieve any information as to why it is familiar. Such a model views déjà vu as metacognitive: familiarity may be erroneously triggered, but then the search for contextual information does not return supporting recollective information. Instead, there is the certainty that the familiarity is false, which is presumably supported by an evaluation that the current situation/location/perceptual input is novel. Note that this is not the same as the butcher on the bus, where familiarity is high but the recollected specifics are (momentarily) absent. It is rather that top-down information is generated which actually opposes the feeling of familiarity.

4

CLASSIFYING DÉJÀ VU

I believe that the terms false memory and paramnesia should be abandoned as they have the double inconvenience of being vague and imprecise – because it is not certain that these are memory phenomena. In order to maintain clear expression, not implicating any theory, the term illusion de déjà vu is used.

Arnaud (1896, p. 306)

Much early scholarly work into déjà vu considered how many types of déjà vu there are. This need to classify the experience and create terms that apply to specific types of experience presumably stems from the fact that the experience is difficult to describe and has perhaps been hitherto poorly described. As early as the nineteenth century, Arnaud was already showing an awareness of alternative terms, and discussing which terms would be the most suitable. Arnaud also suggested that there were two different forms of déjà vu:

One proposes two types: First, a mild type compatible with healthy states in which the illusion has a very short duration, stops suddenly and is rectified immediately; and second, a more severe type of longer duration and in which the resolution is incomplete or null. This last form is obviously pathological.

Arnaud (1896, p. 456)

This chapter starts by outlining and defending a contemporary definition of déjà vu. The question of how many types of déjà vu there are is addressed with reference to memory theory, proposing the idea that there are possibly two forms of déjà vu experience which map onto familiarity (déjà vu) and recollection (déjà vécu), respectively. Finally, a few related experiences, such as *presque vu* and *jamais vu* are briefly discussed.

A contemporary definition

The contemporary study of déjà vu has been shaped by Brown (2004), who wrote an exhaustive account of the phenomenon, reviewing work from many domains and fields, and summarising his research both in popular articles and a review in *Psychological Bulletin* (Brown, 2003) which has been cited 118 times (Google Scholar, December 2016). In this influential review, Brown borrows Neppe's (1983) definition, "any subjectively inappropriate impression of a present experience with an undefined past" (Neppe, 1983, p. 3). Brown's own definition is a "clash between two simultaneous and opposing mental evaluations: an objective assessment of unfamiliarity juxtaposed with a subjective evaluation of familiarity" (Brown, 2004, p. 2). Most work published subsequent to Brown's (2003) article has drawn upon Neppe's and Brown's definitions, and as such we can be sure that the field is on the whole conforming to the same operationalisation of the déjà vu experience.

O'Connor and Moulin (2010, p. 165) place more of an emphasis on the clash in evaluations and the metacognitive nature of déjà vu:

> The sensation of déjà vu arises as a conjunction of two streams of cognition: the phenomenological experience of recognizing a current situation and the awareness that this feeling of recognition is inappropriate. Most importantly, the overall evaluation of the déjà vu-eliciting situation sides with the higher-order metacognitive awareness of inappropriate recognition.

This definition emphasises that we must be aware of the false nature of the familiarity, and the second sentence specifies that the false familiarity must be resolved in favour of it being found to be false. This is subtly different from Brown's definition because his definition implies some sort of 'objective' truth to the feeling of falseness. The 'objective' assessment of unfamiliarity is not objective at all, but we resolve the experience towards this subjective assessment of unfamiliarity and not the other subjective assessment, that of familiarity. In short, there is no objective information encoded in human memory: it is possible that one feels that something is familiar but believes this feeling to be false (i.e. déjà vu) even when, indeed, they have actually ('objectively') already encountered something before.

How many types of déjà vu are there?

One theme that characterises parapsychological work on déjà vu is the drive towards classifying the experience, and generating subtypes. For instance, Neppe's view (at the time of going to press) is that there are 35 different of déjà vu experiences:

> Only 11 recognized kinds of déjà vu by 1979; 19 new terms developed by Neppe, including two independently by Funkhouser; 5 more esoteric terms from 1885 to 1910 were discovered in 2008.
>
> *(Neppe, 2015 – www.scholarpedia.org/article/Deja_Vu)*

Neppe's subtypes include déjà gouté (already tasted), déjà lu (already read), déjà rêvé (already dreamt) and déjà rétrosenti ("already sensed as a reanimation of living into the past going backward in time. This balances déjà pressenti in the time distortion context"). Neppe also considers that there are four subtypes of déjà vu:

- Psychotic Déjà Vu,
- Temporal Lobe Epileptic Déjà Vu (TLE déjà vu) specifically in temporal lobe seizures,
- Subjective Paranormal Experience Déjà Vu in subjective paranormal experients,
- Associative Déjà Vu in ostensible normal – the common or garden subtype in ordinary individuals.

(Neppe, 2015 – www.scholarpedia.org / article / Deja_Vu)

These quotes represent a quest to carefully but unparsimoniously document the many different types of déjà vu experience. They are not a theory-driven account of cognitive function that could explain the experience, but a bottom-up collection of personal experiences and descriptions which mostly just refer to one modality or another. They tend to refer to the trigger of the experience such as 'déjà visité' for visiting a place and finding it familiar. The classification of déjà vu like this seems fraught with difficulties (although there may be some cognitively interesting reason why some triggers occur more than others – for some data see Table 4.1). Imagine we have déjà vu whilst drinking a cup of coffee. Is the déjà vu associated with the taste of the coffee (déjà gouté) really any different from the déjà vu induced by the smell of the coffee (déjà senti)? There are two problems here. The first is that most descriptions of déjà vu by most research participants emphasise that the experience encompasses the whole situation and all modalities, even if often people will identify a particular trigger, such as a conversation feeling familiar. For instance, this healthy participant from Fortier and Moulin (2015) described the experience thus:

> Usually if I have déjà vu, it is during a conversation with another person. I will feel that the environment, the content of the conversation and even the exact movements of our bodies has happened before.

Thus, it seems unlikely that separate elements of our experience would become decoupled from what Gennaro, Herrmann and Sarapata (2006) describe as the 'unity of consciousness'. A second problem is more critical and concerns human memory theory. Human memory is not organised as separable memory systems according to content or modality, but by duration and retrieval type (see Tulving, 1985). That is, if déjà vu is a glitch in the memory system, or any cognitive system, it should respect the delineated cognitive processes according to biologically real domains. Although perceptual inputs are different for audition and visual perception, for instance, by the time these inputs are integrated into the long-term episodic memory system, they are fused, such that there is very little interference or

TABLE 4.1 Triggers for déjà vu and physiological and psychological factors associated with the déjà vu experience – subjective report of frequencies from retrospective questionnaire data (taken from Wells et al., unpublished)

Trigger	Number (and percentage) of healthy participants reporting trigger (n = 229, mean age = 26.45)
Environmental/situational triggers	
Conversation	124 (54.1%)
Familiar location	109 (47.6%)
Familiar people	94 (41.0%)
Unfamiliar location	49 (21.4%)
Unfamiliar people	42 (18.3%)
Psychological/physiological factors	
Tiredness/sleep deprivation	63 (27.5%)
Stress	31 (13.5%)
Anxiety	24 (10.5%)
Recreational drugs	12 (5.2%)
No particular trigger	61 (26.6%)

competition between the modalities, and we can think of a memory as a mental construct which binds together different modalities into a coherent whole. Thus, while it may be possible to consider different forms of déjà vu experience, these should be based on neurologically plausible differences in the underlying processes involved in the separate subtypes.

For instance, given that there are studies which point to there being different neural substrates for face versus object recognition, one possibility (which has not received any scientific attention) is that people could have a distinct form of déjà vu related to the processing of non-familiar faces. In fact, studies have reported pathological versions of exactly this type of problem – whereby all faces are recognised as being familiar ('hyperfamiliarity for faces') even when they are strangers (Ward et al., 1999, "seeing film stars everywhere"). In this way, brain damage leads to a specific problem with face recognition, and a chronic form of 'false fame'. Finally, one piece of evidence that speaks against modality-specific forms of déjà vu would be the report of déjà vu in people who are congenitally blind (O'Connor & Moulin, 2006). First, the fact that people who are blind have déjà vu means that the experience is not solely visual. Second, rather than a fractionation of the experience according to the trigger in the environment or modality, the published report of déjà vu in a person who is blind, again points to an integration of different sensory sources (O'Connor & Moulin, 2006, p. 247):

> Hearing and touch and smell often seem to intermingle in the déjà vu experiences. It is almost like photographic memory, without sight obviously. It may be more accurate to say multi-dimensional memory, as if I was encountering

a mini-recording in my head, but trying to think, "Where have I come across that before?"

A theory-driven proposal: déjà vu and déjà vécu

In cognitive psychology, to consider the question of how many types of déjà vu there are, we will refer to another taxonomic question: how many types of memory are there? If we are to believe that there are separate forms of déjà vu for faces, places and conversations, it would be good to appreciate whether it is possible that there are indeed separate memory or neural systems responsible for processing these types of stimuli in the memory system. In fact, whereas it can be argued that there are specific neurological and cognitive systems responsible for faces, or for language, for instance, these differences are less meaningful when it comes to human memory: whereas some interesting differences between visual and verbal materials exist, the emphasis in long-term memory is more on the common processes and brain regions involved in encoding and retrieval. We do not talk about 'conversation memory' as a specific part of memory, and so, given that déjà vu is a memory phenomenon, we should not entertain a special kind of déjà vu for conversations, which is different from other types of information that can enter into episodic memory.

There is very little to suggest that a credible difference could exist between varieties of déjà vu in this sense. However, when considering the phenomenology of déjà vu, in terms of its intensity, duration, emotional character and so on, it may be possible to generate a theory-based account of déjà vu subtypes. Certainly, it does seem that déjà vu can be of different forms and intensities, regardless of the trigger or modality. One feature that may help us better define and classify the déjà vu experience is *prescience*. Prescience describes the feeling of being able to predict the future. This is sometimes a feature of déjà vu, but is not always a feature. Likewise, sometimes with déjà vu we feel like we may be able to retrieve some specifics of the current 'repeated' situation. Using such differences, it might be possible to generate a classification of déjà vu subtypes based on the theory outlined in the preceding chapter, that there are recollection and familiarity subprocesses involved in human recognition. Here, the possibility that déjà vu might be split into familiarity and recollection subtypes is assessed.

Moulin, Conway, Thompson, James and Jones (2005) and O'Connor et al. (2010a) argue for two principle forms of déjà vu – based on familiarity (déjà vu) and recollection (déjà vécu). This idea drew heavily on Funkhouser's (1995) terminology and reasoning. Funkhouser (1995) proposed that there are three types of déjà vu, differentiating a brief fleeting experience (déjà senti – literally 'already felt') and a more fully developed experience (déjà vécu – literally 'already visited'), as well as claiming a separate type of déjà vu for locations and places (déjà visité). The third type is not of interest to us, because it again refers to a specific trigger (place) rather than delimiting a certain kind of mental experience. Table 4.1 shows that places (familiar more so than unfamiliar) are common triggers for the déjà vu experience.

Moulin et al. (2005) deliberately borrowed from Funkhouser's (1995) fractionation of déjà vu and his characterisation of it as a more complete, complex mental experience of reliving the current moment. Notably, to describe déjà vécu he uses the passage from Dickens' *David Copperfield* mentioned in Chapter 2 (Dickens, 1850, p. 236):

> We have all some experience of a feeling, that comes over us occasionally, of what we are saying and doing having been said and done before, in a remote time of our having been surrounded, dim ages ago, by the same faces, objects, and circumstances of our knowing perfectly what will be said next, as if we suddenly remember it!

This stresses contextual detail and feelings and thoughts that come to mind during the experience of déjà vu. As such, it parallels recollection where, in remembering an event, we are able to draw up contextual information and the specifics of a previously experienced event. There is also the notion of prescience; the feeling of being able to predict what will happen next. In contrast, Funkhouser (1995) describes *déjà senti* as a less tangible sensation, and differentiates it as being 'primarily or even exclusively a mental happening' with no precognitive aspects. To illustrate this sensation he draws on a quote from Hughlings Jackson (1888, p. 202):

> [W]hat is occupying the attention is what has occupied it before, and indeed has been familiar, but has been for a time forgotten, and now is recovered with a slight sense of satisfaction as if it had been sought for.

This passage describes a mental event that is incomplete, with an absence of recollective detail, and the 'reliving' of a situation. It is akin to the lower-level epistemic feelings described in the previous chapter – a more pure form of familiarity.

O'Connor et al. (2010a) outline the difference between a familiarity and recollection type of déjà vu experience, although without using the term déjà senti, largely because, despite Funkhouser's (1995) observant classification, the literature had already converged on a description of déjà vu that emphasised familiarity. The primary reasoning behind the existence of two forms of déjà vu was based on the logic that either familiarity or recollection can contribute to recognition memory – and hence both should probably contribute to false recognition or illusions of recognition. O'Connor et al. argued that the reproduction of thoughts, contextual information and memories to support the false impression of having experienced a previous moment before suggested a glitch in the recollective part of recognition, not familiarity.

This dual-process definition, whilst plausible, has received limited empirical support, except in epilepsy (see Chapter 7), even though the separation into déjà vu and déjà vécu has gained some interest. It could be that déjà vu and déjà vécu lie on a continuum whereby strong feelings of familiarity lead to sensations of recollection and the retrieval of specifics – which may be confabulated – in support of the erroneous familiarity. In the epilepsy literature déjà vu and déjà vécu are separable experiential phenomena, a distinction identifiable qualitatively in the context of spontaneous and provoked epileptic activity. However, it is not clear how possible it is to differentiate feelings of remembering and familiarity in the déjà vu experience, and this has never been systematically researched in healthy groups.

In short, déjà vécu can be thought of as a more striking form of déjà vu, possibly made more frequently for novel than mundane events, and always accompanied by feelings of mental time travel, and reproducing the present as if it is contextual information from the past. Other researchers (e.g. Milton, Butler, & Zeman, 2011; Kalra, Chancellor, & Zeman, 2007) have used this distinction between a strong, reliving of the past based on recollection-like mechanisms, and others have used the term déjà vécu to describe something stronger than the mere feeling of familiarity (e.g. Bancaud, Brunet-Bourgin, Chauvel, & Halgren, 1994). In sum, however, the phrase déjà vécu continues to be used without precision and without consistency between researchers and different types of research (notably in epilepsy and healthy populations). Until consensus is reached about its definition, and indeed until there is sufficient evidence for its existence as a separate type of experience (especially in healthy groups), it will be a term which possibly confuses déjà vu research more than it contributes to it. A proposed concrete definition is provided in Chapter 7 in the context of temporal lobe epilepsy.

If nothing else, the attempt to classify déjà vu demonstrates the need to tighten up the terminology of déjà vu, particularly if we appeal to what is known about the human recognition memory system. For instance, Spatt's (2002) account of a parahippocampal system being at fault in déjà vu experiences is summed up thus: "This memory system is responsible for judgments of familiarity. The result is that a momentary perceived scene is given the characteristics of familiarity that normally accompany a conscious recollection" (p. 6). This quote confounds familiarity and recollection. A better phrasing would be *the scene is given characteristics of familiarity without complete retrieval*.

Pathological and healthy déjà vu

For clinical applications, it is of importance to know whether there are differences between healthy déjà vu experiences and pathological experiences. This is in fact a theme that has dominated research into epilepsy and psychiatric difficulties. For the purposes of cognitive neuropsychology, however, it is less important to distinguish between healthy and unhealthy experiences. In fact, the whole premise of cognitive neuropsychology is that we can learn about healthy cognitive function and the brain by studying dysfunction and disorder. To this end, it is assumed that the experiences of déjà vu generated by damaged or diseased brains are the same as those experienced by healthy people. This rationale stems from attempts to understand the human memory system by using case studies of amnesia, for example (for a defence of this approach see Rosenbaum, Gilboa, & Moscovitch, 2014). The patterns of performance produced by people with severely impaired memory help us better understand the divisions between separate memory systems and provide a biological basis for such a distinction (e.g. studies on forgetting in amnesia; Squire, 1981). According to this approach, the experience of the amnesic may be unusual and deficient, but the nature and quality of forgetting is assumed to be the same in the amnesic and the healthy participant: it is only that the amnesic experiences more forgetting. The same approach can be used for déjà vu – we assume that the déjà vu in temporal lobe epilepsy is more frequent but otherwise no different from the déjà vu experienced by healthy people. This is a simple assertion, but not so clear-cut as a quantitative analysis of memory, as we rely on subjective report.

One critical issue in comparing healthy and pathological forms of déjà vu is awareness, an issue that was identified by Arnaud (1896). Bertrand et al. (2017) propose that it is the delusional nature and the idea that the patient cannot or does not correct the impression of familiarity that should be used to define a sensation of familiarity as pathological. For instance, although people with temporal lobe epilepsy may experience déjà vu as part of an epileptic seizure, one should not describe this as pathological déjà vu even though it is clearly produced as part of a disease process. The rationale is that healthy déjà vu and epileptic déjà vu do not differ in their phenomenology or duration, and epileptic patients do not act upon their déjà vu experiences, but indeed can correct them and identify them as momentary memory errors.

Because the very definition of déjà vu necessitates two mental evaluations and a recognition of the erroneous nature of the familiarity, any situation where the experient lacks insight or is delusional is pathological. If a patient really does believe her life to be repeating and maintains this belief despite evidence otherwise, this is clearly not like 'healthy' déjà vu. Therefore, the term recollective confabulation is favoured for such delusional, pathological phenomena that have typically been described as 'chronic' déjà vu experiences or 'déjà vécu'. In essence, it is suggested that if someone is aware that they are suffering from déjà vu, it is not a pathological form.

Other associated phenomena

Jamais vu

Déjà vu has been described as being related to other experiential and familiarity phenomena. One related phenomenon is 'jamais vu', which is often described as being the opposite of déjà vu, coming from the French ('never seen'). Jamais vu occurs when we have a sensation that something we know to be very familiar suddenly seems unreal or unfamiliar to us. Descriptions of this experience in daily life include faces and places, but also procedural acts like playing a musical instrument or driving a car. One can be performing a repetitive act and suddenly have a complete loss of fluency as if becoming lost in a very familiar environment. Perhaps the most common example is with the spelling of words. Occasionally with familiar words we have the sensation that we cannot remember how they are spelt, or the visual written form of a word suddenly looks strange or 'wrong'. This experience has been described as 'word alienation' (see Brown, 2003).

Jamais vu has been described as a symptom in epilepsy and migraine (e.g. Bigal, Lipton, Cohen, & Silberstein, 2003) and its relationship with delusional syndromes has also been evoked in the literature (e.g. Ellis, Luauté, & Retterstøl, 1994). In such cases, it is usually mentioned alongside déjà vu. The literature on jamais vu is radically different from that on déjà vu, however, as there are very few scientific studies on the topic, and no common definition or theory has been advanced. This is perhaps surprising because jamais vu, in the form of word alienation or semantic satiation, has proved rather easy to induce in the laboratory using paradigms of repeated presentation or 'dissociative staring'. In a very early experiment, Severance and Washburn (1907) examined the 'loss of associative power' in words that were stared at for three minutes. They used words "of six letters, printed in long primer type, cut out of the same periodical and placed upon a background of white paper". Their six participants were all women, and had had "a fair amount of introspective training". They noted how the words became strange, lost their meaning and became perceptually fragmented over time. For instance, for the word 'blood',[1] the following reports were given:

24 seconds:	"… b and d look like each other turned backwards, hence meaningless."
60 seconds:	"o's look unfamiliar, staring."
72 seconds:	"b and d look like p and q upside down."
179 seconds:	"a collection of letters"

Severance and Washburn (1907, p. 183)

Similarly, Titchener (cited in Smith & Klein, 1990) remarked upon this phenomenon, but in spoken form: "Repeat aloud some word – the first that occurs to you; house, for instance – over and over again; presently the sound of the word becomes meaningless and blank; you are puzzled and a morsel frightened as you hear it" (Titchener, 1919, pp. 26–27).

More recently, similar experiences have been described in experiments interested in dissociative or 'compulsive' staring (e.g. van den Hout, Engelhard, de Boer, du Bois, & Dek, 2008). In their research, van den Hout and colleagues sought to understand the cognitive basis of obsessive-compulsive disorders, particularly repeated checking behaviours. They state that when behaviours are repeatedly carried out, then this is counterproductive for memory confidence – we are less confident for materials that we have repeatedly checked. First, van den Hout and Kindt (2003) showed that when healthy participants repeatedly 'checked' (20 times) a stimulus (a virtual gas stove) they showed effects of repeated checking. Actual memory accuracy was unaffected, but the vividness, detail and confidence in memory (as measured by subjective rating scales) were greatly reduced. In a follow-up study (van den Hout et al., 2008) focused on perception and the effect of staring. First, participants looked at a gas stove for ten seconds and then completed a questionnaire about it. Next, they were asked to stare at the centre of the gas ring for ten minutes, and were asked "not to talk, avert their gaze, or blink their eyes" (p. 1301). Their main interest was subjective measures of uncertainty, finding that staring at the gas stove significantly increased perceptual uncertainty, captured in the phrase: "I realized that I saw it, but the image was not clear somehow" (p. 1303). For obsessive-compulsive disorder, these results suggest that, at least in part, repeated actions or checking may alter subjective experiences of confidence and perception. They suggest that momentary feelings of unfamiliarity may be conceptually similar to the lack of reality induced by unusually sustained processing of information.

Repeated checking has been linked to the concept of semantic satiation (e.g. Giele et al., 2013), as has jamais vu (e.g. Brown, 2004). Semantic satiation has been described as "the subjective experience of loss of meaning of a word as a result of prolonged inspection and repetition of that word" (Smith & Klein, 1990, p. 852), but it is mostly often applied to more specific, experimental contexts, applying particularly to semantic priming designs. Balota and Black (1997) suggest that semantic satiation occurs because massed 'excessive' processing of a stimulus leads to habituation or satiation: in this way it offers a natural limit to the effects of semantic priming and spreading activation within the memory system. Balota and Black examined semantic satiation in younger and older adults using a semantic memory paradigm. Participants repeatedly saw a word (e.g. dog) twice, 12 or 22 times, then had to make a semantic relatedness judgement on a pair (such as, dog–cat or dog–chair). For younger adults, semantic satiation was shown in that the relatedness effect (the well-documented decrease in reaction times to make a decision for related trials) reduced for the trials where the word was shown more times. For older adults, the same satiation was not found. Interestingly, the third experiment in their paper looked for a similar satiation effect using phonologically related materials (same–claim, same–dime) but found no effect. Whilst satiation effects do not appear to be produced for phonological representations, semantic satiation has at least been shown for processing of faces (Lewis & Ellis, 2000).

For future research into jamais vu, there are two critical considerations. First, it is not known whether repeated exposure is critical for jamais vu in daily life. It seems that jamais vu is a sensation that can be experienced without dissociative staring or repeated exposure. Indeed, when it has been described in temporal lobe epilepsy, it seems to be just as unpredictable and esoteric as the déjà vu experience. Second, the critical issue for jamais vu appears, as with déjà vu, to be its strange, subjective phenomenology. The research into semantic satiation and compulsive staring, for instance, seem to emphasise objective cognitive performance and subjective experience, respectively. In Balota and Black's experiment, for example, it is not sure whether participants felt any unusual sensations during the task, even if their cognitive performance was altered. Thus, future research should ascertain the similarity and differences between everyday versions of the jamais vu experience and those that are experimentally induced by repetition. Moreover, future research should examine whether underlying changes in the dynamic activation of semantic concepts leads to changes in phenomenological experience: does semantic satiation give rise to the feeling of jamais vu?

In sum, there has been very little scientific investigation of jamais vu, but it can be thought of as related to similar concepts induced by repetitive processing, such as word alienation, dissociative staring and semantic satiation. It is thought to occur less frequently in daily life than déjà vu, and although déjà vu and jamais vu are both experienced in the same pathologies, it has still not been reliably demonstrated if the frequency of the two experiences are correlated in healthy groups or not (see Brown, 2004). The fact that it represents a dissociation between a subjective evaluation of unfamiliarity for something which is known to be familiar means that it is likely, at least, to be related to the déjà vu experience conceptually. Of particular interest is the finding that older adults are less susceptible to semantic satiation, and the examination of the experience of jamais vu in older adults is a priority.

Presque vu

There has been even less research into presque vu, translated as 'almost seen'. The links with the déjà vu experience are even less clear, but if nothing else, it also receives interest from those researchers who are leaders in the field of déjà vu. For instance, Cleary (2008, p. 356) describes it as "the feeling that one is on the verge of an epiphany". She invokes research into decision making and suggests a feeling of familiarity may, in problem-solving situations, precede the point at which a problem is solved, leading to the sensation. In this way, the feeling is related to the 'aha' moment, or the sensation of insight which is associated with solving a problem (e.g. Kounios & Beeman, 2014). In the first study of its kind, Kostic, Booth and Cleary (2015) used aphorisms (e.g. the apple doesn't fall far from the tree) and vignettes which exemplified those stories (e.g. *Ben grew up to be very similar to his father. They both watched action films and loved reading political magazines. He followed in his father's footsteps in other ways, too: they both worked as lawyers in the same firm*). They found that participants were likely to report presque vu after failing to identify the story-aphorism match on the first attempt but before succeeding on the second attempt. This ingenious experimentation is undoubtedly of value for theories of problem solving and demonstrates the role of familiarity in sensations of insight.

One issue is whether, defined and operationalised like this, presque vu describes a real-world 'glitch' in memory processing, as do déjà vu and jamais vu. It seems to be a more anodyne version than is captured in the quote from Joseph Heller's *Catch 22* (1961) for instance: "there were other moments when he almost saw absolute truth in brilliant flashes of clarity that almost came to him: presque vu". Also, unlike jamais vu and déjà vu, there is no false sensation or conflict in evaluations when defining presque vu as Kostic et al. have.

To have a form of presque vu that is in keeping with the false feelings in jamais vu and déjà vu, we would have to accept a definition of a feeling of profound insight into something that was in fact false. William James (1882) once described a set of experiences that had this 'false' insight. Whilst intoxicated on nitrous oxide, he noted down several profound fragments and phrases, such as "Reconciliation— econciliation! / By God, how that hurts! By God, how it doesn't hurt! Reconciliation of two extremes. / By George, nothing but othing! / That sounds like nonsense, but it is pure onsense." He described these thoughts as coming from a 'delirium of theoretic rapture'. James (1882, p. 226) writes of his experience of intoxication:

> With me, as with every other individual of whom I have heard, the keynote of the experience is the tremendously exciting sense of an intense metaphysical illumination. Truth lies open to the view in depth beneath depth of almost blinding evidence. The mind sees all the logical relations of being with an apparent subtlety and instantaneity to which its normal consciousness offers no parallel; only as sobriety returns, the feeling of insight fades, and one is left staring vacantly at a few disjointed words and phrases, as one stares at a cadaverous-looking snow peak from which the sunset glow has just fled, or at the black cinder left by an extinguished brand.

At least anecdotally, it seems that in stress and fatigue, as with the déjà vu experience, we may be prone to having such momentary profound insights that turn out to be false. This might including waking up in the night with ideas thought to be really important or novel, or sudden realisations of how the world works, which on closer examination are false or facile. In truth, whether the subjective experience of presque vu is a useful one in cognition or in clinical research is an issue that needs more attention.

Summary: a dual-process metacognitive account of déjà vu

Chapter 3 outlines an account of recognition memory that posits that there are two levels of analysis in recognition memory. A feeling of familiarity is produced in response to a mismatch between the state of knowledge and the processing of the stimulus: in his or her butcher's shop, the butcher does not give rise to a strong feeling of familiarity. It is the mismatch between the context and familiarity of the face that produces the strong experience on the bus. A metacognitive evaluation of the memory trace raises this mismatch to consciousness: we are aware of the out-of-context familiarity. A parallel account of déjà vu can be advanced. Déjà vu can also be thought of as an experience of which the key phenomenology is of familiarity (see also Martin, Fiacconi, & Köhler, 2015). However, it is not merely a feeling of false familiarity, because this would be experienced as confusion, uncertainty, or indeed, we would just make the attribution that we are indeed encountering something we have encountered before. Instead, a key component of the experience is the combination of familiarity with the certainty that the familiarity is false. In Whittlesea's terms, the intensity of the familiarity, in the short time it persists before it is overcome by a rational explanation, is magnified by the certainty that the feeling is false.

This dual-process definition of déjà vu is shared by most contemporary theorists, and it neatly maps onto our understanding of the metacognitive system and the notion of epistemic feelings that guide and interpret the activity of the memory system. It is also a useful definition because excess familiarity alone is not enough to be described as déjà vu. If we are delusional and cannot rationally oppose the feelings of familiarity, then this state should be described as pathological. In this way, by definition, one could never have an experience of déjà vu without knowing it; it is a metacognitive experience.

Note

1 The use of the word blood, given as an example, appears to be at odds with the brief presentation of the method, which states that six-letter words were used.

5

THEORIES OF DÉJÀ VU FORMATION

> Theories are like toothbrushes: everybody has to have one; no one wants to use anybody else's.
>
> *Anonymous*
> *(cited by Alan Baddeley, at the International Conference on Memory,*
> *Sydney, 2006)*

This chapter starts out by reviewing the popular and historical theories of déjà vu formation, before moving onto contemporary scientific theories. The first two are the source amnesia and Gestalt similarity accounts, which both draw their support from a handful of experiments on healthy participants. These experiments are reviewed in more detail in Chapter 10, and it is recommended to read these two chapters together. Third, there is the decoupled familiarity hypothesis, which takes as its support findings from neuropsychological populations, most notably temporal lobe epilepsy, which again is covered in more detail in its own chapter (Chapter 7). It will be seen that these three theories fall into one of two categories of explanation: that déjà vu is caused by a particular stimulus, and is therefore 'bottom-up', or that déjà vu is merely a neurological event without a specific trigger in the environment. Briefly, as has been developed over the first four chapters in this book, the idea is that déjà vu is a memory phenomenon and, as such, should be researched with recourse to the theoretical state of the art in memory research. This chapter presents the three key memory theories of déjà vu and introduces the reader to the literatures on which these theories are based, although this experimental and clinical work is expanded on in subsequent chapters.

Popular theories of déjà vu formation

Dual-pathway accounts

Aside of metaphysical or religious explanations, possibly the most popular explana-tion of déjà vu amongst lay people is the dual pathway, or 'split consciousness' idea. There is a visual version of this idea, that déjà vu is caused by information from one eye being processed in advance of the other, the 'optical pathway delay' theory (e.g. Osborn, 1884). This idea has been dispatched with the most minimal of empirical work – the demonstration of déjà vu in one blind case study (MT; O'Connor & Moulin, 2006). This perhaps makes the more specific point that if we are to con-sider dual-pathway accounts, they cannot focus purely on visual perception. The fact that congenitally blind people experience déjà vu means that it is not a purely visual experience, and our theories need to explain the phenomenon at a higher level of analysis.

More generally, the dual-pathway theory (e.g. Wigan, 1844; Titchener, 1919/ 1928) posits that consciousness somehow becomes split. Typically, this theory invokes the idea that a signal between one hemisphere and the other becomes delayed, such that information arrives a moment too late to consciousness, and is out of sync with another signal which has already arrived and relayed the same information.[1] The main problem with this theory is that it no longer tallies with information about how the brain processes information, and it is somehow a throwback to early anatomical ideas about the hemispheres. One easy test of the idea would be to examine déjà vu incidence in people with absent or dysfunctional corpus collosa, but this – to the best of my knowledge – has never been examined. These dual-pathway accounts usually discuss two separable streams of 'conscious-ness' (e.g. Penfield & Perot, 1963). Given that such vague theories of consciousness tend to be difficult to sustain scientifically and require further specification into component parts with identifiable neural processes (e.g. Dennett, 1991), describing déjà vu like this is problematic – it is little more than a poorly specified redescrip-tion of the phenomenon. However, that does not mean that there is not dissociation between two processes, as Spatt (2002) states:

> Cognitive neurosciences have demonstrated that cognitive processes can be dissociated, that they often work in parallel, and that they do not converge on a "central observer." Normally all of these processes work together in a way that gives us the impression of a unitary process. Only when something goes wrong does the distinctness of these processes become observable.
>
> *Spatt (2002, p. 9)*

That is, it is clear that some kind of dissociation exists in the déjà vu experience – but in dual-process theories of recognition memory (see Chapter 3), there are enough requisite processes to produce the dissociation required for the feeling of déjà vu – we do not need to posit anything as vague as a 'dual' or 'split' *consciousness*.

In some cases, therefore, this dual pathway account is an appropriate one: it's just that what the pathways are, and in what system they are working, needs more examination. However, as Spatt points out, there is a serious problem with the dual-pathway theory as often described. If there was a doubling of consciousness with dual pathways in the brain, this should really lead to a brief sensation that something had *only just* repeated. In fact, in déjà vu, it usually feels that the repetition is from an undefined or distant past.

Psychoanalytic accounts of déjà vu

A further set of popular theories stem from the psychoanalytic approach, and centre on the fact that déjà vu is caused by the 'memory' of material previously encountered in a dream (often described as a 'precognitive dream') or fantasies. Freud discusses various memory phenomena in the *Psychopathology of Everyday Life* and suggests that déjà vu derives from repressed desires and fantasies (he actually uses the phrase 'déjà vu'). In a lengthy section (pp. 198–206, Penguin edition, 1939), Freud explains various forms of experiential phenomena, including déjà vu and precognitive dreams. His view is that déjà vu is recognition of unconsciously processed information, which, as we will see below, is not unlike many contemporary theories:

> It is in my view wrong to call the feeling of having experienced something before an illusion. It is rather that at such moments something is really touched on which we have already experienced once before, only we cannot consciously remember it because it has never been conscious.
>
> *Freud (1939, p. 203)*

Unsurprisingly, whereas Freud emphasised repressed dreams or 'daydreams' in the formation of déjà vu, for Carl Jung it was centred on the collective consciousness – in that sense each theorist takes forward déjà vu as proof for their own theory. Jung claimed that déjà vu was caused by the partial retrieval of memories from the 'collective consciousness', and described it as an 'anti-epiphany' (Arnold, 2002):

> On a jagged rock above us a slim brownish-black figure stood motionless, leaning on a long spear, looking down at the train. Beside him towered a gigantic candelabrum cactus.
> I was enchanted by this sight – it was a picture of something utterly alien and outside my experience, but on the other hand a most intense *sentiment du déjà vu*. I had the feeling that I had already experienced this moment and had always known this world which was separated from me only by distance in time. It was as if I were at this moment returning to the land of my youth, and as if I knew that dark-skinned man who had been waiting for me for five thousand years.

> The feeling-tone of this curious experience accompanied me throughout my whole journey through savage Africa … I could not guess what string within myself was plucked at the sight of that solitary dark hunter. I only knew that his world had been mine for countless millennia.
>
> *Jung (1961, p. 283)*

Echoing the ideas of Freud and Jung, people continue to think that their experiences of déjà vu are dream-like, and seek to explain them by saying that they encountered a similar or identical experience or situation in a dream. In contemporary research, Funkhouser and Schredl (2010) have argued that déjà vu connected to dreams is a separate experience – this work is reviewed in Chapter 6.

Although the psychoanalytic theories no longer offer much to memory explanations of déjà vu, the idea that déjà vu is related to dreaming is something that warrants further explanation. There is nothing particularly troublesome for a memory account of déjà vu in the idea that previously dreamed material leads to feelings of familiarity. Indeed, in this regard dreams are no different from any other previous experience. Dreams and imagined events, just as real autobiographical episodes, can all be represented in the memory system and if, as developed below, partial or impoverished memories for previous events lead to the experience, then there is no reason why it is not possible that dreams are involved in déjà vu formation. Indeed, Gerrans (2014, p. 1), in a philosophical review states that: "Comparing the way the mind responds to the experience of hyperfamiliarity in different conditions such as delusions, dreams, pathological and non-pathological déjà vu, provides a way to understand claims that delusions and dreams are both states characterized by deficient 'reality testing'". Reality testing is a particular form of memory for the source of information, and this is in fact a current theory of déjà vu formation (see below). Here, it is stressed that there is little to suggest that dreams are the *only* cause for the déjà vu experience. However, there is no reason why they should *not* be a source of information which generates a subsequent déjà vu experience. Of course, the argument here is not for the existence of precognitive dreams, but rather an overlap, or perceived overlap, between materials previously generated in a dream and the current situation. As will be developed in Chapter 6, however, a major challenge for research in this field is to overcome the criticism that the participants merely justify their déjà vu with a post-hoc rationalisation based on the recall of a dream – using one subjective and nebulous entity to explain another.

Erroneous pattern-matching

A final popular explanation is that of erroneous pattern-matching. This is an idea that has been popular with scientists, but has received very little empirical support, mostly because nobody involved in empirical work with humans has raised it as a possibility. This report taken from the media, from Nobel prize-winning neuroscientist Tonegawa, came from his overview of a study about pattern-matching, using a genetic model of Alzheimer's disease in mice (which affects the growth of the dentate gyrus):

> "These animals normally have a distinct ability to distinguish between situations," Tonegawa said, like humans. "But without the dentate gyrus they were very mixed up." ... Déjà vu is a memory problem, Tonegawa explained, occurring when our brains struggle to tell the difference between two extremely similar situations.
>
> *Mosher (2007)*

Tonegawa's paper (McHugh et al., 2007) makes an undoubted contribution to the field of memory. It considers a very fundamental aspect of memory – that we might match 'patterns' of activation in the brain. That is, the reason we recognise something is because it makes a pattern of activation in the brain that we can match to existing representations. We return to Tonegawa's quote and ideas in Chapter 6, but here it is worth noting that the pattern mismatch account as articulated by Tonegawa does not differentiate common-or-garden false positives with the experience of déjà vu. The idea of similarities between a previous experience, scene or event is, in fact, something that is discussed below and is a plausible account of déjà vu formation. It is even possible that this involves the dentate gyrus and pattern-matching processes, but it is probably too early in the development of the cognitive neuroscience of déjà vu to tell. However, the main issue with the pattern-matching account is that it does not offer enough specification. We still have to explain the critical difference between making a false positive response due to familiarity and the ability to know that a feeling of intense familiarity is in fact false. This implies a higher-order interpretation of memory processes in déjà vu, raising an interesting question: could a mouse experience déjà vu?

Contemporary memory theories of déjà vu formation

In Brown's (2003) review, he proposes four categories of scientific accounts of déjà vu. First, there are the dual-processing accounts, whereby two cognitive processes are momentarily out of synchrony. This account is somewhat vague in that these desynchronised processes could be perceptual or any other realm of cognition, and indeed, in terms of memory, this proposition is an adequate description of déjà vu: the sensation of familiarity is out of synchrony with the knowledge of the current situation: *it feels like I've been here before, but I know it is my first time in New York.* Brown's second category of explanation is neurological, such as minor seizure activity (even in healthy people) or the disruption of neuronal transmission – not unlike the optical pathway delay discussed above. Again, at some level, we must imagine that déjà vu has a neurological basis, even if it does not have a neurological cause, so this may be a question of considering what level of explanation we wish to pursue. There is a conceptual overlap between Brown's proposal of this neurological category and the decoupled familiarity hypothesis discussed below, as the neurological account suggests that the cause is ultimately not something in the environment, but a temporary fault in the brain. However, specifying the problem as neurological does little to specify the candidate cognitive mechanism involved. For that reason, it is probably safe, even if we consider the problem to be broadly neurological, to focus on the memory system as the neurological location of the experience. The understanding of the brain–behaviour (or biology–psychology) relationship is called into question when one overlooks the brain in cognitive explanations, or cognition in brain-based explanations, as was articulated by Brown and Marsh (2010, pp. 57–58):

> If a déjà vu experience can be identified as a likely result of one possible mechanism, this does not necessarily rule out others … Similarly, forgetting where you put your car keys could be traced to biological (fatigue, stress, low blood sugar) as well as psychological (distraction, multitasking) circumstances. Proving one cause for a particular incident does not rule out other possibilities.

Brown's third category is memory, more specifically 'implicit familiarity of unrecognised stimuli', whereby the activation of a stimulus in the environment is somehow enhanced such that it feels familiar without the experient knowing why it is familiar. This explanation has been influential in the experimental work that followed Brown's review, and is presented in detail in this chapter and in Chapter 10. It has been influential because it delivers a readily testable theory of déjà vu formation, something which, at least at first glance, seems easy to reproduce in the laboratory. Brown's final category of explanation is attentional, which too is somewhat related to the memory account above. Brown describes this as 'unattended perception followed by attended perception' and so emphasises perceptual mechanisms, but the same proposal could be made for memory too. That is, we encounter something but only superficially encode it, and then encounter it (perhaps even directly after) and find it familiar because of the prior processing of the information. Put like this, the generation of déjà vu arises, again, because of memory systems that are operating in an unattended or desynchronised fashion. Even though inattention may be the root cause, we would still have to consider this as a memory phenomenon, even if we merely describe the initial inattention as a failure to adequately encode the information in perception into memory.

Thus, the argument here is that these four categories of explanation all draw upon contemporary memory theory. The principal argument for this issue is that even for the attention account, for example, the test of the theory is with using an experiment that has the characteristics of an implicit memory (priming) paradigm. Brown's four categories all relate in some way to memory function, and the next section in this chapter specifies this memory account of déjà vu in more detail. Here, it is proposed that there are three broad memory theories of déjà vu formation that draw on different literatures, but which are all sustainable according to current explanations of human memory. They are not necessarily mutually exclusive accounts of déjà vu – as indicated above. In order these three accounts can be divided into the source amnesia account (e.g. Brown & Marsh, 2008), the Gestalt similarity hypothesis (e.g. Cleary et al., 2012; Dashiell, 1937) and the decoupled familiarity hypothesis (e.g. Illman, Butler, Souchay, & Moulin, 2012; Penfield, 1955; Spatt, 2002).

Source amnesia for familiar stimuli

A famous early quote about déjà vu from Nathaniel Hawthorne describes how it may be produced by the prior exposure to information that is subsequently forgotten. In *Our Old Home: A Series of English Sketches* (1863), Hawthorne describes visiting the kitchen at Stanton Harcourt:

> Now – the place being without a parallel in England, and therefore necessarily beyond the experience of an American – it is somewhat remarkable, that, while we stood gazing at this kitchen, I was haunted and perplexed by an idea that somewhere or other I had seen just this strange spectacle before. – The height, the blackness, the dismal void, before my eyes, seemed as familiar as the decorous neatness of my grandmother's kitchen; only my unaccountable memory of the scene was lighted up with an image of lurid fires blazing all round the dim interior circuit of the tower. I had never before had so pertinacious an attack, as I could not but suppose it, of that odd state of mind wherein we fitfully and teasingly remember some previous scene or incident, of which the one now passing appears to be but the echo and reduplication. Though the explanation of the mystery did not for some time occur to me, I may as well conclude the matter here. In a letter of Pope's, addressed to the Duke of Buckingham, there is an account of Stanton Harcourt (as I now find, although the name is not mentioned), where he resided while translating a part of the "Iliad". It is one of the most admirable pieces of description in the language, – playful and picturesque, with fine touches of humorous pathos, – and conveys as perfect a picture as ever was drawn of a decayed English country-house; and among other rooms, most of which have since crumbled down and disappeared, he dashes off the grim aspect of this kitchen, – which, moreover, he peoples with witches, engaging Satan himself as headcook, who stirs the infernal caldrons that seethe and bubble over the fires. This letter, and others relative to his abode here, were very familiar to my earlier reading, and, remaining still fresh at the bottom of my memory, caused the weird and ghostly sensation that came over one on beholding the real spectacle that had formerly been made so vivid to my imagination.
>
> *Hawthorne, 1863 (iBook edition)*

Source amnesia has been described in a number of experimental contexts, but mainly stems from neuropsychological research on amnesia. Several authors have noted that people with memory impairment might be able to acquire and retrieve (new) information, but not be aware of how they acquired it. Schacter, Harbluk and McLachlan (1984) describe source amnesia as 'retrieval without recollection'. They carried out experiments on people with amnesia (Experiment 1) and healthy undergraduates (Experiment 2), whereby participants were presented with fictional characteristics of well-known and unknown people by one of two experimenters. The amnesics showed source amnesia after retention intervals of seconds or minutes: on over a third of trials where they retrieved a target item (item recall), they failed to recollect that either of the experimenters had taught the fact to them. The healthy undergraduates demonstrated that even when item recall was equivalent to that of amnesics, they exhibited less source amnesia – typically, they might not remember which of the experimenters had presented the information, even though they could report the source of the information more generally. In line with the account of 'something more' in recollection in Chapter 3, the idea is that when we have complete recollection, we are able to retrieve something of the source of the item, as was explained in Perfect et al. (1996). A special category of source information is the ability to later distinguish between previous episodes that were real or imagined – described as 'reality monitoring' (e.g. Johnson & Raye, 1981).

The idea is that material is familiar because it has been encountered before; déjà vu arises because we forget the source of the information, or perhaps the source of the information was never consciously known. If processing at encoding is sufficiently shallow, or the interval between encoding and retrieval sufficiently long, we may find information highly familiar without being able to remember why. For instance, we may have read about, or seen in a movie, the exact same corner of the street in New York where we experience déjà vu when being there for the first time, but we cannot recollect why or how we have this familiarity, so interpret the feeling as déjà vu.

The source amnesia account of déjà vu is concrete enough to lend itself to empirical investigation. Invoking such a theory, Brown and Marsh (2008) have produced an illusion comparable to déjà vu in the laboratory. In their study, in a first phase, participants briefly processed photos of locations on their own university campus, or on another campus (where they have never been). At encoding they were instructed to concentrate on another task, which ensured a superficial encoding of the pictures (just detecting in which of four quadrants was a small cross). In a later session, participants viewed the pictures again, this time saying whether or not they thought they had been to those places or not. Brown and Marsh found that participants who were exposed to pictures without processing them deeply were more likely to report that they had visited that location. If this simple finding were extended to the real world, where you may arrive at a location and find it familiar, but not know why, it may feel something like déjà vu. However they do not mention déjà vu. explicitly until the discussion of the paper, suggesting that it arises when: "part or all of a particular situation may actually have been previously experienced but not explicitly recollected" (Brown & Marsh, 2008, p. 190).

In an early article on memory and unconscious processes Jacoby and Whitehouse (1989) examined false recognition influenced by unconscious perception. This article is notable for citing Titchener's (1928) paramnesia as an illusion of memory that is produced by "a disjunction of processes that are normally held together in a conscious present" (p. 425), which is held by many to be a description of déjà vu, as explained by Jacoby and Whitehouse. The idea, much like the Brown and Marsh (2008) experiment, is that superficial processing at encoding can lead to subsequent familiarity (what Titchener described as a 'preliminary glance' which later gave rise to a 'feeling of familiarity'). Although Titchener's account of déjà vu is usually described as a 'splitting of consciousness', Jacoby and Whitehouse used this as inspiration for an experiment using subliminal presentations of words. They presented a long list of words that people were instructed to remember for a later test. A standard recognition memory test followed, except that when the words were presented for a recognition decision, they were preceded with a flashed, masked word. This word either matched the test word, or was a context word that did not match the test word. In a baseline condition, there was no context word. There was a between-subjects manipulation of presentation duration and instructions, such that participants in one condition were aware of the context word (200 ms), and unaware in the other condition (50 ms). Thus, there was a situation (in both conditions) where the familiarity for a distracter or target word had been increased. Jacoby and Whitehouse's emphasis was on whether the priming of the recognition decision influenced false positives – and this is most pertinent to our discussion of déjà vu. They found (Experiment 1) that the probability of making a false positive following a prime with the identical word was .36 in the unaware condition and .24 in the aware condition. There was an interaction, too, such that when the primes did not match the word, the unaware group was less likely to make a false positive (.19), but the aware group was more likely to identify a new word as old (.29). In their discussion, Jacoby and Whitehouse emphasise their theory of fluency and memory, stating that the priming effects shown are evidence for fluency of processing a word as being interpreted as a memory signal – that of familiarity. That is, their account, like the Whittlesea material covered in Chapter 3, is one of attribution. The results cannot be interpreted by priming alone, but as a reflection on why something feels familiar: hence the difference in effects for the unaware and aware conditions. If you know that your memory has been manipulated, you are less likely to show this effect of the prior presentation of the word (again this is directly comparable to Goldinger & Hansen's (2005) results). In a final sentence, Jacoby and Whitehouse sum up their findings:

> We are not really certain that our experiments and arguments are totally in line with the ideas that Titchener had in mind. But, then, the attribution of ideas to a source is always open to error, even when the source that is in question is one's own past.
>
> *Jacoby & Whitehouse (1989, p. 135)*

As a general principle, the Jacoby and Whitehouse article seems to offer an important proof of concept that subliminal or incidental processing of a stimulus could affect later processing of that stimulus. It is not clear if any of their participants experienced anything like déjà vu, and it is not really mentioned in the article. It would have been interesting, in a post-experimental questionnaire, to examine the subjective experience of the attribution process in memory during the recognition task.

This experiment raises an important issue – the distinction between false positive errors and déjà vu. Although both may arise from feelings of familiarity, the familiarity in the Jacoby and Whitehouse article is uncorrected – the participants merely increase their false positive rate, presumably because they are not aware of the source of the familiarity of the words. However, in a déjà vu experience, we adjust our interpretation in the other direction: we do not make a false positive, because at the same time as feeling that something is familiar, our attribution is that this is a fault. So in that sense, the familiarity part is just half the story. If we really found something very familiar but could not oppose such a feeling metacognitively by the retrieval of contrary evidence, we would simply make a false positive error – I *have* been here before. Thus, two important points come out of the Jacoby and Whitehouse paper: (1) it is not clear if this 'familiarity' illusion is the same as déjà vu (more generally) and (2) it is not known if the participants did actually feel déjà vu (in this article specifically).

The Gestalt similarity hypothesis

The difficulty with the source amnesia account is that identical materials have already been previously perceived (albeit perhaps subconsciously) in all the laboratory analogues. This means that, in fact, the feeling of déjà vu is not (at least objectively) false: there is indeed an underlying familiarity for an item, even if it was seen for only 50 ms. It is not clear how this might work in the real world because (a) déjà vu can occur for completely novel scenarios, and (b) it is difficult to imagine how the subliminal activation of concepts and ideas arises in the real world. The key feature of the similarity hypothesis is that there is some overlap between a perceptual experience (which is responsible for triggering the déjà vu) and a previously stored representation, not unlike the pattern mismatch idea above. That is, an identical repetition of a stimulus is not necessary to produce it.

The Gestalt similarity hypothesis is broadly the same as the source amnesia account above, except that the feeling is triggered by similarity, not merely forgetting (or superficial encoding). As an example, Knight (1895) experienced familiarity whilst in Tibet, and subsequently suggested that this was due to the vivid descriptions of Lepta in Swift's *Gulliver's Travels*, a similarity which was not retrieved initially. This seems perhaps like an account of familiarity akin to the butcher on the bus phenomenon (described in the previous chapter) and, unlike the Hawthorne quote above, we are not sure if this feeling, as it lasted for 'some time', was really like déjà vu at all.

> For some time I was greatly puzzled while wandering through this region. It all, in a way, seemed so familiar to me. Surely I had somewhere, long ago,

lived amid this curious people and in such a weird land as this – but when and where? Was I myself a Ladaki re-incarnated in England by mistake? was I a degraded Mahatma, now recognising feebly once more the long-lost country of my origin? The idea was not a pleasant one, and I felt quite relieved, at last, when the explanation of this mysterious feeling flashed across me. Yes; I had lived before among these people. I remembered that when a small boy I had read 'Gulliver's Travels,' and that the voyage to the flying island of Laputa had made a great impression on my imagination. I had conjured up that kingdom to my mind just such a perspectiveless, artificial, unreal-looking land as this; and just such a people as these queer Ladakis had those no more queer people, the Laputans and the sages of Balnibarri, appeared to my fancy.

Knight (1895) (iBook edition)

Contemporary views of this explanation place an emphasis on configural similarity. The 'Gestalt' in the title refers to an overarching 'form' or 'structure' into which perceptual elements can fall:

déjà vu is elicited by familiarity with the arrangement of the elements within a scene. For example, when visiting a friend's home for the first time, one may have a strange sense of having been in that living room before. Perhaps the arrangement of the furniture in the new friend's living room (e.g., the way that the couches, tables and lamps are arranged) maps onto an arrangement that was seen before, perhaps in the person's doctor's office waiting area. The inability to recall the doctor's office waiting area as the source of this familiarity leads to the experience of déjà vu.

Cleary et al. (2012, p. 969)

The critical issue is developed in the last sentence of this quote: the experient must be unaware of the source of the familiarity, and this leads to the inherent conflict in feelings in the experience – in this sense, it is like the source amnesia account above. Again, the beauty of this account of déjà vu is that it lends itself to an existing laboratory task, the recognition without identification paradigm, which is where it is possible to make a stimulus familiar in such a way that the participant is not aware of the source of the familiarity (e.g. Cleary et al., 2012; Cleary, Ryals, & Nomi, 2009; Cleary & Reyes, 2009; Cleary, 2008).

In perhaps its most elegant manifestation (Cleary et al., 2012), participants 'study' rooms in a virtual reality environment (where the experimenter provides a label, such as 'bedroom'). Participants then encounter similar and dissimilar rooms in a test (Experiment 1) or similar, dissimilar and identical rooms (Experiment 2). Participants report whether they can recall the label, followed by a rating of familiarity for the room and a report (yes/no) as to whether they are experiencing déjà vu. Cleary and colleagues arrange the test rooms such that half match the studied rooms configurally, and half do not. In Experiment 1, they report that participants can recall the label of nearly half the configurally similar rooms, leaving a set of rooms which are similar in some way, but where the similarity is undetected. These similar rooms can be compared to the rooms which do not resemble previously encountered rooms. The experience of déjà vu was measured for these rooms with a yes/no question, with 27 per cent of similar rooms giving rise to déjà vu, significantly higher than for the dissimilar rooms (17 per cent). Furthermore, the familiarity ratings were higher for the configurally similar scenes, and an item-by-item correlation showed that the more familiar a room feels, the more likely it was to give rise to a feeling of déjà vu. Experiment 2 produced similar results, with again participants reporting déjà vu experiences on about a third of items.

The decoupled familiarity hypothesis

An alternate (but not opposing) view is that déjà vu arises when the sensation of familiarity becomes decoupled from the current outputs of memory processing, such that there is a false feeling of familiarity independently from what is actually being perceived in the environment. This false feeling is then corrected by intact recollection mechanisms, as described in Chapter 3: a top-down correction is applied which counteracts the familiarity that is being sensed. The decoupled familiarity hypothesis has largely been argued from a neuropsychological viewpoint, such that the false familiarity is produced by a random brain event.

The chief support for the decoupled familiarity idea has been neuropsychological, arising from data from neurological populations, most particularly temporal lobe epilepsy (TLE; see Illman et al., 2012). An early presentation of this idea (O'Connor & Moulin, 2008) emphasised that whereas the Gestalt similarity hypothesis was essentially driven by the environment (i.e. is bottom-up), the decoupled familiarity hypothesis is top-down – an error caused by processing problems in the brain. The genesis of this idea was the observation that in cases of TLE, the feeling of déjà vu is essentially unpredictable, and when it does occur, it is felt for all domains and modalities, and does not reduce according to what the experient pays attention to (the same occurs in other pathologies (e.g. Kalra & Zeman, 2007) – see the illustrative quotes in Table 1.1).

Spatt's account of déjà vu in 2002 is perhaps, to date, the clearest neuroscientific theory of déjà vu. He suggests that it is a 'possible' parahippocampal region that is at fault, in keeping with dual-process accounts of memory (e.g. Aggleton & Brown, 1999). His account is unique in that it takes as its main evidence the epileptic literature on déjà vu, and makes a reasoned account of déjà vu in healthy people based on epilepsy. Spatt's theory is that déjà vu is a by-product of the memory system, in the same way that dreams can be considered a by-product of the cognitive system responsible for wakeful activity, and he sums it up thus:

> I argue that [déjà vu] is the phenomenological result of a false activation of connections between mesiotemporal memory structures and neocortical areas directly involved in the perception of the environment. This false activation results in wrongly labelling a momentary perceived scene as familiar.
>
> *Spatt (2002, p. 8)*

Summary: a phenomenon in search of a theory

It has been previously noted that there is probably far too much theorising about déjà vu in the absence of a strong empirical basis for those theories (Moulin & Chauvel, 2010). The number of possible accounts has been reduced to three broad memory theories of déjà vu formation which are sustainable according to contemporary memory theory, and which receive some empirical support. The first two discussed here posit some environmental similarity or superficial processing that triggers the false familiarity (in that sense they are broadly related), and these can be described as environmentally driven or bottom-up theories. The third theory derives from a different literature – that of memory dysfunction and the 'dreamy state', particularly in epilepsy – and is essentially top-down, caused by a temporary glitch in memory processing. Critically, the first two theories are data-driven or bottom-up, in that they are caused by the processing of something in the environment and its relation to a pre-existing stimulus. As such, it should be possible, in theory, to pinpoint 'why' someone has déjà vu at any point. This idea is common with the nineteenth century and psychodynamic theories of déjà vu – there is a reason for why déjà vu is experienced, even if it is an anodyne, perceptual reason, or a resemblance to something in the 'undefined' past. In contrast, the decoupled familiarity hypothesis is a top-down account, and suggests that déjà vu is a random, biological event that is not linked to what is going on in the environment. This has its roots too in historical work, most notably the early ideas of Hughlings Jackson and the research into epilepsy. One major criticism of this top-down account of déjà vu is that it makes déjà vu very difficult to study in healthy groups if the only reason for the 'pure' form of the experience is a momentary glitch in processing in the temporal lobe. Furthermore, it places a heavy emphasis on memory pathology and dysfunction, and is therefore open to the criticism that healthy and pathological forms of déjà vu differ in some way.

One theme that dominates this chapter is the nature of the different accounts of déjà vu. The decoupled familiarity view is grounded in neuropsychological populations, whereas the Gestalt and source amnesia accounts derive from the experimental psychology tradition of North America. As such, it is worth noting that whereas the Gestalt familiarity hypothesis may be better suited to describing déjà vu formation in healthy populations, it is unclear whether it extends to epileptic cases, where it is easier to propose a neurological basis to the problem. The same criticism can be made of using the neuropsychological approach and abnormal brains to theorise about déjà vu in healthy populations. It should be stressed here that the three theories are not necessarily mutually exclusive, and that there may be multiple causes for the déjà vu experience. Even if in daily life it may appear due to fatigue or migraine activity, it may be cognitively identical to cases where it is provoked in the laboratory, or where an overlap with a previous experience leads to the sensation. In any case, a strong theory of déjà vu formation should be able to explain both accounts and both sets of data. Just as with the cognitive neuropsychology of memory more generally, neuropsychological groups (in this case people who repeatedly experience déjà vu) should constrain our theories, and provide the test that proves the rule.

Finally, the non-memory accounts of déjà vu have been skimmed over in this chapter, but they offer an important historical context for the research domain and develop the material given in Chapter 2. Although we would no longer sustain a purely psychoanalytical account of déjà vu, for instance, nor could we yet endorse Tonegawa's specific pattern-matching account, it should be acknowledged that these ideas have some value for current theory. They describe how déjà vu arises because of a failure to recall why and how something is familiar, or suggest that there are similarities between what is perceived and what is stored. The idea of dissociation between processes is an extremely useful way of thinking about déjà vu. Most importantly, even the idea of the two hemispheres working out of sync as being the reason for déjà vu needs further investigation, due to its role in hyper-familiarity feelings for unknown faces (Negro et al., 2015). This suggests that the synchronisation of hemispheres may be involved in at least some familiarity phenomena, but that, at the same time, it is the familiarity circuits of the temporal lobe, which we can understand through memory theory, which are the place to start our consideration of the cognitive neuropsychology of déjà vu.

Note

1 Interestingly, there exists an inter-hemispheric account of a peculiar disorder, that of 'hyperfamiliarity for faces' (e.g. Negro et al., 2015), but it is beyond the scope of this book to address this disorder in too much detail. In short, Negro et al. describe this disorder as "the loss of coordinated activity between the complementary face processing functions of the left and right temporal lobes" (p. 1). A relatively rare disorder, hyperfamiliarity for faces occurs following brain damage and where there is an abnormal feeling of familiarity (usually a chronic problem) for faces, even when there is no recognition deficit for faces, not to be confused with prosopagnosia or Capgras' delusion. Negro et al.'s case (GN) experienced hyperfamiliarity "constantly throughout the day to the extent that for many (unknown) persons met or seen, GN engaged in effortful memory searching, trying to remember the circumstances, episodes and reasons that made the person's face look familiar. The failure to recall such circumstance, and the stress related to it, leaded her to social detachment, as she stopped leaving the house or watching TV. By contrast, her ability to recognize truly familiar faces was unimpaired and correct recognition was associated with retrieval of the specific identity and correct name" (pp. 2–3). Hyperfamiliarity for faces should not be confused with recollective confabulation (Chapter 8) because the experient is aware that their sense of familiarity is false. The relationship between hyper-familiarity for faces, on which there is a growing literature, and déjà vu is not known. For déjà vu it is an interesting disorder because it seems to be a chronic form of false familiarity which, when it occurs, applies only to faces and does not extend to other forms of visual information.

6

INDIVIDUAL DIFFERENCE STUDIES OF DÉJÀ VU

The length of a person's right arm correlates with the length of his right arm about .98, i.e. very near perfection; the length of his nose, however, shows very low correlations on the average with the size of his feet.

Eysenck (1953, p. 31)

Much of the early research in déjà vu was based on an individual differences approach using data collected from large-scale surveys. This work tended to amount to a natural history and definition of the experience rather than theory-driven research. Correlations are found, for instance, between déjà vu frequency and the number of journeys taken away from where you live (e.g. Chapman & Mensh, 1951; Richardson & Winokur, 1967). Correlations have been used to argue about the triggers and causes of déjà vu – such as dreams; and the factors associated with the experience – such as age. This chapter presents the current state of the art in the individual differences approach – beginning by examining the effect of age on the frequency of déjà vu experiences, and also considering other factors shown to commonly correlate with déjà vu experience: such as the recall of dreams. The most recent studies to use this approach have correlated the frequency of déjà vu with the size and connectivity of certain brain structures, an extremely promising development for better understanding déjà vu.

Déjà vu across the lifespan

Consider again the quotes by the Nobel prize-winning neuroscientist, Tonegawa, which he made with reference to aging, Alzheimer's disease and memory impairment. Recall that he was discussing memory performance in mice.

"These animals normally have a distinct ability to distinguish between situations," Tonegawa said, like humans. "But without the dentate gyrus they were very mixed up."

Déjà vu is a memory problem, Tonegawa explained, occurring when our brains struggle to tell the difference between two extremely similar situations. As people age, Tonegawa said déjà vu-like confusion happens more often – and it also happens in people suffering from brain diseases like Alzheimer's. "It's not surprising," he said, "when you consider the fact that there's a loss of or damage to cells in the dentate gyrus."

As an aging neuroscientist, Tonegawa admitted it's a typical phenomenon with him. "I do a lot of travelling so I show up in brand new airports, and my brain tells me it's been here before," he said. "But the rest of my brain knows better."

Mosher (2007)

Tonegawa's observation goes against one of the few consistent findings in déjà vu research: that older people report fewer instances of déjà vu. Some correlations between age and frequency of the experience are given in Table 6.1. The relationship between (increasing) age and (decreased) déjà vu is actually so well-known that Sno, Schalken, de Jonghe and Koeter (1994) used this variable to assess the validity of their individual differences measure of déjà vu (Table 6.4). Additionally, reviewing studies which report mean age, Brown (2004) found that those studies with an older sample had a lower lifetime incidence of the phenomenon, $r(13) = -.44$. This is a critical issue because the theories of déjà vu formation reviewed in the preceding chapter connect it with episodic memory function, and so we might expect it to increase with age, not decrease, since episodic memory function declines as part of the healthy aging process. Thus, the aging effect – if it is genuine – might help us explain the cognitive basis of déjà vu experiences, knowing what we know about memory function in healthy older adults. However, looking at the mean ages in Table 6.1, it can be seen that the samples are not particularly old. Moreover, cohort effects need to be considered.

Cohort effects and déjà vu

One problem with concluding that older adults have fewer déjà vu experiences is that all the studies which examine this issue have been cross-sectional, i.e. comparing groups of people of different ages, rather than longitudinal, following the same individuals over time. In aging research such designs fall foul of cohort effects, whereby the differences that we intend to measure between different age groups actually reflect cultural differences and environmental differences between those groups rather than the internal psychological processes at work in the aging individual, or age per se (Back & Bourque, 1970). The best way to control for cohort effects is to use a longitudinal design, which also has its disadvantages, and

TABLE 6.1 Correlations between age and frequency of experiencing déjà vu

Study	n	Age Mean (standard deviation); range	Correlation with age (r)
Sno et al. (1994)	190	35.8; 18–75	−.22
O'Connor & Moulin (2013)	206	Undergraduates	−.171*
Wells et al. (in prep.)	153 (anx.)	26.8 (9.1)	−.20*
	199 (controls)	25.4 (8.0)	−.25***
Adachi et al. (2007)	113 (schiz.)	39.3 (10.7); 19–67	−.171
	386 (controls)	38.4 (11.6); 18–69	−.38***
Adachi et al. (2008)	227	39.6 (14.0);16–69	−.338***
Fortier & Moulin (2015)	137 (English)	27.61 (9.57)	.16/.17***§
	456 (French)	25.61 (9.67)	
Lacinová et al. (2016)	365	29.05 (11.17); 18–70	†

Notes: *p < .05, **p < .01, ***p < .001; † Lacinová et al. used a logistic regression analysis and found that age was significantly associated with déjà vu; anx. = a population with clinical anxiety; schiz. = a population diagnosed with schizophrenia; § Fortier and Moulin used a negative scale to express the frequency of déjà vu; hence, this is a positive correlation, but in the same direction as all the others: older age, fewer déjà vu experiences.

the differences between cross-sectional and longitudinal designs mirror those of between- and within-subject designs, respectively.

According to a cohort explanation, there could be differences in déjà vu experience across the lifespan due to a shift in cultural or environmental factors influencing the individual, rather than due to cognitive changes. It is possible that fewer older adults report experiencing déjà vu simply because it is a concept with which they are less comfortable. Indeed, one major problem for aging studies is that the belief, or acceptance, of the existence of déjà vu has increased in recent years. Gallup and Newport (1991) reported that from 1978 to 1990, déjà vu experients increased from 30 per cent of the population to 55 per cent. If we take the data on incidence from Brown's (2004) review, we find a relationship between when the survey was conducted and how many people say that they have had the experience, $r(41) = .50$. The possible shift in meaning of the term (e.g. Lazerson, 1994) and the growing popularity of the term was covered in Chapter 2.

Thus, changes in collective societal beliefs may account for the age differences mentioned in previous studies; these findings might not reflect genuine age differences, but rather cohort effects: "older cohorts matured during an era in which belief in déjà vu was not as accepted as it is today" (Brown, 2003, p. 400). That is, perhaps older adults do not understand the term or have not experienced the use of the phrase in relation to cognitive difficulties, and this creates a false impression of reduced déjà vu in old age. Whether déjà vu does increase or decrease with age is an important issue because it may shed some light on the mechanisms of déjà vu formation, and more generally the nature of beliefs about memory function in older adults.

Possible cohort effects in the understanding of the term déjà vu were examined in two studies reported in Moulin et al. (2014). In the first study, Moulin et al. examined participants' estimates of déjà vu occurrence in the last year and more generally in their life. If aging leads to experiencing déjà vu less frequently, we would expect that whereas recent experiences might be reduced, the lifetime incidence should be similar to younger people. For a comparison, the frequency of intrusive memories was assessed (e.g. Berntsen & Rubin, 2002; the relationship between intrusive memories and déjà vu is discussed in the following chapter). There were 74 younger adults (M = 18.59 years, SD = .94, range = 18–24 years) and 56 older adults (M = 71.00, SD = 6.50, range = 60–84 years). Participants completed a simple one-page questionnaire using provided definitions of the experience.

Twenty-two of the older adult participants said that they had not had déjà vu in the last year (39 per cent of the sample). Only eight people in the younger group (11 per cent) said that they had not had déjà vu in the last year. Moreover, the difference between the mean number of déjà vu experiences between the groups was significant, with the older adults having had fewer déjà vu experiences in the last year. There was a marginally significant difference in lifetime incidence, with the older adults reporting fewer instances of déjà vu in the lifespan – despite having lived considerably longer. Brown (2004) found that on average, people between the ages of 15 and 24 experience déjà vu between two and three times a year, whereas in this study the undergraduate sample reported having had it nine times in the last year. In a correlational analysis, within the older group there was a negative correlation between age and the incidence of déjà vu in the last year $r(44) = -.356$, but not lifetime incidence of déjà vu $r(38) = .-072$.

There was no age difference in the rates at which young and old groups experienced involuntary memories. Both young and old participants indicated that on average they experienced an involuntary memory between once a week and once a month, although 11 per cent of both samples reported having an involuntary memory once a day. Interestingly, in the older adult group, the number of involuntary memories correlated strongly ($r(44) = .723$) with déjà vu – such that more involuntary memories were reported with higher levels of déjà vu.

An online questionnaire ($n = 347$) with a mean age of 31.9 years (SD = 17.76, range of 18–90) reported in Moulin et al. (2014) focused on how older adults assess déjà vu in comparison to the tip of the tongue (TOT), another key metacognitive phenomenon (Schwartz & Metcalfe, 2011). It also considered how well older adults could define déjà vu (and whether younger and older groups differ in how they define it). Participants selected which they believed to be the correct definition of déjà vu from a set of three. The correct answer included the dissociation necessary for a déjà vu experience; a second option gave a definition which was about a strange subjective experience but not related to déjà vu; and the third option gave the incorrect but popular conception of a repeated experience. Overall, 54 (15.6 per cent) participants incorrectly defined the déjà vu phenomenon.

Relatively more of the older adults failed to correctly define déjà vu; of the 50 older adults (i.e. people aged 60 years and over), 32 per cent chose the incorrect definition, and the people who incorrectly defined déjà vu had a significantly older mean age than those who correctly defined it.

Participants also used a rating scale to report when they had had their last déjà vu or TOT experience. This rating scale included five points which assessed recency: *in the last day, last week, last month, last six months* and *last year*, and the final point on the scale was used if participants could not remember their last déjà vu experience. Forty-six per cent of the older adult group could not remember their last déjà vu experience. When excluding these people who could not remember their last experience, it was found that the younger people had experienced déjà vu more recently, $r(196) = .240$. This supports the idea that older adults have fewer experiences of déjà vu, but also the idea that they are less able to recall their last déjà vu experience. This either points to them making inaccurate assessments of how frequently it occurs (i.e. they experience it, but forget that they do so), or it is a genuine finding that because they have it less frequently, they have to look a lot further back in order to retrieve the last instance of it.

In terms of the TOT experience, participants had experienced a TOT significantly more recently than déjà vu, and there was a significant correlation between TOT and déjà vu: people who had had a déjà vu experience more recently also reported having had a TOT more recently, $r(306) = .19$. In sum, whereas there is clear evidence for a relationship between age and déjà vu frequency in both studies, there is also evidence that older adults are less likely to endorse the correct definition of déjà vu, suggesting some role of cohort effects in the understanding of the term in the differences in young and old rates of déjà vu.

It is thus consistently found that older adults are less likely to have déjà vu, or that the frequency of experiencing déjà vu decreases with age. Given the three principal memory-based theories of déjà vu, it is perhaps best to think about this age-related change in terms of memory function. The fact that we see a small but measurable age-related decline in episodic memory function and behaviours related to it (e.g. Naveh-Benjamin, Moulin, & Souchay, 2009; Pierce, Simons, & Schacter, 2003) helps us to triangulate on the causes of déjà vu. If nothing else, it suggests that déjà vu is associated with intact or proficient memory function.

Déjà vu could arise less in older adults because it is a complex metacognitive evaluation of a mismatch between two different kinds of information. A relatively large literature points to the fact that older adults have deficits in metacognitive evaluation of episodic memory. As an example, Souchay et al. (2007) examined older adults' capacity to predict their upcoming recognition for a currently unrecallable target word in a cue–target pair using the feeling-of-knowing (FOK) paradigm. Older adults have been shown to have a particular metacognitive deficit for making FOK predictions – they are less able to gauge the likelihood of future recognition than young controls (e.g. Souchay, Isingrini, & Espagnet, 2000; but see also MacLaverty & Hertzog, 2009 for an opposing view). Souchay et al. (2007) examined the relationship between the ability to recollect contextual details from encoding and the accuracy of FOK predictions, finding that older adults with better recollection scores also had more accurate FOK. Extending the finding to a similar but stronger pattern in Alzheimer's disease, Souchay (2007) suggested that a deficit in recollection meant that information pertinent to predicting future recognition was absent or insufficient in older adults, and their predictions were less accurate as a result: metacognitive accuracy in episodic memory relies upon recollection.

Déjà vu can be thought of as an epistemic feeling akin to a FOK, as it shares a similar metacognitive evaluation of the memory trace – this is a hypothesis which itself is supported by the correlations reported above between the TOT (again a metacognitive state related to the FOK) and déjà vu. Moulin et al. (2014) proposed that there was likewise insufficient episodic detail to produce the conviction that the feeling of familiarity was false. That is, older adults may fail to retrieve enough contextual specifics to oppose the feeling of familiarity and generate the clash of mental evaluations that is at the core of the déjà vu.

This would suggest that older adults are more susceptible to false recognition based on familiarity, which is a priority for future research: people who are less likely to have déjà vu should be more prone to having false memory experiences. However, this may prove difficult to test, at least in retrospective questionnaires of real-world behaviours, because we are predicting that people accept experiences and locations as having been previously encountered, *without them realising* that they are false! In the laboratory, at least, there is experimental evidence to suggest that older adults do have a different relationship with their memory system. Gallo, Bell, Beier and Schacter (2006) showed that older adults were less likely to adopt a 'recall-to-reject' strategy to prevent the creation of false memories. It is also known that older adults are more susceptible to produce errors on false-memory paradigms (Gallo, 2010). In particular, because prefrontal cortex function shows a pronounced age-related decline (e.g. West, 1996; Balota et al., 1999) and this area has been proposed to be critical for the retrieval monitoring in memory which can prevent false memories, older adults have helped us better understand the cognitive and neurological bases of false-memory phenomena: age-related increases in false memory are highest in tasks that require retrieval monitoring. In turn, it is proposed that this memory control function – which is possibly reliant on the recall of specifics and which is also possibly part of the brain network which takes in the temporal lobe and the prefrontal cortex – is compromised in healthy aging and leads to fewer déjà vu experiences.

Describing déjà vu – cultural differences?

One concern is that when asked about déjà vu, we do not know what the reference is for participants – how they may define the experience, according to their beliefs, general knowledge or even suggestibility (saying that they have had déjà vu when they have not). Participants' responses may actually reflect uncertainty about what the experience is, or – despite attempts to provide a clear definition of déjà vu – use a definition of déjà vu which emphasises repetition of experiences rather than the clash of two evaluations. This concern about déjà vu just meaning any form of repetition is supported by linguistic studies of the term (e.g. Lazerson, 1994, see Chapter 2) and by dictionary definitions.

There may thus exist cultural and linguistic differences in how the term is used, but there have been very few studies addressing this issue. Fortier and Moulin (2015) compared French and English cohorts on their description of the déjà vu experience using a questionnaire measure. Clearly, the understanding of the term déjà vu is of particular interest in French, as in French it can be both used to describe the infrequent memory error, but also in everyday language to literally mean 'already seen'. Thus, in French there is the suggestion that déjà vu sometimes may actually be the act of seeing something again, and at that, the term déjà vu is not nearly so unusual or interesting. To assess this, an online survey on 593 participants (137 participants answered an English version and 456 participants responded to a French version) was carried out.

Some summary data are presented in Table 6.2. Most people in this sample described déjà vu as brief, infrequent, strange and disturbing, which resonates with most contemporary definitions of the experience. Very slight but significant differences in how the French-speaking and English-speaking samples described their experience of déjà vu were found. French people rated déjà vu as significantly more frequent than the English-speaking group. The French sample was more likely to describe the phenomenon as 'erroneous', and were less likely to question the reality of the phenomenon. That is, French respondents do not use the term as merely having seen something before, but find the experience more disturbing than do the English-speaking group.

The descriptions of the experience were not exactly in line with the hypothesis, because it could be expected that the experience would be more banal in the French group, whereas in fact it appears to be more disturbing. In sum, this article makes a very specific incremental contribution, but it does point to the fact that, at least, there are differences in how people use the term, something that is also a concern in studies comparing different cohorts of people – such as people with and without epilepsy, anxiety, memory impairment, and so on.

TABLE 6.2 Table to show mean dichotomous classifications of déjà vu characteristics, between French and English groups. Cohen's *d* gives an estimate of effect size (adapted from Fortier & Moulin, 2015)

	English group	French group	Cohen's d
Disturbing (1) – pleasant (7)	4.55	2.62	1.28
Frequent (1) – infrequent (7)	4.81	4.39	0.25
Strange (1) – normal (7)	3.17	2.99	0.10
Brief (1) – long (7)	2.42	2.37	0.03
Real (1) – real (7)	3.53	3.49	0.02

Déjà vu, dreaming and the paranormal

Given the parapsychological origins of déjà vu research, it is unsurprising that studies have long continued to examine its relation with other subjective experiences and mysterious phenomena (reviewed by Brown, 2004). In a more recent and straightforward study, Fox (1992) used questionnaire data to examine the relationship between déjà vu and several variables in the context of a study looking at paranormal experiences and beliefs. He concluded that "Déjà vu is more frequent among younger and more highly educated respondents, but it is unaffected by sex, race, income, marital status, and religious preference differences" (p. 417). In this way, his conclusions mirror the consensus view from contemporary studies. Fox asked participants to rate the frequency of five experiences (pp. 419–410): Déjà vu ("Thought you were somewhere you have been before, but knew that it was impossible"); Extra-sensory perception ("Felt as though you were in touch with someone when they were far away from you"); Clairvoyance ("Seen events that happened at a great distance as they were happening"); Contact with the dead ("Felt that you were in touch with someone who had died"); and Mysticism ("Felt as though you were very close to a powerful spiritual force that seemed to lift you out of yourself). Déjà vu was the most commonly experienced (between 33 and 36 per cent had never experienced it across the three different years that the survey data was collected – each time with about 1000 US respondents). Only between 12 and 17 per cent of participants responded that they had never had any of the experiences. Most importantly, using factor analysis, Fox determined that déjà vu was not an experience that shared characteristics with the other four, even though the other four reliably grouped into one sole factor. In fact, apart from for déjà vu, which Fox suggests should not be considered as a paranormal experience in the same way as the other four, his study is rather inconclusive. Whilst some relationship with socio-cultural variables was found for déjà vu, the same was not the case for the other experiences.

The results from a more recent study point to there being equivocal findings on the association between paranormal belief and déjà vu. In a recent study (discussed more fully in Chapter 9), Shiah, Wu, Chen and Chiang (2014) used questionnaires administered to patients with schizophrenia and 422 healthy participants in order to look at schizophrenic symptoms and belief in the paranormal. This study blurs the distinction between superstition and psychopathology, finding that déjà vu scores did not correlate with a paranormal belief scale in schizophrenic patients, whereas they did for the healthy adults. However, the schizophrenic patients were significantly more likely than the healthy adults to believe in psi and have superstitious beliefs, but reported fewer instances of déjà vu. This relationship is further complicated by the fact that superstitious and paranormal beliefs in healthy populations tend to correlate with schizophrenic-like symptoms as measured by clinical tools (e.g. Thalbourne, 1994). One suggestion is that, as with Fox's conclusion, one should not think of déjà vu as a paranormal experience.

In the same vein, dream experiences should not be thought of as paranormal, although the overlap between dreams and déjà vu as cognitive phenomena which impinge on the typical focus of research of parapsychology is clear. Contemporary research (e.g. Fortier & Moulin, 2005) continues to find that déjà vu experiences correlate with several dream variables (e.g. the ability to recall your dreams vividly). Again, a review is provided in Brown (2004). More recently, Funkhouser and Schredl (2010) have focused specifically on déjà rêve [*sic*] 'already dreamt' as a particular form of déjà vu experience. They reviewed the literature by summarising the relationship between déjà vu and dreams in previous published works. They showed that when participants are asked to identify a particular source for their déjà vu experience, between 16 and 74 per cent of participants report identifying that they had dreamt previously about the occurrence. In an empirical study in the same paper, participants reported the frequency of déjà vu in response to the question: "How often do you find yourself in a situation that you have already dreamed in a similar way (déjà vu)?" (p. 61). The responses to this question were then correlated with various published scales for evaluating personality, dreams and demographic characteristics. Participants were 444 undergraduates (in Germany) whose mean age was 23.5. In their study, the highest correlation of any variable with déjà vu was for dream recall frequency ($r = .252$); people who had more frequent déjà vu experiences were also more likely to remember the contents of their dreams. About 95 per cent of participants had had at least one déjà rêvé experience. The big five personality dimensions were not related to déjà vu frequency. However, a measure of 'Absorption' which measures "the capacity of becoming absorptively involved in imaginative and aesthetic experience, e.g. 'I can be greatly moved by eloquent or poetic language'" (p. 61) correlated positively with déjà vu experiences. Likewise, a measure of 'Boundaries' (e.g. Hartmann, 1991) showed that people with 'thin boundaries' were more likely to experience déjà vu. Such people have been characterised as prone to nightmares and "are sensitive and vulnerable, experience mental in-between states, and involve themselves quickly in relationships" (Schredl, Kleinferchner, & Gell, 1996, p. 219).

It is difficult to know what to make of the déjà rêvé research. One complication comes from the fact that it is a subtype of the déjà vu experience (albeit a very frequent one). Furthermore, in the temporal lobe epilepsy literature, déjà rêvé has been used as term to describe the genuine re-experience of dreamed material in seizures and when provoked by electrical stimulation of the cortex (see Chapter 7). There is nothing to suppose that, just like any other autobiographical source, the retrieval of dreamed material is a special kind of memory experience, any more than the retrieval of conversations or locations as particular subtypes of the déjà vu experience. However, it is clear that a substantial proportion of people believe that déjà vu is related to material they have previously dreamed – which is, of course, in keeping with Freud's theory (covered in Chapter 2). Whether Freud can be thought of as the source of this popular belief or whether he tapped into a folk psychological belief about dreams and déjà vu is not clear.

A major problem in this avenue of research is the reliance on retrospective questionnaires for both the assessment of déjà vu and dreams. As Funkhouser and Schredl (2010) point out, the correlation between the two variables may just arise because both rely on the capacity to recall a mental experience that we have experienced lately. Moreover, just as the research into déjà vu and dreaming is after the fact, so too are our experiences. Consider this particularly apposite quote (an extract from one of the participants cited in Chapter 1; Jersakova et al., 2016):

> Another experience was years before I began high school I had a dream about walking down a strange hallway, then years past and the first day of high school came and there the déjà vu feeling was. (Of course maybe I never dreamt it, maybe it was just déjà vu that made me think I dreamt it).

To conclude this section, it could be argued that, when faced with a strange and inexplicable feeling of familiarity, people are drawn to dreams as a way of explaining the sensation, and confabulate a justification based on a previous dream. Coltheart (2017) has recently elaborated a theory of how healthy people generate such justifications that share all the properties of neuropsychological confabulation, based on the 'drive for causal understanding' (Gopnik, 2000; discussed in Chapter 8). According to such a view, the overlap between dreams and déjà vu experiences is merely a post-hoc justification driven by the need to find a 'reason' for the strange experience of déjà vu. In fact, even Freud emphasised that precognitive dreams were more apparent than real, describing how, in contrast to déjà vu, they are an illusion, because the conviction of having had the dream before is not felt until the moment where the apparent dream comes true. It is therefore possible, especially amongst those who report remembering their dreams, that the easiest justification (after the fact) for a false sense of familiarity, especially given how strange it is, is that it represents something that has already been dreamt.

Déjà vu and the brain: the correlational approach

Using the same individual differences approach, considering questionnaire performance and possible explanatory variables, we can also examine brain structures. The rationale is that brain morphology or connectivity might explain differences between people in the occurrence of déjà vu. In the first study of its kind, Brázdil et al. (2012) administered a frequently used questionnaire of déjà vu experiences, the Inventory for Déjà vu Experiences Assessment (IDEA[1]; Sno et al., 1994) to 113 healthy participants and measured grey matter volume in temporal lobe structures critical for recognition using source-based morphometry. Using an initial split of the sample according to whether they had ever experienced déjà vu, they identified brain regions whose morphology differed according to déjà vu experience (see Table 6.3). Grey matter volume from these regions was then correlated with frequency estimates from the questionnaire, with the finding that it was negatively related with déjà vu experiences, particularly in medial temporal/hippocampus regions. People who experienced déjà vu had lower grey matter volume in areas of the temporal lobe, and Brázdil et al. naturally emphasised that this was a region critical for recognition memory. In particular, they converged on the parahippocampus

TABLE 6.3 Regions of interest showing significant morphological differences between healthy participants who do and do not experience déjà vu, with coordinates. Z scores ranged from 2.88 to 3.89 (regions presented in order from largest to smallest cluster size) (adapted from Brázdil et al., 2012)

Region of interest	MNI stereotactic coordinates (x, y, z)
Left parahippocampal gyrus/hippocampus/fusiform gyrus/amygdala	−30, −34, −14
Left putamen/caudatum	−20, 10, −6
Right putamen/caudatum	50, −44, 20
Left/right thalamus	0, −16, 6
Right parahippocampal gyrus/hippocampus/ amygdala	−36, −4, −2
Left superior temporal sulcus	−52, −46, 8
Right insula	
Left insula	38, 14, −6
Right inferior parietal lobule/superior temporal sulcus	22, −6, −22

as showing pronounced differences in grey matter volume between their healthy participants with and without déjà vu, and they note that this is where electrical stimulation in patients with epilepsy is most likely to lead to déjà vu (reviewed in Chapter 7) and that this had been a region previously thought to contribute to the déjà vu phenomenon (Spatt, 2002).

The study of Brázdil et al. thus added some empirical support (for the first time) for the notion that in healthy people, as in epilepsy, the parahippocampus, and more broadly the medial temporal lobe, is involved in déjà vu formation. There are, however, a number of criticisms of the study. First, Labate and Gambardella (2013) published a commentary in which they essentially questioned whether the healthy participants were indeed healthy. Since Brázdil et al. (p. 1242) had concluded that "the role of 'small seizures' in the genesis of non-pathological déjà vu experiences deserves consideration", they reasonably pointed out that a subtle epileptic disorder should be ruled out, citing their work on 'a common, often unrecognized clinical entity', benign TLE. This form of epilepsy is characterised by seizure onset beginning in adulthood and notably epileptic déjà vu "that often represents the only predominant ictal symptom" (Labate et al., 2011).

A more major problem is that Brázdil et al. (2012) clearly showed that with a decrease in grey matter volume in the critical areas there was an increase in déjà vu frequency. This is problematic, as in single case studies of people who have had their temporal lobe resected in epilepsy, the findings are in the opposite direction. This topic is covered in the next chapter. In brief, using a parallel rationale, but looking at groups of people with TLE who do and do not experience déjà vu, Martin et al. (2012) found that the patients who have déjà vu actually have a *greater* volume of tissue in the similar medial temporal area. Happily, both studies converge on the same area of the brain, but the diverging results with regards to volume and déjà vu experience point to the need for more research into this area, most notably considering fine-scale recollection and familiarity structures in more detail.

This was partly the motivation for a follow-up to Brázdil et al.'s initial study (Shaw, Mareček, & Brázdil, 2016). In a similarly novel and technically complex study based on the same imaging and questionnaire data from the same participants, they aimed to consider the functional status of the temporal lobe rather than its structure. Because the experience is so infrequent and brief, and difficult to produce in laboratory conditions, Shaw et al. used a proxy for measuring function directly, taking advantage of the fact that brain structure varies in regions that interact frequently in functional networks. Thus, they measured 'grey-matter covariance', but again focusing on the regions identified above, and exploring how the grey matter covariance is related to the frequency of experiencing déjà vu. The pattern of results obtained was then examined with reference to the Brainmap database (e.g. Laird et al., 2009), such that the structures involved could be related to functional networks. A more complex pattern emerged than the initial study, with two dissociable patterns of grey matter covariance emerging, one of which "involves medial temporal lobe structures primarily, among which grey matter becomes more positively correlated with greater déjà vu frequency" (Shaw et al., 2016, p. 1077). Critically, they interpret these findings with reference to the difference between recollection and familiarity, and their finding of two proximal networks in temporal lobe structures related to déjà vu, one of which shows greater covariance and the other less covariance associated with déjà vu possibly pointing to the sort of dissociation between recognition memory processes which are evoked in cognitive descriptions of the déjà vu experience.

Déjà vu and correlations with recognition memory performance

Because we can apparently find neurological variables which correlate with the frequency of déjà vu, and moreover, because we can pinpoint those zones to the function of memory, it should, in theory, be possible to use the same approach as Brázdil but show systematic differences on behavioural memory tasks according to the frequency with which people experience déjà vu. O'Connor and Moulin (2013) set out to test this hypothesis: given that we can observe differences in temporal lobe regions according to the frequency of déjà vu experiences, we might expect that there is some behavioural corollary. Two hundred and six undergraduate participants took part in a standard recognition memory paradigm that asked for evaluations of recollection and familiarity with a remember–know procedure (see Chapter 3), and these scores were compared with the self-reported incidence of déjà vu. An important part of the design was that recognition memory for high- and low-frequency words was compared. A robust finding in the recognition memory literature is that high-frequency words are less likely to be recognised with recollection than more distinctive low-frequency words (e.g. Yonelinas, 2002). Thus, it acts as a check that participants are making their subjective evaluations in line with known properties of the task.

This task replicated the anticipated differences between remembering and knowing and between low- and high-frequency words. (The mean proportion of hits to high-frequency targets (.757) was significantly lower than to low-frequency targets (.879). The questionnaire measures yielded relationships between variables that replicated those from previous individual differences research. There was a significant negative correlation between déjà vu incidence and age, $r(204) = -.171$, and a significant positive correlation between déjà vu incidence and travel frequency, $r(203) = .216$. The critical issue was the relationship between these questionnaire measures and the experimental recognition memory task. Correlation analyses were carried out on recollection and familiarity parameters and self-reported déjà vu incidence from the post-experimental questionnaires. (Scatterplots illustrating the correlation data are shown in Figure 6.1.) As is clear from the graphs, there were no significant correlations between either recollection or familiarity déjà vu and déjà vu incidence. Overall, there was no association evident in these correlation analyses between the tendency to differentially employ recollection (or familiarity) and the tendency to experience déjà vu.

In sum, the recognition memory test replicated standard word frequency effects, with performance reliably above chance. The individual difference measures replicated the typical correlation between déjà vu frequency and age and frequency of travel. In short, a well-powered memory experiment and a correlational task replicated well-known associations found in the déjà vu literature, but which pointed to there being no relationship between those people who have more déjà vu experiences and the performance on a memory test.

The Brázdil et al. (2012) study led to the prediction that we might see systematic differences in recognition memory according to the frequency of déjà vu experiences. The behavioural study does not support the idea that the propensity to experience déjà vu is due to a marked change in the functional capacity of the temporal lobe. One consideration is that in their regions of interest analysis, Brázdil did not examine many structures outside the temporal lobe. The temporal lobe is often referred to as part of a memory network taking in the frontal lobes and it is the interplay between these two regions that has been implicated in déjà vu, but as elucidated in the section above on older adults, the prefrontal cortex, as part of a larger network which includes metacognitive control and monitoring of memory retrieval operations, may well be involved in the generation of the sensation. There thus exists the possibility that other brain regions also capture the differences between those who do and do not experience déjà vu.

In terms of the behavioural study, O'Connor and Moulin (2013) focused on memory measures rather than considering a more metacognitive approach which considers people's relationship with their memory – such as the capacity to use a strategy of 'recollection rejection' to overcome false memory, for instance. Future

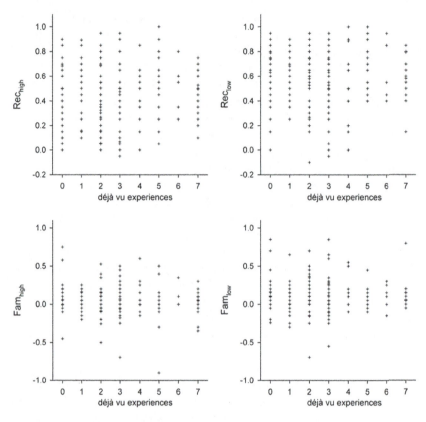

FIGURE 6.1 Scatterplots showing the (lack of a) relationship between recollection and familiarity for high- and low-frequency words and déjà vu. Reported déjà vu incidence is plotted on the x-axis. y-axes plot Rec parameters (top; calculated as "Remember" responses to targets minus "Remember" responses to lures) and Fam parameters (bottom; calculated as "Familiar" responses to targets minus "Familiar" responses to lures). Separate Rec and Fam parameters were calculated for responses to high-frequency (left) and low-frequency (right) words.
Taken from O'Connor and Moulin (2013).

research should consider this metacognitive aspect in studies of individual differences. It is possible that it is how people consider and interpret their memory system, rather than some memory capacity, which best captures the individual differences in the déjà vu experience. Moreover, the use of words in their experiment, whilst useful in that word frequency effects can be used to verify the recollection and familiarity responding, may not generate déjà vu – repeating the same experiment but with scenes (as have been used in most experiments on déjà vu, see Chapter 10) is a priority for future research. Chapter 10 reviews one study (Sugimori & Kusumi, 2014) which has produced a significant correlation between rates of déjà vu in the real world and responding on a particular type of memory task, suggesting that the search for a laboratory analogue of déjà vu is not a fruitless task, and that the individual differences in experience of déjà vu in the real world may be captured in the laboratory.

Summary: the future of retrospective survey methods

It is clear that several factors are related to déjà vu experience in healthy groups, including age, travel frequency, the recall of dreams and the volume of the temporal lobe. Brown (2003) also concluded that both education level and socio-economic class correlate with the frequency of experiencing déjà vu. This is an esoteric collection of variables, and difficult to explain. The pattern of data is complicated by the fact that, given the structural differences in the integrity of the temporal lobe between those who do and do not report frequent experiences of déjà vu, we do not see a behavioural effect using laboratory measures of recollection and familiarity. We might expect people with differences in familiarity and recollection responding to have a characteristic profile of déjà vu experience, as has indeed been shown in TLE (the focus of the next chapter). It remains a research priority to consider the recognition memory system in more detail in searching for individual differences explanations of déjà vu.

The aging data perhaps offer a clearer contribution to the formation of déjà vu. Like the data comparing English and French speakers presented at the beginning of this chapter, it does point to there being some differences in how groups use and understand the term déjà vu, which is of course problematic for research in this area. Nonetheless, the fact that, after allowing for these differences, there does seem to be a reduction in déjà vu experiences in older adults, helps us triangulate on possible mechanisms of déjà vu formation, especially because the report of déjà vu seems to be correlated with other infrequent mental phenomena, such as intrusive memories and the TOT experience. In this way the relationship with age and memory helps us triangulate on a metacognitive account of déjà vu – déjà vu is not a memory error in the sense of forgetfulness, despite Tonegawa's claim at the beginning of this chapter. It would appear that a loss of memory function leads to a reduction in déjà vu experience, but this probably relates to differences in familiarity and recollection, and the metacognitive evaluation of both in healthy older adults. Thus, these indications from the individual differences domain need to be taken up in experiments comparing groups of younger and older participants, using the paradigms described in Chapter 10. The questionnaire data strongly suggest that we should find a reduction in déjà vu experiences in older adults in laboratory settings.

One conundrum to address here is the relationship between déjà vu and travel frequency: people who travel more are more likely to experience déjà vu, which, unlike aging, appears to have little to do with memory function. However, Whittlesea and Williams' (1998) observation about the phenomenology of familiarity between friends and strangers may help us understand these data. The more we travel, the more we are exposed to novel environments. Presumably, in novel environments we are more likely to detect the clash in evaluations necessary in the déjà vu experience: we can find something familiar, but be very sure that we have never encountered anything like this particular moment before. In familiar locations, the feeling will be less frequent, just because the evaluation will be that we have indeed been here before. The mismatch in the experience and its evaluation will therefore be stronger in novel locations. Again, this robust questionnaire finding can be taken forward in experimental work, such as the comparison of false familiarity for mundane and distinctive scenes (Brown and Marsh, 2008; reviewed in Chapter 10).

In concluding, it should be noted that many of the studies which use questionnaires to classify groups of people according to their experience of déjà vu use IDEA (see Table 6.4; Sno et al., 1994). The IDEA is split into two parts. If on the first part, a respondent indicates, according to a provided definition, that they have had déjà vu, they then answer specific questions about their view of a specific déjà vu occurrence. Because this tool predates many of the recent developments in memory research and the resurgence of interest in déjà vu, it is perhaps time to

TABLE 6.4 An overview of Sno's IDEA (Inventory of Déjà vu Experiences Assessment; Sno et al., 1994)

Part A	Déjà vu experiences
Questions about incidence and frequency of various mental phenomena and variables associated with déjà vu	Derealisation Jamais vu Precognitive dreams Depersonalisation Paranormal qualities (e.g. clairvoyance, telepathic qualities, etc.) Dream recall Travel frequency Daydreaming
Part B Questions about the qualities and characteristics of a specific déjà vu experience	• Questions about triggers, contexts and circumstances of the experience (e.g. 'place', 'conversation' – 'can you remember exactly where and when you had the same experience or feeling before?') • Retrocognition • Elapsed period • Duration • Pervasiveness • Time of day • Precognition • Depersonalisation • Repetition • Derealisation • Effects of the experience (e.g. 'indifference' or 'surprise') • Attribution of the experience (e.g. 'reincarnation' or 'memory deficit') • Preceding affect • Influencing factors (e.g. headache, blackout)

consider a more theoretically driven measure for classifying and collecting déjà vu experiences. In particular, a measure which could draw parallels with other meta-cognitive and memory phenomena, as well as considering separable contributions of recollection and familiarity to déjà vu, would be more useful. On a related note, the studies here overwhelmingly address the frequency and not the intensity (or some other quality) of the déjà vu experience. As such, it is possible that the field is missing some critical relationship between dissociative experiences and the quality of déjà vu, for example.

Finally, contemporary questionnaire studies of déjà vu point to it being an interesting and complex real-world phenomenon. Viewed from a memory perspective, it seems that understanding déjà vu in the real world, as experienced by certain kinds of people, may tell us something about how memory works, and how people understand and experience their own memory. In comparison with other memory mistakes and illusions, déjà vu has largely been overlooked in this regard, but given its relationship with age (which is proposed to stem from episodic memory deficits) and its link with metacognition, it can be proposed that déjà vu is actually a healthy, positive mental experience which makes the experient aware of – and possibly corrects – a brief failure in the memory system.

Note

1 The critical question used was: "Have you ever had the feeling of having experienced a sensation or situation before in exactly the same way when in fact you are experiencing it for the first time?"

7

DÉJÀ VU IN EPILEPSY

He who is faithfully analysing many different cases of epilepsy is doing far more than studying epilepsy.

Hughlings Jackson (1888)

Research into temporal lobe epilepsy has delivered the largest scientific literature of déjà vu. This is partly because there is a clinical significance to the experience of déjà vu; it can be a useful diagnostic entity. For people with epilepsy, déjà vu is sometimes far from being a curious by-product of the disease, as this quote testifies:

Before being diagnosed with epilepsy, I was experiencing the feeling of déjà vu almost continuously every day. Since being on medication I only have a rare sensation of déjà vu – which isn't a mild seizure, but the type of déjà vu that everyone experiences. ... When I was experiencing déjà vu almost continuously before taking medication, it made my life difficult as completing normal tasks became harder to complete. I felt like I was being constantly distracted by the déjà vus.

Research participant (Illman et al., 2012)

As such, to better care for and diagnose people with epilepsy, it is necessary to explore the triggers, incidence and neurological sequelae of 'epileptic' déjà vu. However, it is also the case that because déjà vu occurs infrequently in healthy participants, and although it may not be any more frequent in people with epilepsy in general, in some people with epilepsy, and in some conditions, it is far more predictable a phenomenon than in the general public. As such, epilepsy, particularly of the temporal lobe, has offered a means to investigate déjà vu empirically. In this chapter this research will be reviewed, examining single cases, neuroimaging and questionnaire work, and focusing on studies of direct electrical stimulation of the cortex, where déjà vu has been provoked artificially in patients. A key theme that will be addressed will be whether the organisation of the temporal lobe memory system and the experiences of people with déjà vu can enable the separation or classification of déjà vu experiences. Note that epilepsy contributes to our under-standing of déjà vu both directly, through the occurrence of naturally occurring déjà vu in the disease, and indirectly, both through surgical interventions reducing or producing déjà vu in patients, and through pre-surgical stimulation procedures through which we can learn more about the activation of different structures in the brain.

Déjà vu in temporal lobe epilepsy

Hughlings Jackson (1888) coined the phrase 'dreamy states' to describe the peculiar mental states that occur in epilepsy, referring to them as "double consciousness" (see Chapter 2 for a more detailed discussion of his cases). Hughlings Jackson is consid-ered the first to have pinpointed such phenomena to dysfunction of the temporal lobe, and he emphasised how they needed to be better understood: "These are all voluminous mental states and yet of different kinds; no doubt they ought to be clas-sified" (p. 200). Hughlings Jackson did not use the term déjà vu to describe these peculiar sensations, but it is clear that one aspect of this dreamy state is the feeling of déjà vu. (For more about the history and significance of memory research in epilepsy in the nineteenth century, see Berrios, 2012.) Contemporary descriptions of a dreamy state converge on the same notion of a disturbance to consciousness, uneasiness and dreamy qualities (see Gloor, 1990).

What Hughlings Jackson described as the dreamy state came to be described as a 'simple partial seizure' (SPS). The classification of seizures states in epilepsy is a complex issue and in a state of flux. As of 2017, The International League Against Epilepsy (2017) has reclassified seizure states, and the simple SPS is now referred to as a focal-aware seizure. This is a helpful classification because it emphasises two critical scientific concepts important for our purposes. First, the seizure is focal because it affects only a specific part of the brain and does not discharge more generally. Second, it places an emphasis on the experience of the seizure: people who have these kinds of seizure are aware of what is happening and the resultant changes in consciousness. Despite the clear advantages of this new term (and the broader classification of seizures by anatomical and psychological considerations), here we will continue to use the terminology *simple partial seizure* to reflect these temporary disturbances that are focal in nature and for which the participant is aware.

Electrophysiological measures of déjà vu

The history of déjà vu research in epilepsy developed in parallel with our ability to measure electrical activity in the conscious ('awake') brain. Epileptic activity can be described as a result of the abnormal electrical synchronisation of neuronal activity

in a particular zone in the brain. It is unsurprising, therefore, that many of the investigations of déjà vu in TLE centre on electro-encephalography (EEG) technology.
Many such studies (reviewed below) use specific-depth electrodes (which can both
measure and administer current) into the brain. Less invasive methods use surface
EEG recordings.

In a study typical of this approach, Weinand et al. (1994) took long-term recording of electrical activity using subdural strip electrocorticographic methods (which
involves measuring activity from underneath the skull on a matrix or grid of electrodes). They report results of the tiny minority (1.3 per cent, eight of 610 of their
patients who underwent this procedure) of people for whom the seizure started
with an 'aura' of déjà vu. In their eight patients, they recorded activity for a mean
of 3 days and only measured a mean of three seizures per participant in this period
(range 1–6). Here we see how infrequent déjà vu can be even in the minority of
people who have it in a 'predictable' fashion; it is an approach that requires extreme
patience. Weinand et al. (1994) found results which contribute to a debate first
started by Penfield (e.g. Mullan & Penfield, 1959) and followed up by Halgren,
Walter, Cherlow and Crandall (1978) concerning the hemispheric location of déjà
vu. Penfield had argued that the anatomical origin of déjà vu was in the non-dominant (non-language) hemisphere (typically the left hemisphere in right handed
people). Weinand et al. found "consistent lateralization of ictal déjà vu to the temporal lobe in the hemisphere non-dominant for handedness" (p. 1059). Of note,
by this point the location of déjà vu as originating in the temporal lobe was no
longer of doubt. However, as shall be shown below, the debate about which hemisphere is involved in déjà vu has largely dropped from view as we have been able
to look at neural structures with more precision and also consider discharge and
after-discharge across the two hemispheres; as our ability to measure the electro-
physiology of the brain becomes more detailed, so our reasoning about déjà vu
becomes more complex.

The incidence of déjà vu in temporal lobe epilepsy

One might expect, then, that déjà vu is experienced more commonly in temporal
lobe epilepsy (TLE) than in the normal population. Several researchers have examined the incidence and nature of déjà experiences in epilepsy compared to healthy
participants. A key clinical issue is whether there is any diagnostic value to the frequency or nature of déjà vu in TLE.

A large-scale questionnaire study by Adachi et al. (2010) addressed the incidence
of déjà vu in healthy and epileptic participants. They administered the Japanese
Inventory of Déjà vu Experiences Assessment (IDEA; based on Sno et al., 1994).
In their sample of 312 patients, 143 had TLE; these were matched with a control
group of 402 healthy adults. Intriguingly, they found that significantly *fewer* patients
had some form of déjà vu (63.1 per cent), compared with controls (76.1 per cent).
This does not tally with the idea stated above that due to temporal lobe dysfunction
people with TLE are predisposed to a memory-based déjà vu experience.

At first glance, this suggests that there is nothing unique about the déjà vu experience in epilepsy. However, Adachi and colleagues were also motivated to investigate whether the subjective experience of déjà vu could be predictive of seizure activity. They asked patients to differentiate between instances where they were aware the déjà vu was part of seizure activity (seizure recognition form – SR) and those when it occurred as a non-epileptic subjective event (non-seizure recognition – NSR). The SR form was experienced by 24 per cent of patients and most commonly in TLE, whereas 55.6 per cent had the NSR form, and 16.3 per cent encountered both. Out of those patients experiencing both types, it was found that the SR form tended to occur more frequently at night, was reported as occurring more recently, and was associated with negative affect and more dissociative features; hence, there were several phenomenological differences between the two. Despite the finding that déjà vu is less common in epilepsy more generally than healthy people, it is nevertheless more predictable and consistent in patients experiencing the phenomenon frequently as part of their SPS (many times per month; Warren-Gash & Zeman, 2014), and it is for this reason TLE is critical for understanding déjà vu.

A critical issue is thus *when* the person with epilepsy experiences déjà vu. Some people have it as part of their seizure manifestation, and diagnostic schedules indicate that déjà vu can be experienced as part of an SPS. These cases are undoubtedly of most interest for the study of déjà vu. However, outside abnormal electrical firing of the temporal lobe, one might expect there is the same type and frequency of déjà vu as in healthy groups. Or, as suggested above by Adachi et al. (2010), the experience of déjà vu outside of seizure activity may actually be reduced due to low-level structural abnormalities or damage in the temporal lobe. In any case, as will be discussed, the minute differences in the precise areas of dysfunction and damage in the temporal lobe mean that even in TLE there is heterogeneity in the experience of déjà vu.

Johanson, Valli, Revonsuo and Wedlund (2008) carried out a thorough review of subjective experiences in SPSs which gives an idea of the incidence of déjà vu within seizure manifestation. Immediately following an SPS, participants called a telephone number and attempted to describe what was felt during the ictal and post-ictal period. Their study is typical of an approach which aims to classify and better understand the changes in consciousness in partial epileptic seizures. In this way, they respond directly to Hughlings Jackson's plea: "no doubt they ought to be classified". They surveyed 262 reports of seizures generated by 56 participants. Within these reports, 36 per cent of all accounts (reported by 22 experients) included 'hallucinatory' experiences, of which 18 per cent were misperceived memories, such as *déjà vu* (e.g. "I felt I had walked along this road before") and a *combination of déjà vu and prescience* (e.g. "I had a strange feeling that I knew what the people were going to say"), but some were flashbacks, which Johanson et al. interpret as episodic memories (e.g. "I saw pictures from a party I went to a long time ago"). Based on these data, an estimate would be that approximately 7 per cent of all seizure-related changes in consciousness include déjà vu-like experiences. However, Johanson et al.'s sample included people with different epileptic foci (only 47.5 per cent of the sample had TLE), and as such the incidence would probably be higher within TLE.

It should be noted that epilepsy can lead to a variety of different alterations of consciousness and perception, as well as déjà vu. For a full discussion of 'hallucinations, illusions and delusions' that occur as part of seizure manifestation in epilepsy, see Kasper et al. (2010). They refer to a range of subjective experiences, including déjà vu, from vertigo to hearing voices, and the feeling of somebody nearby ('sensed presence').

Differences between healthy déjà vu and déjà vu in TLE

Whether or not healthy déjà vu and déjà vu in TLE represent the same phenomenon is critical for our use of TLE to understand the phenomenon in healthy people. Adachi's finding of a lower incidence of any déjà vu in patients (above) therefore provides evidence that, on the one hand, déjà vu is a 'healthy' phenomenon, actually occurring less frequently in people with damage to the temporal lobe. Also, it is clear that memory dysfunction alone does not lead to déjà vu given that other forms of memory impairment which stem from temporal lobe atrophy also do not lead to higher levels of déjà vu, e.g. Alzheimer's disease or healthy aging.

Fukao, Murai, Yamada, Sengoku and Kusumi (2005) compared the qualitative characteristics of déjà vu in 15 TLE patients with 115 university students. They found that 75 per cent of students experienced déjà vu. Déjà vu was experienced more for places than people in both controls and patients, but there were qualitative differences in the circumstances under which it occurred. Ictal (that is, occurring during a seizure) déjà vu was more likely to occur in familiar locations; for people, it was unrelated to the degree of familiarity of the person; it generally did not evoke feelings of surprise; and it was more likely in a state of mental relaxation. In controls, however, déjà vu was more likely to occur for unfamiliar locations and people, cause surprise and to happen more often in a state of mental fatigue. Common characteristics between the two types included the average duration of the phenomenon (in the order of seconds) and a feeling of nostalgia. In contrast to Adachi et al., the authors did not find déjà experiences to be associated with negative emotion.

More recently, Warren-Gash and Zeman (2014) explicitly aimed to test whether there are differences in healthy and TLE déjà vu. They surveyed 50 epileptic patients who experienced ictal déjà vu, and compared their experiences with 50 non-epileptic neurological controls, and 50 medical students. They used Sno et al.'s IDEA to investigate déjà vu function and found very few differences between control and TLE déjà vu experiences, apart from associated fear, blackouts and headaches. Warren-Gash and Zeman's conclusion was:

> epileptic déjà vu was similar to physiological déjà vu, but was distinguished
> from it by its frequency and its associated features – the 'company it keeps'
> *Warren-Gash and Zeman (2014, p. 147)*

Warren-Gash and Zeman (p. 147) present the following account from a person with TLE:

> "At work I was on the phone and a colleague asked 'are you ok?' The conversation seemed familiar; I felt warm and had a metallic taste in my mouth. I had to sit down."

This account includes familiarity but also features other sensations and phenomena (a metallic taste, warmth) which would be very unusual in a healthy person's déjà vu. A development of this idea is shown in Figure 7.1. In short, where discharge is sufficient in the seizure activity we may expect adjoining regions to contribute to the intrinsic cognitive and physiological sensations caused by the SPS, but there will also be metacognitive and psychological reflections on the feeling of déjà vu. As an example, someone with TLE may well experience fear during a déjà vu experience because they know déjà vu to be associated with seizure. Whereas for a healthy person a déjà vu may be of little or no significance – or be an interesting glitch, as captured in the second quote at the beginning of this chapter – in TLE, higher-level interpretations and feelings may also affect the experience. On one level the associated experiences may be neurological in origin, reflecting a larger network of brain regions activated in the SPS; on another level, they may include thoughts and interpretations due to having epilepsy. Aydemir, Tekcan, and Özkara (2009) examined how people with epilepsy remember their first seizures (as an example) and showed that they retain very vivid, emotive accounts.

At present, there is therefore evidence to suggest that déjà vu is comparable in TLE and healthy groups, except for a set of related phenomena and experiences that are associated with but are not a part of déjà vu. However, one major limitation of this work is that it relies upon a retrospective, questionnaire-based report of previous experiences, which may induce bias and distortions, and also lack

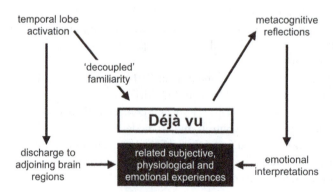

FIGURE 7.1 'The company that it keeps'. Neurological and psychosocial contributions to the quality déjà vu experience in TLE.
Adapted from Fortier and Moulin (2015).

phenomenological detail and specificity, in line with the critique of the IDEA (Sno et al., 1994) in the previous chapter. It is thus a major research priority to develop more precise and theoretically driven measures of déjà vu, and perhaps even more importantly, start measuring experiences online through smart phones, etc., as was carried out by Johanson et al. (2008). There are however some data on how brains differ between people with epilepsy who do and do not experience déjà vu, compared to healthy controls who do experience déjà vu, and it is this topic which is now discussed.

Structural neuroimaging of déjà vu in TLE

With this approach, the rationale is broadly the same as the Brázdil et al. (2012) study presented in Chapter 6: can we find structural differences in the brain that correlate with the frequency with which people experience déjà vu? Hypometabolism during fluorine-18 fluorodeoxyglucose positron emission tomography (FDG PET) has been shown to be a good indicator of the brain regions involved in the genesis and discharge of ictal events in TLE. The first study to utilise this method in assessing the functional anatomy of déjà vu was conducted by Adachi et al. (1999), who used a semi-quantitative analysis to compare the metabolic activity in a range of neuroanatomical areas in patients with and without seizure-related déjà vu. Patients were selected from a series of surgical candidates for intractable epilepsy; the sample included 14 patients with non-lesional unilateral TLE experiencing déjà vu habitually alongside SPS, and 17 patients not experiencing déjà vu matched for a number of epilepsy-related variables. Upon initial qualitative analysis, the groups' FDG PET images were indistinguishable, as a similar number of patients in each showed either normal uptake or diffuse hypometabolism of temporal areas in the left and right hemispheres. Using principal component analysis, they derived a factor (the 'visual network') that primarily included mesial temporal structures, the parietal cortex and other visual association areas where significant hypometabolism was found predominantly in the left hemisphere of déjà vu patients, regardless of the side of seizure onset. Interpreting their findings, the authors suggest that déjà vu may result from initial activation in mesial temporal structures, followed by spreading discharge into visual pathways; the activation of such a network helps explain the mnestic quality associated with the distorted visual cognition during déjà vu experiences. The approach of having two groups of patients with TLE who do and do not experience déjà vu has inspired other similar studies with the same design.

More recently, Guedj, Aubert, McGonigal, Mundler and Bartolomei (2010) conducted a similar FDG PET study, but used a voxel-based analysis to identify specific structures within the medial temporal lobes responsible for déjà vu, rather than the regional analysis adopted by Adachi et al. This study was theoretically guided by existing knowledge regarding the proposed specialisation of medial temporal structures in familiarity. The sample included two matched groups of eight TLE patients with and without déjà vu as part of their seizure manifestation. A matched control group of 20 neurologically intact healthy subjects was also used. In comparison with healthy participants, the déjà vu group displayed significant ipsilateral hypometabolism in parahippocampal regions (entorhinal and perirhinal cortices), the superior temporal sulcus, superior temporal gyrus. More fine-grained analysis of MTL regions also displayed hypometabolism in the amygdala and hippocampus. In comparison, TLE patients without déjà vu only displayed a significant hypometabolism within the hippocampus compared to controls. Several further voxel-based analyses were used in comparing the results between the two patient groups, all yielding the same pattern whereby TLE patients with déjà vu showed significant ipsilateral hypometabolism of the perirhinal and entorhinal cortices (parahippocampus) and superior temporal gyrus compared to patients without déjà vu.

The results support the finding of significant hypometabolism in the medial temporal lobe found in Adachi et al.'s (1999) PET study, but do not corroborate their suggestion of the involvement of the parietal cortex. The metabolic findings are interpreted by Guedj et al. as lending support to the thesis that the parahippocampal regions are specifically and independently involved in familiarity-based recognition, and hence déjà vu experiences.

In TLE, déjà vu appears to manifest alongside emotions of fear and occasionally pleasant feelings of nostalgia, as indicated above. Because the amygdala is proposed to be the key structure in emotional processing, Van Paesschen, King, Duncan and Connelly (2001) examined whether abnormal amygdalae in patients with intractable TLE have any localising value for SPS using MRI with amygdala relaxation time mapping (AT^2). They interviewed 50 patients before AT^2 mapping and obtained descriptions of SPS manifestations, which were classified into 15 types. As well as emotions such as fear, these also included déjà vu, which was defined as "a stereotypical feeling of familiarity, recognition, or reminiscence that the patient recognized as abnormal" (p. 858). Importantly, they excluded patients with evidence of multifocal seizure onset. Patients with an abnormal AT^2 reported a higher median number of SPS to those with normal AT^2 (six compared to three). Stepwise logistic regression analyses showed that déjà vu; cephalic (e.g. light-headedness) and warm sensations; gustatory hallucinations; and indescribable strange sensations were the best predictors in discriminating between those with abnormal AT^2 and those without. Of these, déjà vu emerged as the best predictor of abnormal AT^2.

Labate et al. (2015) used volumetric analysis to compare the brains of 32 people with TLE who experienced déjà vu, 31 people who did not experience déjà vu with TLE, 22 healthy controls who did experience déjà vu and 17 controls who did not experience déjà vu. To split the groups they again used responses on the IDEA. All groups underwent awake and asleep EEG, and whole-brain voxel-based morphometry was calculated for all participants. TLE patients with déjà vu and without déjà vu were matched for hippocampal sclerosis. Based on previous work (notably Brázdil et al.'s (2012) study), Labate et al. conducted specific analysis of prespecified regions: thalamus, hippocampus, basal ganglia, parahippocampal gyrus, visual cortex, temporal cortex, the sensorimotor cortex, the orbitofrontal cortex and the insular cortex. The groups in this study were elegantly designed as 2 × 2 (epilepsy versus healthy control and déjà vu versus non-déjà vu). As might be expected, there were main effects of disease status: there were lower grey matter volumes in several areas of the brain: the right primary motor/premotor cortex, the right insular cortex and the right thalamus. However, analysed like this, there were no main effects according to whether people experienced déjà vu, and no significant interactions either. Labate et al. continued their analysis by splitting down within groups separately. Like this, comparison of TLE patients with and without déjà vu revealed an abnormal *increase* of grey matter volume in the left hippocampus, parahippocampal gyrus and left visual cortex in patients having déjà vu. In the healthy control group, they found only a difference within the left insular cortex, where healthy controls having déjà vu showed *lower* grey matter volume. These results complicate those of Brázdil et al. (2012) reviewed in the previous chapter, but at least converge on the same regions, although the visual cortex finding is without precedent. There is of course a difference in methods and sample sizes between the two studies. Labate et al.'s finding of larger volume in critical areas for memory is consistent with studies that look at neuropsychological test performance using recollection and familiarity, reviewed below. In terms of comparing brain structures, this study points to there being different neural correlates of the experience in healthy and déjà vu groups. Although that does not necessarily mean there are functional differences or phenomenological differences between healthy and epileptic déjà vu, it does at least raise the possibility that the two are not directly comparable.

The structural imaging data in TLE thus point to the parahippocampal regions being critical areas: the hypometabolism in these areas points to a subtle structural abnormality that is related to déjà vu experiences. Groups of patients with TLE who do not experience déjà vu show metabolic differences from controls in this region. The conceptualisation of the parahippocampus as being involved in déjà vu is in keeping with current models of the temporal lobe and differences in recollection and familiarity. Because these studies are based on resting-state metabolism to make inferences about the structure of the brain, it is difficult to assess whether there is under- or over-activation of these critical brain structures. However, other neuroimaging measures, presented below, and cognitive neuropsychological investigations allow us to triangulate on this critical issue.

Intracortical brain stimulation studies

Wilder Penfield (e.g. Mullan & Penfield, 1959; Penfield & Perot, 1963) appears to be the first to have described how stimulation of the conscious brain can give rise to feelings of déjà vu, as covered briefly in Chapter 1. Direct stimulation of the brain is carried out in the context of epilepsy surgery. The idea is that the surgeon can apply current to various zones in the brain to map out important functions in the brain, but also to provoke the sorts of experiential phenomena experienced spontaneously in seizures. If the surgeon can stimulate a similar feeling in the patient as they experience in daily life, it indicates that they have identified a critical epileptogenic zone. In theory, the same stimulation of the brain could be carried out experimentally on healthy subjects, but for obvious ethical and practical reasons, this is not done. The careful consideration of the reports given by patients receiving this procedure (to whom researchers are indebted) can help us triangulate on the cause of déjà vu and its location in the brain, with the caveat that this is a very unusual procedure carried out on an unhealthy brain.

A somewhat typical experience report by a patient is given byVignal et al. (2007):

> "I'm reliving something … but I can see you clearly … It's as if what is happening now has already happened to me, it's like an old memory that I am in the middle of living out" (p. 92).

Penfield described déjà vu as an *interpretive illusion*, and classed vivid recollections of past memories separately as *experiential hallucinations*. He concluded that both of these types of experience were dependent on activation of the lateral temporal neocortex, in particular the superior temporal gyrus. Following Penfield's early work, a number of other studies emerged, all finding that stimulation of the MTL was able to provoke déjà vu in patients either directly (e.g. Halgren et al., 1978), or from after-discharge spreading from lateral areas to the amygdala (Gloor et al., 1982). The lateral site of administration in Gloor et al.'s (1982) study was the middle temporal gyrus, which did not support Penfield's earlier finding.

Bancaud et al. (1994) were the first to specifically link the dreamy state to contemporary memory theory whilst using intracortical brain stimulation. They report the assessment of 16 TLE patients involving the recording of subjective seizure manifestations during intracortical stimulation, chemical activation and spontaneous ictal events. Depth electrode stereotaxic EEG (SEEG) was performed to localise patients' seizures, including a variety of lateral and medial temporal stimulation sites. The authors categorised the 57 experiences generated by patients into four different types of dreamy state: memories of complete scenes; vague reminiscences; 'déjà vu–déjà vécu'; strangeness–familiarity; and non-classifiable. Of these, memories, reminiscences and déjà vu–déjà vécu were recorded the most. In terms of 'visual hallucinations', reminiscences and memory flashbacks were distinguished based on the vividness of detail reported by the patient. Interestingly, despite the visual quality of most dreamy states, rarely did patients report visual disturbance with the current perceptual environment. Instead, the visual element of these subjective experiences was essentially a memory, and Bancaud et al., like Hughlings Jackson, argue that elaborate visual hallucinations are distinct from the memory experiences in déjà vu and dreamy states.

Bancaud et al. found that dreamy states were provoked primarily by stimulation of the anterior hippocampus, followed closely by the temporal neocortex, and to a lesser extent the amygdala. Spontaneous seizures with dreamy states always involved the amygdala, anterior hippocampus and neocortex, the same sites always being implicated following stimulation of the anterior hippocampus. Stimulations to the amygdala and hippocampus involving dreamy states almost always spread to the neocortex (17/20; three amygdala stimulations failed to spread), but stimulation of the temporal neocortex only spread to these mesial temporal structures 8/15 times.

When taking into account the frequency with which each of these structures was involved in dreamy state seizures (either as the isolated stimulation site, or site of after-discharge), the temporal neocortex had the most, followed by the anterior hippocampus and lastly the amygdala. Bancaud et al. (1994) found the superior temporal gyrus an effective site, more so than the middle temporal (MT) gyrus. Laterality effects were not found for MT structures or temporal neocortex.

The authors concluded that the lateral and medial temporal lobe are equally likely sites of localisation, with lateral neocortical structures almost always being involved also, at least in the spread of activity in the initial 10 s following stimulation. For dreamy states to occur, all of these structures must be involved, but the findings suggest it is about ten times more likely to evoke a dreamy state from the medial temporal structures (anterior hippocampus/amygdala) than temporal neocortical sites. Interestingly, ipsilateral MTL stimulation was actually more difficult to generate dreamy states than on the non-epileptic contralateral side (also demonstrated by Halgren et al., 1978), thus lending support to the idea that déjà vu is actually part of 'healthy' brain activity.

Bartolomei et al. (2004) assessed the role of parahippocampal structures (perirhinal and entorhinal cortices) in déjà vu. They analysed the experiences generated from 240 stimulations in the rhinal cortices, amygdala and hippocampus in 24 patients. Overall, the subjective manifestations of stimulations in the rhinal cortices did not differ from those found in other mesial temporal areas, and no convincing effect of laterality was found. However, the frequency of different subjective phenomenon did differ between entorhinal and perirhinal cortices, and between rhinal cortices and other limbic structures; in particular, déjà vu and other memory phenomena. Stimulation of the entorhinal cortex was found to provoke déjà vu most often, whereas the perirhinal cortex was associated more with memory reminiscences; very few stimulations in the hippocampus and amygdala produced either of these responses. Overall, then, Bartolomei et al. displayed that illusions of familiarity were more likely to arise from stimulation of parahippocampal structures; they suggest that the previously reported involvement of other MTL structures may have arisen due to the localised discharge to the rhinal cortices. With these data, it appears that there is something of a continuum between decoupled feelings of familiarity and retrieval of autobiographical images and events from prior experience.

This issue was examined by Barbeau et al. (2005), who present an in-depth analysis of one patient who provided well-described experiential phenomena. Having established the roles of subhippocampal structures in dreamy states, they were motivated to address the issue of how the mnestic content of experiential phenomenon may map onto episodic and semantic memory systems. During SEEG investigation, this patient only reported experiencing experiential phenomena following stimulation of contacts located in the perirhinal region. Barbeau et al.'s findings point to the continuum between feelings of familiarity and more fully formed memories retrieved in context. For instance, they report how a first stimulation was associated with the subjective report of an image of a lake and some bushes, which the patient recalled as being a place he frequents. A second, higher-intensity stimulation in the same region resulted in the same pattern of after-discharge, and this time the patient experienced a visual image which he later confirmed was his brother's friend. These visual images related to decontextualised memories of people and places he had seen very often; essentially, these can be thought of as semantic memories or conceptual self knowledge organised into generalised events (see Conway, 2005).

Vignal et al. (2007) further attempted to delineate dreamy states with reference to the empirically established fractionation of long-term memory. They investigated 16 patients, looking to compare any differences between provoked and spontaneous experiences. They found that 45 per cent of dreamy states were evoked by amygdala stimulation, 37.5 per cent by the hippocampus and 17.5 per cent by the parahippocampal gyrus. There was a preference for dreamy states to arise from right-sided MTL stimulation, and in no cases was déjà vu reported from stimulation of the left MTL. Further, they found that both déjà vu and visual hallucinations were produced by an after-discharge to other medial temporal structures, and not the middle or superior temporal gyri as others have previously found. This was found for provoked and spontaneous seizures, and interestingly, after-discharge to temporal neocortex was associated with a lack, or termination, of dreamy state. Furthermore, in spontaneous seizures not involving the dreamy state, the after-discharge always spread to the whole temporal neocortex.

Vignal et al. (2007) also attempted to resolve some of the past inconsistencies in the classification of the subjective phenomena. They note the distinction made by Penfield and Perot (1963) between déjà vu (involving the altered perception of the present environment) and 'experiential hallucinations' (essentially involving a past memory). They also use the term déjà vécu throughout their report, but not necessarily with the same precision as the definitions given in Chapter 4; their patients were French speakers, and spontaneously used the terms déjà vu and déjà vécu to describe their experiences. No precise definition is given of their definition; it can be assumed that the déjà vécu reports here are synonymous with déjà vu. At the least, the results are clear that the experiences are predominantly visual and most of the memory 'hallucinations' were about people. Vignal et al. again suggest there is actually a continuum between the déjà vu experience and the production of 'hallucinations', as they were often reported to coexist during dreamy states (p. 96): "It is sometimes difficult to determine from the patients' descriptions whether a particular sensation is one of isolated déjà vécu or whether this is accompanied by a more elaborate hallucination, perhaps even for patients themselves." They propose that epileptic discharge restricted to the entorhinal cortex may result in a 'pure' sensation of déjà vu, but as activity spreads to other hippocampal structures and the amygdala, widespread functional activation of the fronto-temporal autobiographical memory network may result in a more intense visual mnestic experience. It is perhaps unhelpful to refer to these memory phenomena as 'hallucinations', and this may be a response to the aggressive criticism of Penfield's early work (e.g. Loftus & Loftus, 1980; see Chapter 2); the term hallucination distancing the patients' experiences from the now-discredited 'video-recorder' view of memory. Although it can be difficult to verify whether the material generated by such artificial stimulations is a genuine event from the past, it is experienced as a memory, and as such may be no different from other intrusive and false-memory phenomena, such as involuntary memories and 'mind-pops' (e.g. Kvavilashvili & Mandler, 2004).

There is thus a rather complex set of findings from the intracortical stimulation studies, with some inconsistencies between authors and methods. In sum, though, a number of interesting ideas come from this literature. First, the déjà vu experience seems to centre on activations that start in the parahippocampal (familiarity) region of the MTL. The extent to which one feels déjà vu or retrieves a memory seems dependent on the extent of the spread of the activation. A few of the above studies suggest that as it is easier to provoke déjà vu in the hemisphere opposing the site of the epileptic focus, this points to déjà vu being a healthy phenomenon rather than a pathological one. In short, the déjà vu found to be localised to the rhinal cortices may represent a lower-level disruption of familiarity circuits, but as additional temporal lobe structures (hippocampus, amygdala) are recruited, a more intense sensation of déjà vécu occurs, sometimes with vivid visual distortion and associations with past memories leading to a feeling of having already lived the current experience. For the memory researcher, a critical finding is the relationship between the magnitude of stimulation, discharge within 3D space within the brain and the phenomenology of the experience. For instance, Vignal et al.'s Patient 11 received two stimulations from the same electrode. At 2 mA there is a feeling of déjà vu, but at 2.6 mA there is the retrieval of visual imagery of a popular TV quiz show 'Who wants to be a Millionaire?'.

The work into such stimulations is fraught with problems of sample size and interpreting the subjective reports generated by patients. A priority in this area is to take the definitions of familiarity and recollection and experimental approaches in order to better understand the experiences generated. For instance, patients could be first trained on remember/know memory experiments to use standardised definitions before answering questions about their memory experiences. Regarding the brain, by definition, these are some of the more severe cases of epilepsy, cases that have typically not responded well to anti-epileptic medication, and people who may have subtle but real damage to the temporal lobe, such as sclerosis. As such, it may be difficult to understand the complex after-discharge and connectivity patterns measured by the electrodes. On the other hand, the consistency of the recent findings and the adoption of the theory-driven approach means that the idea that we can learn nothing from stimulation studies (Neisser, 1967) no longer holds.

In fact, technological advances mean that stimulation of the brain is becoming less invasive and of use in a number of different pathologies (e.g. Parkinson's disease, depression, and Alzheimer's disease; see Lee, Fell, & Axmacher, 2013, for a review), and we are set to learn more about déjà vu as a result. A pioneering article (Hamani et al., 2008) centred on a man who had deep brain stimulation (DBS) to treat morbid obesity using electrodes implanted in the ventral hypothalamus. The authors reported an unwanted effect on memory (including déjà vu sensations), which is not unlike the studies reported here:

> Unexpectedly, the patient reported sudden sensations that he described as déjà vu with stimulation of the first contact tested ... He reported the sudden perception of being in a park with friends, a familiar scene to him. He felt he was younger, around 20 years old. ... As the stimulation intensity was increased from 3.0 to 5.0 volts, he reported that the details in the scene became more vivid.
>
> *Hamani et al. (2008, pp. 119–120)*

Hamani et al. present detailed results of a neuropsychological evaluation of the patient, comparing memory performance with stimulation or no stimulation (in a double-blind fashion). The proportion of recollection in a remember/know procedure using recognition of word pairs increased from .17 to .38 when stimulation was turned on, suggesting that electrical stimulation of the hypothalamus using DBS modulates limbic activity and improves recollection, presumably through connections to the hippocampal memory system. In terms of the déjà vu experience when first setting up the DBS, there is again the idea of a continuum between déjà vu feelings and retrieval of vivid information, one which seems to share a relationship with the electrophysiological data. Similarly, Kovacs et al. (2009) report a non-epileptic case where DBS led to déjà vu: a 22-year-old woman treated with DBS of the left internal globus pallidus for hemidystonia. The globus pallidus is a subcortical structure, part of the basal ganglia complex.

Finally, it should be stressed that stimulating the temporal lobe leads to a whole host of strange phenomena and not just déjà vu, some of which are identified by patients as being material they have previously seen in dreams (often referred to as déjà rêvé). Again, it is hard to prove whether this is actually the case, or whether this explanation is an attempt to justify the generation of such bizarre imagery in such strange circumstances.

Case reports of déjà vu in TLE

The cognitive neuropsychology of memory owes much to the testing of single cases, and the use of detailed case reports of people with déjà vu is no exception. For example, O'Connor and Moulin (2008) report the case of a 39-year-old man (MH) who had never had déjà vu until he developed TLE after contracting encephalitis; he subsequently experienced prolonged periods of déjà vu before complex partial seizures (CPSs), during which he was initially frightened and disturbed. During testing he said that he "went through a period of looking away from what I was recognizing, hoping that this would get rid of the déjà vu. I now know that looking away, or at other things doesn't help, because the déjà vu follows my line of vision and hearing" (p. 145). This case suggests that, at least in epilepsy, the déjà vu is not limited to one percept in the environment. Rather than déjà vu being driven by the mismatch of current experience with similar previous perceptual experiences, O'Connor and Moulin concluded that it is an erroneous epistemic feeling arising from the alteration of normal higher-order processing; the decoupled familiarity hypothesis.

Another case points to the continuum between déjà vu and the retrieval of memories. Milton et al. (2011) describe a 66-year-old TLE patient with transient epileptic amnesia (TEA). TEA is characterised by interictal memory difficulties such as with autobiographical memories (e.g. Illman, Rathbone, Kemp, & Moulin, 2011; Kemp, Illman, Moulin, & Baddeley, 2012). The brief memory attacks in this group are often reduced following low-dose anticonvulsant treatment, but the interictal memory difficulties persist. Milton et al.'s (2011) patient presented with the clinical characteristics of TEA, including an extensive loss of autobiographical memories from his past that remained following treatment. He had never previously experienced déjà vu, but following his treatment period reported approximately 6–7 episodes that had the characteristics of déjà vécu-type experiences, i.e. he felt like he was *reliving* his current experience rather than just mere familiarity. Strikingly, after these episodes he then reported the spontaneous retrieval of a number of remote memories that had previously been inaccessible. His wife verified these memories. Formal testing of one of the recovered memories revealed that it retrieved with the same level of contextual richness, or episodicity, as matched controls. This case report mirrors the findings from stimulation studies, whereby patients report experiencing a déjà vu experience alongside the retrieval of visual memories from their past (e.g. Vignal et al., 2007).

Although déjà vu in TLE is experienced in the context of a neurological condition, it is not pathological in nature as they are generally short-lived and recognised as discrete illusory events by the patient. In contrast, a handful of case reports document the occurrence of more debilitating or persistent forms of déjà vu in epilepsy. Murai and Fukao (2003) report a 23-year-old male TLE patient who experienced déjà vécu-like interictal psychotic episodes. Initially, he only reported experiencing déjà vu auras, but this had developed into a reduplicative paramnesia in which he persistently felt like he was reliving an isolated four-year period of his life. This constant cycle of interpreting his current world as a replay of past events became so debilitating that the patient had attempted suicide on a number of occasions. Takeda et al. (2011) also describe a TLE patient with persistent déjà vu, but not associated with any psychiatric symptoms. Subsequent imaging revealed hyperperfusion of the left medial temporal area during blood perfusion single-photon-emission computed tomography (SPECT) and integration of MRI data identified the hyperperfused area to be in the left entorhinal cortex. The patient's persistent déjà vu was assumed to be a result of epileptic activity, and he was subsequently administered 15 mg/day diazepam for three days, which almost completely abolished it. SPECT was carried out again during this period, this time showing no sign of hyperperfusion in the medial temporal area. Takeda et al.'s single case was notable because of the persistence of and distress caused by the déjà vu experiences. This is one of a number of cases which point to an overlap between psychiatric presentations of delusional beliefs probably triggered by intense and recurring feelings of déjà vu (or déjà vécu, see below).

Finally, déjà vu is proposed to be relatively rare in children (this would be an interesting subject for study in contemporary research, and according to Brown's (2004) review, this has never been directly examined). Brown, however, concludes that the weak literature on this question suggest that "the metacognitive awareness of false familiarity may not be fully developed until the second decade of life" (p. 66). However, déjà vu is possibly of even more clinical interest in younger groups, as pointed out in a case report by Akgül, Öksüz-Kanbur and Turan (2013). They report the case of a 13-year-old female who described her experiences as: "this weird feeling that whatever happens to me in daily life, I feel that I have experienced it before" (p. 552). Nausea and palpitations but no other epileptic signs accompanied these feelings. Only after two days of constant EEG monitoring was any epileptiform abnormality (in the temporal lobe) detected – indeed, the changed rhythmic activity in brain waves occurred whilst the patient had her usual feeling of familiarity and repetition.

These case reports point to the heterogeneity of déjà vu experiences in TLE, and suggest that in some cases, déjà vu symptoms may be more permanent and traumatic. In general, they make some important theoretical points about déjà vu. First, at least in epilepsy, it is an unpredictable physiological event that does not appear to have any specific environmental triggers. Second, déjà vu may lie on a continuum with other memory-based phenomena.

Recollection, familiarity and déjà vu in TLE

To conclude this chapter, the experimental work of Martin et al. (2012) is presented. They have produced the work which best exemplifies how the cognitive neuropsychological approach can yield insights into déjà vu formation. One of their participants gives a particularly clear description of déjà vu:

> It's a really strange feeling. I'll feel like I've been somewhere before – like I'm looking at a snapshot of a scene that I've seen previously. The strange bit is that I also know that I have not been to that place before.
>
> *Martin et al. (2012, p. 2981)*

Of all contemporary literature into the déjà vu phenomenon in TLE, Martin et al. have perhaps the most strongly theory-driven approach, converging on the constructs of familiarity and recollection by using multiple paradigms to pinpoint the cognitive processes at play. Martin et al. (2012) took a sample of seven patients who 'consistently' reported déjà vu as part of an aura of their CPSs (TLE+) and a control group of six TLE patients who had never experienced déjà vu at any point (TLE–). There were also 26 healthy controls. First, as above, Martin et al.'s sample also points to déjà vu being mostly about scenes and a visual phenomenon, and also the idea of 'spreading' déjà vu to whatever is occupying attention:

It's highly visual. Things will suddenly become very familiar. There isn't a progression from vaguely to highly familiar; it's just highly familiar. It's initially object-specific, but when I focus my attention on something else it too becomes familiar. I will even search the room for something that isn't familiar but everything seems to be so.

Martin et al. (2012, pp. 2984–2985)

The novel contribution of this study was to run tests of recollection and familiarity using the two commonly used procedures from the recognition memory literature (see Chapter 3 for more details). In Experiment 1, the participants conducted a recognition memory test where they reported their subjective state at the point of endorsing an item as old (remember/know procedure), just as carried out with the undergraduate sample (O'Connor & Moulin, 2013, reported in the previous chapter). The stimuli used were images of indoor scenes. Experiment 2 used an exclusion procedure with repeating lures (e.g. Jennings & Jacoby, 2003). This is a recollection task that depends more on an objective measure of performance rather than a report of phenomenology. The task is to detect studied target items from distracter items, which repeat. Recollection is required to differentiate the repeating lures from the originally studied targets, as both will feel familiar.

Martin et al. found characteristic differences between their groups of TLE patients who did and did not experience déjà vu. The TLE+ and TLE– groups both showed deficits in recognition memory generally relative to the control group, measured with d', but they did not differ significantly from each other. The same pattern was found for familiarity responding: i.e. the TLE groups were both impaired but did not differ significantly from each other (although familiarity responding was above chance in the patient groups). Interestingly, the recollection measure did yield contrasting results. The TLE+ group had a *superior* recollection performance to the TLE– group, and their recollection was not different from healthy controls. That is, people who reported déjà vu were distinguished by the fact that they had more accurate memory when responding that they 'remembered' a previously seen target. The findings of Experiment 2 corroborated this pattern – the TLE groups showed a general deficit in recognition memory performance, and again the TLE+ outperformed the TLE– on the recollection component of the task, in this case being able to discriminate repeating distracter items from previously studied targets. Moreover, volumetric MRI showed that the déjà vu (TLE+) group had more intact ipsilateral medial temporal structures.

In sum, the Martin et al. data point to the role of recollection in the déjà vu phenomenon. This means that in TLE, to experience déjà vu one needs to have an intact recollection function to detect that the familiarity is false. Sufficient recollection resources and intact temporal lobe structures are needed to create the mismatch between familiarity and recollection. This is a key finding in the déjà vu literature because it points to a delicate imbalance between recollection and familiarity, with impaired familiarity and intact recollection; a pattern of memory impairment which is relatively rare. Importantly, in a patient (MR) with selective damage to

TABLE 7.1 Patient MR's false-positive errors for items assigned to 'know' across four different recognition tasks

	MR *z scores*
Familiar words	17.00
Unfamiliar faces	3.33
Pseudowords	0.71
Familiar faces	2.50

the entorhinal cortex, Brandt, Eysenck, Nielsen and von Oertzen (2016) show the same pattern. MR experienced several seizure types, amongst which she had SPSs with déjà vu. On cognitive testing, she showed intact recognition based on recollection. For instance, 82 per cent of familiar words that were correctly recognised were 'remembered'. However, her recognition memory decision making was impaired when she used familiarity, and she also showed a liberal bias in her responses, making many more false-positive errors. Her *z* scores for false positives across four different types of recognition memory are given in Table 7.1.

Whilst the subject of investigation of MR was not specifically déjà vu, the authors do note that she does experience a great deal of déjà vu, and this would be expected given Martin's previously published results. The article converges on a critical idea to have emerged from the TLE literature, that it is the dissociation of recollection and familiarity which generates déjà vu. Intact recollection processes play the role of interpreting the familiarity signal and are involved in detecting the clash in memory processes at the heart of the déjà vu experiences (even though it might be hypothesised that this monitoring of conflict is traditionally thought of as being a prefrontal cortex activity). Why the parahippocampal hypometabolism in this patient would lead to an excess of familiarity responding is unclear (and the more so for familiar words). However, from the stimulation studies that converge on the same region, it may be supposed that there is some form of over-activation or uncontrolled synchronisation of this zone which leads to decoupled familiarity.

It is also worth pointing out that the idea of needing intact recollection and impaired familiarity to generate déjà vu supports what is found with older adults (who have the opposite pattern) and who experience less déjà vu. On the other hand, Brázdil et al.'s finding that the brains of healthy participants who have déjà vu have smaller temporal lobe structures needs reconciling with this account, but to do so will need a finer-grained analysis of parahippocampal and hippocampal structures.

Classifying déjà vu experiences in TLE

To better understand déjà vu in TLE, and to distinguish the 'company that déjà vu keeps' from experiences and cognitive processes that might be central to the experience, a few authors have tried to subdivide the experience, although there has been a general lack of a coordinated effort in terms of definitions used by one team and another. Here a few proposals are made to consider prescience, déjà vu, déjà vécu, and involuntary memories as related phenomena which might enable us to better differentiate subtypes of déjà vu and their neurological bases.

Prescience

Sadler and Rahey (2004) have carried out probably the only systematic review of prescience as part of the seizure presentation of TLE. They described their use of the term thus:

> A patient was encountered whose seizures begin with a profound sense of being able to predict imminent events in her environment. This experience fulfills the definitions of precognition ("antecedent cognition or knowledge; foreknowledge") or prescience ("knowledge of events before they happen"). These experiences can be distinguished from the more common psychic phenomenon of déjà vu
>
> *Sadler and Rahey (2004, p. 982)*

As an example of the possible dissociation between prescience and pure 'familiarity only' déjà vu, consider first Kovacs et al.'s (2009) patient: "she felt that the situation seemed familiar. No visual or auditory illusions or hallucinations accompanied the déjà vu ... the patient felt neither the ability to predict the future or unreality about current circumstances" (p. 191). Then consider Sadler and Rahey's descriptions given by their Case 1, for example:

> "They start with a rising feeling in my stomach, and a feeling of déjà vu, by which I mean I feel like all of this has happened before. At the same time I have a different feeling that I know what is going to happen next. For example, one day I was talking to a customer in my store, and I had the pro-found sense that I knew what he was going to say next. On other occasions I have looked at a customer just as the seizure is starting and I have a feeling that I know which compact disk he is going to go over and pick up."
>
> *Sadler and Rahey (2004, pp. 982–983)*

In fact, the separation between déjà vu and prescience is not always that clear, in both healthy people and people with epilepsy. Quite aside of differences in the use of the term and the precision of classifying patient descriptions *post hoc*, there are several reasons why they may be difficult to separate. First, logically, if a person feels they can predict the future, one interpretation of this feeling is that they have there-fore experienced the current moment/place/decision/conversation before. This logical problem leads to a chicken-and-egg problem with the association between familiarity and prescience, but one might imagine that it is the low-level decoupled familiarity which is intensely experienced which triggers the interpretation of a prior experience for which one is able to predict the future, rather than the other way around. First we experience familiarity. If this feeling of familiarity persists over a few seconds and through the unfolding of events, it would be reasonable to feel as if we could predict the future and what is about to happen. According to this view, déjà vu experiences with prescience would be more intense and longer-lived than the 'pure familiarity' kind.

A second way of interpreting the relationship between familiarity and prescience comes from the characterisation of the adaptive nature of memory. The memory system has presumably evolved in order to make decisions about upcoming events on the basis of prior experience (e.g. Klein, Robertson, & Delton, 2010):

> For an organism to behave more appropriately (i.e., more adaptively) at a later time because of experiences at an earlier time, the organism must be equipped not only with mechanisms that retrieve ontogenetically acquired information, but also with mechanisms that use this information to make decisions and to plan behaviour.
>
> *Klein et al. (2010, p. 14)*

More generally, in recent years, episodic memory has begun to be seen as part of a system that reconstructs events from past or the future (e.g. Schacter, Addis, & Buckner, 2007). As such, it is normal that prescience and familiarity should be connected in this way. According to this view, we are able to sense the future in that we use an overlap with past experiences to detect what is coming next. In this fashion, familiarity with what is happening in the present may enable, through triggering recollection of specific prior experiences, or by signalling an overlap in prior events and the current experience, a 'prediction' about what is to happen next.

In part, the episodic feeling-of-knowing (FOK) paradigm (e.g. Souchay et al., 2000) shows how these kinds of contingencies operate. If in a study phase we have learned the word pair (House–Wine) and at test we are unable to recall the word *Wine* when prompted with *House*, we are often able to sense the impending retrieval of the information (what is coming next) and reliably predict our future performance. It has been demonstrated that this capacity to predict future performance is based on the familiarity with the cue word (House) – the stronger the degree of familiarity for the cue, the more likely we are to predict we will recognise the other part of the cue later (e.g. Koriat & Levy-Sadot, 2001). Similarly, for solving difficult problems, Metcalfe and Wiebe (1987) have shown that participants can make meaningful 'warmth ratings' which are informative about the time course of problem solving and may signal the upcoming solution to a task. These two examples, however, are somewhat removed from the bizarre and often mystic experience of being able to predict what will happen next.

More work needs to be carried out on prescience in order to find an analogue in healthy people (see also 'presque vu' covered in Chapter 4) and a laboratory task which evokes such strong feelings of prediction of the future. Studies show, incidentally, that episodic FOK is unimpaired in temporal lobe epilepsy (e.g. Howard et al., 2010), even where there is enough disruption in the temporal lobe to produce an episodic memory deficit. However, nothing is known about the relationship of FOK and prescience or déjà vu in TLE, even though the relationship between FOK and delusional memory/recollective confabulation has been researched in other pathologies (see Chapter 8). It seems reasonable, however, to conclude that prescience may signal the involvement of stronger feelings of familiarity, including an attempt to resolve or make sense of the familiarity, and may therefore signal a higher intensity of experience, and possibly even a discharge into a larger network.

Déjà vu and déjà vécu in TLE

Illman et al. (2012) assessed whether the distinction between déjà vu and déjà vécu (discussed in Chapter 4) might be helpful in classifying TLE patients' experiences, and indeed whether in the epilepsy literature there was any evidence of such a distinction. This is perhaps an ambitious aim given the lack of consensus with regards to a definition of déjà vu, and the reliance on a retrospective classification (and particularly on the IDEA which makes no distinction between recollection and familiarity). It is research a priority to use this classification, *a priority*, when asking patients about their déjà vu either retrospectively in questionnaires, or as it occurs spontaneously or under stimulation.

Illman et al. proposed that there is some evidence that déjà vu and déjà vécu are separable experiential phenomena; a distinction identifiable qualitatively in the context of spontaneous and provoked epileptic activity. Moreover, there is some suggestion that the differences in phenomenology are attributable to the functionally independent neural substrates of memory on which their genesis relies. The research reviewed here suggests that parahippocampal areas are involved in the familiarity felt in déjà vu, but also that the more extensive the network implicated, the more complex and complete the déjà experience is (e.g. Vignal et al., 2007). By this view, we could see that mere familiarity results from the activation of a more restricted network, but with extra recruitment or after-discharge to connected areas, the more recollection-like the sensation becomes, and ultimately, partial retrieval may result and even uncontrolled retrieval of visual imagery and emotional content (sometimes referred to as a hallucination).

This straightforward view of the neurological picture of déjà vu/déjà vécu does not receive uniform support. Takeda et al.'s (2011) TLE patient (mentioned above) with persistent and unpleasant experiences seems to describe something more intense and déjà vécu-like: "Whatever happens to me in daily life, I feel that I have experienced it before. I feel like I'm living again the same life that I have lived before" (p. 196). Neuroimaging revealed hyperperfusion of the left medial temporal area and integration of MRI data identified the hyperperfused area to be in the left entorhinal cortex. Takeda et al.'s patient's description of his experience would appear to be consistent with the definition of déjà vécu. Critically, however, the imaging evidence suggested localised dysfunction in the entorhinal cortex was responsible, which is not in line with our view of the larger, broadly speaking, hippocampal network involved in more intense and elaborate versions of the experience (recollection-based déjà vécu).

Moreover, a case reported by Lee, Owen, Khanifar, Kim and Binder (2009) found that frequent episodes of déjà vu were the result of neurocysticercosis localised in the amygdala; following right-sided amygdalectomy sparing the hippocampus, the patient's episodes of déjà experiences ceased. As indicated by the DBS procedure carried out on the hypothalamus (Hamani et al., 2008; above), the convenient hippocampal–parahippocampal story linking déjà vu and déjà vécu does not always hold, and indeed the amygdala and the hypothalamus have both been seen as critical structures in déjà vu formation. It does seem unlikely that such a complex phenomenological experience can be explained by a single structure, and certainly, the most informative study would come from a comparison of all available investigation methods (SEEG, imaging) on groups of patients experiencing different kinds of déjà experiences. Unfortunately, such patients are uncommon and invasive brain recording methods cannot be used *ad hoc* for research purposes. Again, this calls for a need for a better characterisation and description of déjà vu experiences, and perhaps a comparison within individuals with experimental methods.

In an attempt to tighten up the classification of different types of déjà vu, given the notion of differences between familiarity and recollection and the continuum with the retrieval of images from autobiographical experiences, Illman et al. (2012) produced a summary table (see Table 7.2) suggesting a possible classification of déjà vu experiences.

TABLE 7.2 A proposed classification of déjà vu experiences in TLE (adapted from Illman et al., 2012)

Characterisation	Déjà vu	Déjà vécu	(Episodic) Involuntary memory
	Familiarity alone: 'prior occurrence'	Recollection: 'prior experience'	'Specific prior episode'
Feelings			
Familiarity	Yes	Yes	Yes
Prescience	None	Possibly	None
Mental time travel	None	Yes	Yes
Content			
Emotion	None	Possibly	
Visual images	None	None	Yes
Source/context	None	Possibly	
Narrative-like coherence	None	None	Possibly
A defined past	No	Yes	Yes
Recall/reproduction of material	None	Partial	Complete
Time course	Shorter	Longer	–

Summary: insights from temporal lobe epilepsy

Recent research has shown a rapid growth in the number of scientific articles discussing déjà vu in TLE and this chapter has outlined a number of key findings. First, studies of provoked déjà vu by intracortical stimulation point unequivocally to it being a phenomenon associated with erroneous firing in the temporal lobe, and suggest it may lie on a continuum with intrusive/involuntary episodic memory retrieval. Most importantly, the work of Martin et al. (2012) points to déjà vu being the result of an imbalance between recollection and familiarity mechanisms, but that intact recollection was necessary to experience déjà vu. The field has in part been driven forward by single cases and classic neuropsychology, examining cognitive models in reference to specific, measurable mechanisms (such as the difference in recollection and familiarity). This research shows how single cases can continue to illuminate the cognitive neuropsychology of memory (Rosenbaum et al., 2014).

On the other hand, the neurological data are less clear-cut, as a very complex picture emerges when trying to make generalisations across methods and disease types. Moreover, the existing data are largely based on single case studies or series across different laboratories, and with different languages spoken. There is little standardisation of definitions, and little sharing of information. Moreover, the predominant models for understanding the brain, and the technologies for measuring activation and structure, have shown massive improvements and changes in the last few years. As pointed out in O'Connor and Moulin (2010), the search for a déjà vu 'module' or 'zone' in the brain is now considered a fruitless task.

O'Connor and Moulin (2010) outlined several factors to consider when localising déjà vu in the brain, centred on the idea that memory should be thought of as a network of activations rather than a region or a zone. Indeed, spreading activation is frequently considered by those reporting stimulation studies, but O'Connor and Moulin point out that these analyses considering the local topography of the brain by adjoining electrodes do not consider the overarching role of the functional connectivity network, for instance the role of the prefrontal cortex. Considering spreading functional network activation provides the opportunity for a more distributed set of nodes, which may be located in areas distant from a critical 'déjà vu region', but may nonetheless be responsible for the experience of déjà vu. This is seen in the globus pallidus stimulation, which caused contralateral mesial temporal activation in Kovacs et al. (2009). These considerations of a precise functional network in which activation is localised is important given that the displacement of functional connectivity 'seed' regions by millimetres, even within the same brain structure, can lead to the identification of vastly different networks or the identification of differing regions on the borders of the same functional network (O'Connor, Han & Dobbins, 2010b). This is perhaps most critical when comparing activation and experiences resulting from artificial electrical stimulation in adjoining regions.

The congruence of the localised activation with the activation in the rest of the functional network is potentially the most nuanced consideration, an issue that stems from the familiarity–recollection pattern in behavioural data. Recent studies have found that different patterns of intra-network correlations are associated with different behavioural states (e.g. Cohen & Maunsell, 2009; Fair et al., 2009). Aberrant activation of a certain region may therefore differ not only when compared with baseline activation, but also when compared with the pattern of activation within other regions of the same functional (memory) network. Within such a framework, the clash in evaluations of the déjà vu experience is intuitively plausible; mesial temporal structures may aberrantly indicate a sensation of familiarity or recollection despite the rest of the hippocampo-cortical network (and probably frontal structures) indicating a lack of recognition. This also may explain how erroneous familiarity is experienced in the context of a functional network which is still able to accurately recollect the past.

In sum, with the development of theories of déjà vu, and cognitive models of the experience, it will be important to continue to make reference to TLE. In this fashion, TLE represents an important case where the neuropsychological data can test the cognitive models. One perhaps philosophical or conceptual issue to iron out will be that whereas theories of déjà vu that stem from epilepsy research assume that it is an event which is generated by misfiring in the brain, and is thus top-down, experimental cognitive psychology experiments aim to provoke déjà vu by stimuli in the environment. Perhaps one way of addressing empirically this issue would be to have patients undergoing electrode implantation and stimulation to also take part in the sorts of experiments that have generated déjà vu-like experiences in healthy people in laboratory conditions. One should imagine similar patterns of electrical activity in the brain for the electrically provoked and environmentally provoked experiences of déjà vu.

8
RECOLLECTIVE CONFABULATION

> He refused to read the newspaper or watch television because he said he had
> seen it before. However, AKP remained insightful about his difficulties: when
> he said he had seen a programme before and his wife asked him what hap-
> pened next, he replied, "How should I know, I have a memory problem!"
>
> *Moulin et al. (2005)*

Recollective confabulation is a symptom of memory impairment that is often
described as being like permanent or persistent déjà vu. People with recollective
confabulation present with striking delusion-like features, such as calling a TV
repairman because their television is constantly repeating, or claiming that other
people – strangers – have very regular habits, doing things at the same time in the
same place every day. Critically, recollective confabulation is not like permanent déjà
vu, because these patients act on their feelings, and are not aware of the fact that they
have a false sense of familiarity. Recollective confabulation can arise as the result of a
number of different pathologies, but has most often been described in dementia and
in older adults. Conceptually, it is important to distinguish recollective confabulation
from déjà vu by stressing that in recollective confabulation the experient is not aware
of the feeling of repetition – patients with recollective confabulation are delusional
in that they act upon it and believe that their life is repeating.

Cases of recollective confabulation

In 2005, Moulin et al. published a paper reporting two patients with dementia
who presented with what was described as being like permanent déjà vu,[1] and
who made a very high number of false positives accompanied with the subjective
report of 'remembering' on tests of recognition memory (patients AKP and MA;
Moulin et al., 2005). These two patients exhibited striking behaviour in everyday life,

withdrawing from almost all novel activities, complaining that they had experienced them before, and their beliefs were resistant to reasoning from their carers or contrary evidence. They did not present with any other delusions or strange beliefs, nor did they report that they could predict what would happen next, just that they had already experienced events. The problem did not appear to be one of mere familiarity, either, because the patients were prone to spontaneously generate confabulated material to justify their feelings of repetition. Moreover, these justifications seemed to be 'memory-like' in their nature. As an example, AKP (Moulin et al., 2005) justified having read the newspaper before by telling his wife that he had got up before she was awake and had read the newspaper as it was unloaded at the newsagents, before returning back to bed. As such, these patients displayed what is described as recollective confabulation, as typified by the response AKP made to the question of why he thought he had been previously interviewed for a radio show:

> The surroundings are the same, and that – without being offensive – your sight against the filing cabinets and so on, and the heater, it looks familiar. Since then, [my] memory got slightly worse, that's all. Besides, you asked the same questions. Why I remember them, and whether they are really the same, I don't know, but it seems like it.
>
> *Patient AKP in Moulin (2013, p. 1542)*

As with delusions, these feelings of repetition and the associated confabulated justifications were almost completely immune to reason. They were held with very high conviction, as described by Mr K.'s son (O'Connor, 2007, p. 214):

> When we travelled round France, my father saw a hospital and said, "I have been here before, I visited this hospital to see my friend." He then told the story of his previous visit to confirm his memory. When he was asked how this could be possible when he had never visited France before, my father said, "I know that I have never been here when I consider my personal history seriously and logically, but I still strongly feel that I have been here before."

Table 8.1 gives an overview of published cases of recollective confabulation. To these, the case of Louis (Arnaud, 1896) should probably be added (see Bertrand et al., 2017, for a translation and interpretation). Like the patients in Table 8.1, Louis suffered a delusion that may be described as being like constant déjà vu; he believed himself to have encountered newspaper articles before, and confabulated a source for the information. In Arnaud's paper, he describes how Louis claimed to have already met the people he met in a very distinctive context: watching the funeral procession of Louis Pasteur. Louis' delusion was persistent and he was somewhat anosognosic, not appearing to understand the nature of his memory problem. However, he did have some awareness, as summed up in this quote from the

TABLE 8.1 Summary table of patients with recollective confabulation (adapted from Moulin, 2013)

Case	Age	Diagnosis	Example behaviour (caregiver report)
Moulin et al., 2005			
AKP	80	MCI	Wife finds a £1 coin in the street, AKP claims he put it there for her to find; complains that he has watched or read the news before
MA	70	Alzheimer's disease	On a trip to an electrical store to mend the washing machine, MA reported that she'd been to the exact same office before and sat in the same chairs with the same people
Moulin, 2013			
HF	80	Alzheimer's	HF and his wife recently moved to a new area, and when they visited the hospital for the first time, HF was certain that he had been there before and had sat in the same chair
YM	77	Alzheimer's	YM's daughter reports that YM comments that she has seen things or has been places before when she hasn't
DW	79	Alzheimer's	Déjà vu mainly only occurs for television programmes, and is most notable for premieres
PA	77	Fronto-temporal dementia	Wife reports that he has a tendency to stare at people and feels he recognises strangers, for example a man at the bus stop who he thought he knew from Cambridge
JE	82	Alzheimer's disease	Déjà vu occurs when visiting novel places
RH	79	Alzheimer's disease	Symptoms of déjà vu are most prevalent at night, thinks he has repeatedly got up in the night. Reports thinking that he knows and recognises everybody. Feels as if he has already watched TV programmes and can predict what happens
LH	81	Alzheimer's disease	Practically all of the time when watching television LH will think he has seen the programmes before and cannot be persuaded otherwise
ACC	89	Depression	Momentary experience, but often feels that he has seen a whole TV programme before
IB	75	MCI	IB reports having been places before when she has not. Also described having already seen a plastic bag in the hedge before, and of having read a newspaper before that she had already purchased

TABLE 8.1 *(cont.)*

Case	Age	Diagnosis	Example behaviour (caregiver report)
FH	76	Alzheimer's disease	FH's wife said that it often happened that when walking down the road, he would say "I saw that person dressed the same, at exactly the same time last week"
PG	77	Alzheimer's disease	PG's partner commented that he had episodes of déjà vu, particularly for places. When visiting new places for the first time, or seeing a place on television to which PG had never been, PG would comment that he remembered going to them
JM	84	MCI	JM wrote to the BBC complaining that everything on TV was a repeat. She also called a TV repairman to come to fix her TV due to it repeating everything
Craik et al., 2014			
VL	81	Probable Alzheimer's disease	"While passing through a small town VL noticed a shabbily dressed man standing on a corner and exclaimed, 'You'd think that man would have other things to do – he's always standing on that corner!'" (p. 369)
Shanks et al., 2014			
HF	74	Amnestic MCI	"On meeting him for the first time he said, 'I am certain that I have seen you both before, four or five weeks ago.' His wife affirmed that he believed everything had happened or been seen by him already, even when she knew this was not possible. The experience included events, conversations, meeting strangers, TV programs, newspapers, and the content of books." (p. 408)
Turner et al., 2017			
EN	38	Severe closed head injury (aged 26 in 1994)	"His father reported significant problems consistent with déjà vécu. He said that EN had delusions about events re-occurring, especially with large sporting events that he was watching on television. When EN saw these events on television he insisted that he had already seen them before. He always reported that he had seen them in 1994 when he was in the Brain Injury Unit of the hospital where he had been treated following his accident." (p. 143)

Notes: MCI = Mild Cognitive Impairment.

question and answer session reported in the 1896 article, where he evades the issue of reporting the nature of subsequent events:

> M. CHARPENTIER – M. Arnaud's patient claims that all his impressions were already felt by him. We could try to control his statements by real points of reference. I remember a sufferer who stabbed his wife; he maintained that he had received the injury, and showed his scar.
> M. BRIAND – In the case of abnormal events, we could ask the patient what was the outcome.
> M. ARNAUD – I tried. He evades this by responding: I don't remember; my memory is bad.

Patient AKP's response to a similar question quoted at the beginning of this chapter is remarkably alike. Contemporary recollective confabulation patients show behaviours and describe experiences that are very similar to those reported by Arnaud. These patients refuse to read newspapers or watch television programmes. Like Louis, they identify public events (such as the Bali bombing in 2002; Moulin et al., 2005) as having already occurred. Turner, Shores, Breen and Coltheart (2017) have even identified that memory of such public events may be particularly prone to recollective confabulation (see below).

One clear difference between Louis and all but one contemporary case of recollective confabulation is aetiology. Table 8.1 shows that nearly all patients have been older adults, and most have had a dementia-like presentation. (A somewhat broader spectrum of age and diagnosis is shown in Table 8.2, which summarises the unverified reports of carers from email correspondence.) It is difficult to pinpoint the cause of Louis' neurological damage. His age, the reported onset after repeated fever and the reference to headaches are in keeping with a diagnosis of neuroinflammation, possibly due to cerebral malaria or other tropical disease. Arnaud reports repeated episodes of fever, which when experienced in malaria can, in rare cases, lead to neurological symptoms (e.g. Idro, Jenkins, & Newton, 2005). At the most severe, cerebral malaria leads to severe neuroinflammation, coma and psychiatric symptoms and cognitive changes, even memory impairment (e.g. Najjar, Pearlman, Alper, Najjar, & Devinsky, 2013). There is also some overlap with the case reported by Murai and Fukao (2003) in the previous chapter. Their 23-year-old male TLE patient experienced déjà vu-like interictal psychotic episodes. Initially, he only reported experiencing déjà vu auras, but this developed into a form of delusion in which he persistently felt like he was reliving an isolated four-year period of his life. This constant cycle of interpreting his current world as a replay of past events became so debilitating that the patient had attempted suicide. The level of distress and the idea of a repeating period of life are very similar to Louis. However, the cases of older adults with recollective confabulation, whilst presenting with depressed mood and a lack of engagement with many activities, are not particularly distressed by their symptoms and certainly do not show

TABLE 8.2 Further descriptions of recollective confabulation as reported by correspondence with carers (adapted from O'Connor et al., 2010)

Age	Diagnosis	
74	Memory difficulties	"Chronic déjà vu. I can't find any explanation, or correlation with any of her physical ailments … it gets worse during stress … but has become chronic (multiple times a day). It is bothering to her and worrisome to me. It is triggered by both novel events and mundane, common occurrences, but much more prevalent with change of environment."
85	Early dementia	"She doesn't read or watch TV because 'she's seen or read them all before'. She even told me that CBC must be on strike because they are running re-runs … we were out for a drive and were about 20 km from home. We passed a couple walking along the side of the road and mom said she had seen them earlier that morning when she was out for her walk around the block. I tried to explain that it was doubtful that it could be the same couple but she insisted that she could describe the coat the lady was wearing and proceeded to do so."
Unknown	Stroke	"One of the most striking features of her brain injury was this newfound sense of having seen every single show on television before, years ago, when she was younger. This was, ironically I suppose, coupled with an inability to remember what had happened at the beginning of the show by the time the program ended. She also developed a tendency to make up memories from her past that had never actually happened (childhood events and the like) and recounts them very detailedly, never realising that they are in fact false."
78	Unknown	"My parents decided to not let the déjà vus interfere with their winter vacation and went to Florida. My Dad reported that the déjà vus were stronger and more frequent. Museums, restaurants, beaches, stores and people never visited, were all seen/felt/done before. They were worse than when at home … At the flower show a week back, we were standing there, looking at a display and she said 'oh I saw that before, last night on TV, I think', then, she saw a lady pass us and said, 'you've seen her, she's on TV. I know I've seen her before'."

TABLE 8.2 (*cont.*)

Age	Diagnosis	
86	Unknown	"In the last two years of her life (she died at 88) I would have to say that she essentially lived in almost a constant state of déjà vécu whenever she was removed from her narrowly defined daily routine (in an assisted living residence). Whenever she spent time with me, for example, there was continual reference to 'the trees have sure grown taller,' total strangers on the road had 'gotten fat and, look, he has a new dog,' and every stranger she met was assured that she knew them already. Newspapers had been read before, she had repairmen in to find out why the television kept showing programs she had seen before, newly published books had been read years before, etc."

the type of agitation and frustration reported by Arnaud. As such, Louis may remain something of an outlier in terms of recollective confabulation.

Another case which is a little different from the collection of recollective confabulation patients presented in Table 8.1 is EN (Turner et al., 2017), who, like Louis, is far younger than the majority of the published contemporary cases. Most notably, EN's recollective confabulations are limited to public events. Below is a transcript of an interview between Martha Turner (MT) and EN.

> EN: I saw the tsunami and I said "That happened when I was in hospital in Sydney!" And I said – "We're finally catching up!". I thought "get over the déjà vu, I'll be able to start living a normal life now!"
> MT: So when did the tsunami actually happen? What year?
> EN: Well I reckon I saw it when I was in hospital in 1994.
> MT: And they were showing reports of the 1994 tsunami more recently?
> EN: Yeah. They were finally showing in the country what I saw in hospital in 1994.

Turner et al. also asked EN if his experiences were like déjà vu:

> MT: Have you heard the term déjà vu? Is there any difference between that and the kind of thing you experience?
> EN: Well everyone says "you only think you've seen it before". But I'll swear black and blue that I have seen it before.
> MT: So with these kinds of events … with the sports and everything else, you're sure that you've seen it before?
> EN: Yeah I'm 100% sure that I saw it when I was in hospital.

EN did not have dementia but was assessed 12 years after a severe head injury sustained after a fall from a cliff. It is noted that he presented later with an 'apparent delusional condition' and that he had experienced severe memory difficulties and a lack of awareness into his condition since his discharge. The head injury was described as combining hypoxic and diffuse axonal damage, with a depressed fracture of the left frontal bones. The case of EN, along with what we can glean from Arnaud's report of Louis, stresses that recollective confabulation is a symptom which may arise as the result of several different pathologies. Indeed, spontaneous confabulation more generally can result from a range of different aetiologies, from the more well-known, such as Korsakoff's syndrome (e.g. Kopelman, Thomson, Guerrini, & Marshall, 2009), to the lesser known, such as immunologically mediated dementias such as non-paraneoplastic syndromes (e.g. Rosenbloom, Smith, Akdal, & Geschwind, 2009). As with recollective confabulation, dementia, particularly Alzheimer's disease, can present with confabulations (e.g. Attali, De Anna, Dubois, & Dalla Barba, 2009), although it is not thought to be a typical part of dementia. Even amongst the older adult recollective confabulation patients, unknown or varied causes can produce the same symptoms (such as stroke, or mild cognitive impairment, see Table 8.2). Indeed, it is possibly even the case that the unusualness of recollective confabulation and its similarity to delusional states may hamper the diagnosis of a more 'neurological' presentation of memory impairment in Alzheimer's disease, given as it leads to an atypical presentation. In any case, recollective confabulation, like delusional memory and confabulation symptoms more generally, seems to arise from several different neuropathologies.

Another way in which EN differs from the other cases is that as well as having recollective confabulation only for public events (particularly sporting events), his prior study episode is always reasoned to be his previous stay in hospital. He traces back all his feelings of familiarity for the present to a specific period in 1994 when he was previously hospitalised. In contrast, the other patients tend not to have well-defined specific periods in which they first experienced the repeating events, and their sensation is in fact of continued repetition of a non-specified past, for example: "He's here every time we come to this place!" (VL, Craik et al., 2014, p. 369). AKP read car number plates and stated that the drivers had "very regular habits", "always passing by at the exact same time every day". Such sensations also referred to the mundane: when shopping with his wife, AKP would say that it was unnecessary to purchase certain items, because he had bought the item the day before. There is some attempt by patients to understand the feeling of repetition and rationalise a specific study phase. Often, the previous episode is just the day before, but both AKP and Arnaud show a tendency to report that events are repeating at exactly a year's interval, a judgement cued by knowing the date. For instance, AKP, when signing his consent form for his research visit, claimed that it was also on the 6th of December the previous year that he had been visited to conduct research, supporting his claim that it was, again, at that time, St Nicholas' day.

Recollective confabulation and recognition memory decision making

In neuropsychological testing, all of the patients reported in Table 8.1 had demonstrable impairments on standardised tests of memory. In particular, research has focused on the measurement of recognition memory, and a summary of patient scores on recognition tests is shown in Figure 8.1. In this graph, false positives are given on the x-axis, whereas hits are plotted against the y-axis. It can be seen that with the patient scores tending to be more rightward than the control means for the same tasks, the patients make many more false positives (and often fewer hits, also). In terms of z scores, the patients make at least 3 standard deviations' times the amount of false positives on the same task. There are of course differences according to the type of task used, and the patient tested, but the general pattern is one of

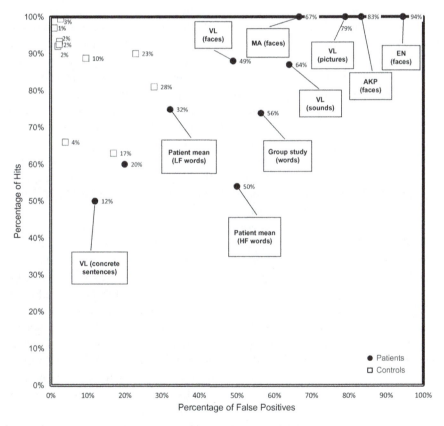

FIGURE 8.1 Rates of false positives (as a percentage, x-axis) and hits (as a percentage, y-axis) for recognition memory tasks in patients with recollective confabulation. For references and patient initials see Table 8.1.

Notes: control data are for age-matched control performance on the same tasks. Patient means are taken from Moulin (2013).

making high amounts of false positives. For example, AKP made a high number of false positives whether tested with forced-choice or source-memory designs, and for words, pictures of objects, and faces. Similarly, VL made significant amounts of false positives for all types of materials, including sentences and sound effects of environmental sounds.

Moulin et al. (2005) reported that AKP and MA also made false positives for low-frequency words, such as *dirge* or *puck*, when it is unusual to make such errors in healthy groups due to their distinctiveness (Gardiner & Richardson-Klavehn, 2000). Reports from spouses suggested that false recognition was also more pronounced for more distinct events in daily life, e.g. a funeral announcement, a radio interview, a striking piece of world news, seeing a woman have a fit whilst on holiday, or finding money (O'Connor et al., 2010). Initially, it was thought that these errors for such distinctive events were not consistent with the view that it was pre-existing familiarity that was driving the sensation, but the opposite – novelty. The relationship between novelty and recollective confabulation is discussed below.

Based on these experimental findings and observations, Moulin et al. (2005) suggested that the core deficit was one of 'recollective confabulation' and that the more information engaged attention, the more novel that it was, then the more it gave rise to a feeling that the event or stimuli had been encountered before. The initial argument was that because veridical recollection is associated with a subjective feeling of having experienced an event before combined with the retrieval of contextual information and experiences at study, then the false recollection of erroneous contextual details pointed to this being caused by an underlying erroneous feeling of recollection. AKP and MA made such reports spontaneously. For instance, AKP confabulated secret early morning trips to the newsagents to read the newspaper as it was unloaded from the lorry in order to justify his belief that he had already heard about the news in the morning paper.

In favour of this hypothesis, it was found that AKP and MA were very likely to ascribe the subjective experience of remembering (R) to their false positives (as measured using the remember–know paradigm presented in Chapter 3). This is a striking finding. There can be no veridical contextual information present for false positives made to non-studied items, and as such it is usual to observe a higher proportion of familiar (F) than R responses for FPs in healthy groups. This arises because an unstudied item can feel familiar (e.g. Gardiner & Richardson-Klavehn, 2000), but cannot give rise to the retrieval or 'remembering' of contextual specifics. Indeed, in Moulin et al. (2005), the control group's very few false positives were mostly (62 per cent) assigned to F responses or guesses. In comparison, AKP and MA, respectively, assigned 57 per cent and 43 per cent of their false positives to the R response category. Importantly, this did not appear to be merely due to a misunderstanding of the response categories: AKP reported that he 'remembered' the word 'kink' because he "could not hear what it was", and it was indeed the case that the word had to be repeated to him during the study phase, and he made a familiar judgement for the word 'part', reporting "It is so familiar it is hard to tell." More justifications for patients and controls are given in Table 8.3.

TABLE 8.3 Some examples of justifications of R and F judgements for patients and controls, taken from Experiment 3 (Moulin et al., 2005)

	Stimuli – word	Status	Judgement	Justification
Patients	Science	FP	F	"Just rings a bell, a familiar word."
	Bargain	FP	F	"I just feel I saw it, what else can one say?"
	Puck	FP	R	"By association – change the first letter."
	Plaza	FP	R	"Polish is the same, it means beach."
	Enigma	FP	R	"Enigma Variations, it sticks in the mind."
	Edict	Hit	F	"Just a feeling."
	Modernist	Hit	F	"It's vague, I think I saw it before."
	Gondola	Hit	R	"I remember seeing this at the beginning."
	Polka	Hit	R	"Polka is Polish for female."
Controls	Preference	FP	F	"I think I saw it, not remember."
	Employment	Hit	F	"I think I've heard it."
	Arrival	Hit	F	"I'm not sure, it just seems to me."
	Fissure	Hit	R	"I saw rocks opening."
	Handkerchief	Hit	R	"I thought the word is so out of the group, the others are posh."
	Gondola	Hit	R	"Almost certainly, it's a romantic thing."
	Polka	Hit	R	"I made an association with polka dot. It's a Polish word, it means woman."

Notes: FPs = false positives; R = remember judgement; F = familiar judgement.

Is recollective confabulation a problem of familiarity?

A critical issue is whether we should describe the core problem in recollective confabulation as arising from false recollection or false familiarity. It appears that the problem is one of *experiencing* remembering, in the sense that *justifications* for the repetition of the current moment are confabulated rather than the mere sensation of familiarity. However, one priority for research into these patients is to consider whether the underlying memory problem is one of near-continual false familiarity, or a false recollection problem. To differentiate these two is perhaps impossible (and indeed an invalid question if one is of the view that there is only one sole process in recognition memory, see Chapter 3) given their subjectivity, but in an attempt to address this issue, experiments with high- and low-frequency words have been used, where we can make inferences about pre-existing levels of familiarity of the items to which the patients are making recognition decisions. If the decisions are being driven by familiarity, we should see more false positives for high-frequency words, but if the core problem is one of recollection, we might see that there are more false positives for items which are distinctive and therefore more easily afford the classification of being 'recollected'.

To this end, a 30-item yes/no recognition memory test with equal numbers of high- (e.g. *Marriage*) and low- (e.g. *Bayonet*) frequency words was administered to patients and controls (Moulin et al., 2013). Participants were visually presented 30 words intermixed in a pseudo-random order and made a pleasantness judgement for each word. This was followed immediately by a test in which the 30 previously presented targets and 30 word-frequency matched 'new' words were read aloud individually in an intermixed pseudo-random order. Participants indicated whether the word was old or new. If they reported the word as old they immediately made a judgement of their subjective experience based on recollection, familiarity or guessing, as above.

Recognition memory was measured across all items and for all subjective states by analysing the discrimination index, where false positives are subtracted from the hits. The controls outperformed the patients (see Table 8.4). The recollective confabulation group was significantly above chance – responses were not just random. The analysis centred on the pattern of performance across subjective category (familiar and remember) and high- and low-frequency words. Critically, for false positives more false positives were made for high-frequency words in general across both groups. As expected, the recollective confabulation group made significantly more false positive errors in recognition, but each group made on average more high-frequency false positives than low-frequency false positives. If anything, the difference between false positives in the recollective confabulation patients group was higher than in the controls' – they show more of a susceptibility to make false

TABLE 8.4 Group means on the recollective experience task (Experiment 1) for high- and low-frequency words. Controls, $n = 16$; Recollective Confabulation patients, $n = 14$ (taken from Moulin, 2013)

	Controls		Recollective Confabulation	
	High frequency	*Low frequency*	*High frequency*	*Low frequency*
Hits	13.31 (1.49)	(14.00) (0.97)	11.43 (3.43)	11.36 (3.02)
False positives	1.44 (1.86)	0.37(0.86)	8.64 (4.97)	4.93 (3.83)
Proportion of hits R	.81 (.16)	.81 (.22)	.57 (.32)	.53 (.31)
Proportion of hits F	.16 (.13)	.17 (.19)	.32 (.22)	.35 (.27)
Proportion of FPs R	.08 (.16)	.08 (.17)	.33 (.27)	.26 (.28)
Proportion of FPs F	.50 (.43)	.33 (.47)	.43 (.36)	.49 (.37)
Proportion of R correct	.99 (.04)	.99 (.05)	.64 (.26)	.87 (.17)
Proportion of F correct	.64 (.39)	.60 (.49)	.55 (.27)	.62 (.32)

positives for high-frequency words than low-frequency words. This finding suggests that familiarity is driving the tendency to make false positives in this group, something that is completely in keeping with healthy memory errors (Gardiner & Richardson-Klavehn, 2000).

The proportion of hits assigned to remember (R) and familiar (F) for high- and low-frequency words was also analysed. On the whole, participants made significantly more R responses than F. However, the patient group actually assigned fewer Rs and a higher proportion of Fs to their hits. This does not point to an exaggerated tendency to report subjective experience as R, at least for their correct recognition. As with other studies into memory impairment in dementia (e.g. Barba, 1997), these data show that the ability to endorse items as old on the basis of remembering is diminished.

The critical analysis was the examination of false positives assigned to each subjective experience category. There was the expected main effect of subjective state such that more false positives were assigned to familiar than remember. On the whole, this analysis supports recollective confabulation patients making false positives on the basis of familiarity, not recollection. A subanalysis on the patients indicated that the proportion of false positives assigned to R or F, as a group, did not actually differ for high- or low-frequency words.

Performance given the assignment of a particular subjective category was also analysed. That is, if someone assigns an R to an item at test, what is the probability that it is a correct answer? If it is dysfunctional recollection that is behind the experiences of people with recollective confabulation, we might expect low levels of performance for items given an R. On the other hand, if familiarity is impaired, this might be shown in the proportion correct of items assigned to F. The proportion of each subjective category that was correctly recognised was analysed (also shown in Table 8.4). The main effect of word frequency was not significant. There was, however, a higher proportion correctly recognised for R than for F items. Whereas the controls show little or no difference in performance for the high- and low-frequency words (with performance slightly higher on the high-frequency words), the patients perform much better on the low-frequency words than the high-frequency words (75 per cent versus 60 per cent). This is consistent with distinctiveness being used to enhance recognition memory – again, not consistent with a deficit in recollection. The group by subjective state pattern shows both groups having superior performance for R judgements, but this pattern is more pronounced in the control group. This latter analysis permits the comparison of group performance against chance. Whereas healthy controls were significantly above chance for R responses and not for F responses, with no difference according to word frequency, the pattern was the opposite in patients. In patients it had no bearing on their performance whether the item was reported as an R or F – only the objective status of the word determined above-chance responding, with the patients being above chance only for low-frequency words.

Recollective confabulation patients are a memory-impaired group, who on the whole, whilst making a lot of false positive errors, have a pattern of subjective responses in keeping with controls. Their responses are in general in line with the objective qualities of the stimuli used (word frequency). It appears that their problem is one of familiarity – their performance is poor on materials that have a pre-existing level of familiarity, such as high-frequency words, and their subjective report of familiarity has little bearing on their actual performance.

What are the justifications given in recollective confabulation

Thus far, it might be suggested that recollective confabulation patients have a familiarity problem which leads to them justifying this familiarity by falsely 'recollecting' a previous study phase. Immediately, this poses some critical questions about what 'remembering' is, even in healthy populations. It is possible that any form of justified 'remembering' like this is reconstructed, online, during a retrieval attempt. In this way, it is proposed that the patients' making sense of their feeling of familiarity is a natural reaction that has been learned throughout the lifetime. When we have a strong feeling of familiarity, it triggers a search in memory. If we are able to recover some specifics from the study phase, we will use those, but perhaps if not, we will still attempt a justification. This is a proposal that needs some extra experimentation.

It is arguable, however, that the experience of remembering serves some epistemic purpose (as argued in Chapter 3). 'Remembering' indicates what mental state is currently in mind (see Conway, 2009; Wheeler, Stuss, & Tulving, 1997; Moulin & Souchay, 2014). When we experience remembering, we usually have a high degree of certainty that what we have in mind is a memory and not a daydream, fantasy or some other kind of mental construction. It is, of course, possible to have recollective experience for false memories of the autobiographical kind (e.g. Conway, Collins, Gathercole, & Anderson, 1996) or for words presented in lists (e.g. Roediger & McDermott, 1995). Thus, when these recollective confabulation patients report 'remembering' a prior episode, they believe themselves to be remembering but cannot find a mental representation that could stand as a memory. They instead focus on the stimuli most closely associated with their feeling of remembering and confabulate an explanation, usually in the form of a false memory, that accounts for or justifies the feeling. In support, similar mismatches between justifications and objective memory performance are also seen in healthy older adults (Perfect & Dasgupta, 1997). Whereas young people show a high level of concordance between think-aloud reports of processes at encoding and subsequent justifications of R responses, older adults have been shown to justify R responses on the basis of sensory experience that they did not previously report at encoding. Thus, this chronic recollective confabulation may be an extension of a normal memory process.

Recently, Coltheart (2017) has suggested that all confabulation arises as part of a healthy process applied to an abnormal situation. Confabulations more generally (but here it is proposed this is very much the case for reclusive confabulation) are responses to abnormal experiences arising from brain damage (by definition).

However, Coltheart argues that the occurrence of confabulation itself need not be seen as due to any impairment of cognitive processes due to the brain damage. He claims that it is instead "a consequence of a general property of human cognition that is often referred to as 'the drive for causal understanding'" (p. 62). To support his idea, he describes four cases of confabulation from healthy people, people undergoing hypnosis, amnesics and delusional patients.

In healthy groups, Coltheart cites the example of consumers justifying their evaluation of products (de Camp Wilson & Nisbett, 1978), a decision that seems a long way from a recognition memory decision. Wilson and Nisbett presented people with four identical pairs of nylon stockings. Fifty-two passers-by were asked to judge which of the four pairs was of the best quality. After making their choice, participants were asked to justify it with the question "Could you tell me why you chose that one?" Only two people reported any suspicion that the pairs of stockings were identical. That is, 50 people – the vast majority – offered a justification for their choice. "Most of the subjects promptly responded that it was the knit, weave, sheerness, elasticity or workmanship that they felt to be superior" (Wilson & Nisbett, 1978, p. 124). Coltheart points out that these opinions are groundless – objectively false – just like a confabulation, but they act to support the decision-making process and justify it to a third person: he places an emphasis on the 'conversational' role of confabulation. Therefore, the process of confabulation, especially when we seek to understand strong feelings of familiarity, for example, may not be an inherently pathological process. In this way, in some very rare cases, a healthy process of justification of a previous memory is misapplied to the present moment, and this is recollective confabulation. The question then arises as to why the person with recollective confabulation does not reject out of hand the familiarity as false – as we do in healthy déjà vu – but instead intensifies and adds to the problem by confabulating a justification for their false recognition.

Metacognitive accounts of recollective confabulation

O'Connor et al. (2010), Moulin (2013), Craik et al. (2014) and Turner et al. (2017) have all proposed two-factor interpretations of recollective confabulation. These two-factor accounts are all broadly similar in that they address the underlying cognitive deficit (presumably a problem with overactive familiarity) and the interpretation of the familiarity (the inability to reject the familiarity as false and the generation of confabulated recollections of prior events). According to Langdon and Coltheart (2000), the interaction of two factors is necessary for the formation of a delusion, and thus, this account sees recollective confabulation as a type of delusion. According to Langdon and Coltheart there is first a neuropsychological anomaly that alters perceptual or emotional processing and so disrupts the "perceived reality". Second, there is damage to a system of belief evaluation that is responsible for the person's failure to reject the erroneous belief that stems from the first neuropsychological anomaly. As such, this second factor could be seen as metacognitive – a failure to interpret and reject the false feeling of familiarity, and the inappropriate generation of supporting material from memory.

This interpretation of the two-factor account can be tested by considering metacognitive accuracy. Both Moulin (2013) and Turner et al. (2017) have tested metacognition in their experimental work with recollective confabulation patients. Research into the feeling of knowing (FOK) in semantic memory (general knowledge) reveals somewhat unremarkable results, in that patients seem appropriately cautious and do not feel that they 'know' information that they do not know: their metacognition is intact. However, the data for episodic memory points to a deficit. For instance, a second experiment in Moulin (2013) measured how confident the patients were in their episodic memory recognition decisions. This was a two-alternative forced-choice recognition task, which had been used previously (Moulin et al., 2003). Participants first made a forced-choice decision of which of two items was old and then rated their confidence in this decision on a three-point scale. The data from healthy controls and Alzheimer's patients was compared to a group of patients with recollective confabulation.

For overall recognition performance, the older adult control group outperformed both patient groups, and there was no significant difference in performance between the recollective confabulation and control (non-recollective confabulation) dementia patients. Mean proportion correct (and SDs) for the recollective confabulation, non-recollective confabulation control and older adult control groups, respectively, were .64 (.08), .66 (.13), and .92 (.06). For confidence in responses, it was found that whereas the controls assigned most of their responses to the certain category (which is appropriate given their high level of performance), the non-recollective confabulation patients assigned most of their responses to the guess category. The recollective confabulation patients showed a pattern that was somewhat between these two groups: they made significantly more certain responses and fewer guesses than the non-recollective confabulation comparison group.

Thus, the recollective confabulation patients perform objectively worse than controls but have a level of performance which is in keeping with patients with dementia without recollective confabulation. However, subjectively, those who have recollective confabulation show some overconfidence in their recognition memory responses in comparison to the dementia control group. This points to a metacognitive failure. The final analysis concerned the relationship between the subjective and objective indices of memory on this task, presented in Figure 8.2. On the whole, the groups performed significantly better on the items for which they assigned higher levels of confidence. However, the recollective confabulation group showed a somewhat different pattern, with performance being arithmetically lower for the quite sure category, compared to when they were guessing: they were more likely to be correct when they guessed than when they felt quite sure.

To analyse the appropriateness of the subjective reports of confidence, a gamma correlation was calculated for each participant. This is a non-parametric measure of association between people's confidence response and their recognition accuracy (see Nelson, 1984). A gamma correlation closer to one indicates accurate memory

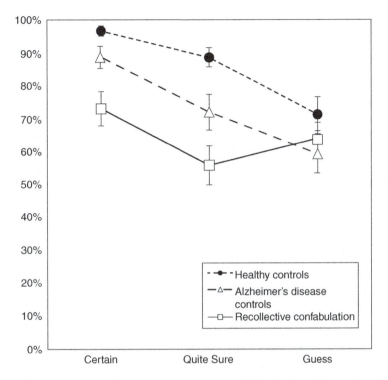

FIGURE 8.2 Proportion of correct recognition at each level of confidence for patients with recollective confabulation, healthy controls and controls with Alzheimer's disease. Error bars are 1 standard error of the mean.
Adapted from Moulin (2013).

monitoring, where a person correctly recognises more items of which they were more certain. A gamma correlation of zero indicates no association between confidence and recognition performance. The mean (and standard deviation) gamma correlations for the control, non-recollective confabulation and recollective confabulation groups, respectively, were .64 (.46), .58 (.35) and .11 (.48). The healthy controls and those with dementia but without recollective confabulation had gamma correlations that were significantly different from zero, whereas the recollective confabulation patients did not produce gammas that were significantly different from zero. Moulin (2013) concluded that the recollective confabulation group have a metacognitive deficit. Whereas the dementia control group are able to accurately assign subjective evaluations to their recognition performance, the recollective confabulation group show a significant impairment in this regard, and actually do not make assessments of their recognition that are above chance. This represents a double deficit in keeping with a dual-factor account: there is a memory deficit (which is comparable to that seen in dementia), but in addition there is a significantly poorer metacognitive evaluation of memory.

Patient EN was not found to have a metacognitive deficit, at least for general knowledge, and was not in fact prone to make 'over-extended' remember judgements on episodic tests. Moreover, to recap, his recognition memory performance was normal for words and objects, whereas recollective confabulation was found across tasks and materials for Moulin's patients and for Craik's patient, VL. Turner et al.'s (2017) account is based on a second factor of 'source monitoring'. When EN was tested for the source of knowledge in experimental tasks, his performance was at chance levels. This is a subtly different form of two-factor account, but one that, as discussed below, at least resonates with the neuropsychological account of recollective confabulation. Shanks, McGeown, Guerrini and Venneri (2014) also propose that source confusion may give rise to recollective confabulation. Further research work with recollective confabulation patients should aim to reconcile these differences, although as well as the differences in tasks used (which is easy to address) there is a clear heterogeneity in patients (which is more troublesome).

Novelty and recollective confabulation

One of the more interesting features of recollective confabulation is that it seems that more striking, less commonplace, distinct events trigger more intense episodes of recollective confabulation. On hearing of the death of a close friend, for instance, AKP claimed that he had already heard the news and he even refused to go to the funeral, claiming that he had already been. These experiences were also frequently experienced on holiday (O'Connor et al., 2010). One patient, Mrs M (reported in O'Connor et al., 2010, and part of the sample in Moulin, 2013) presented having complained to the BBC about the high levels of repeats on television, and also as having called a repairman to fix her television given how it was repeating. Strikingly, Mrs M was unhappy watching new television programmes, in particular, the soap opera, *Neighbours*, but she was happy watching old films that she had already watched before. Ironically, whilst watching DVDs of old films, she said she could happily watch them again, as she had forgotten what had happened. When meeting recollective confabulation patients in their own homes for the first time, they claim to have met the researcher like this before. Interestingly, this comment is not made on subsequent visits.

This emphasis on novelty as a trigger was consistent with research on the relationship between novelty and recollection (e.g. Jeewajee, Lever, Burton, O'Keefe, & Burgess, 2008) – especially in the hippocampus (see O'Connor et al., 2010). In short, the detection of novelty is supposed to trigger the encoding of information that may recruit neurally overlapping regions responsible for recollection (e.g. Tulving, Markowitsch, Craik, Habib, & Houle, 1996). O'Connor et al. (2010) developed a neuroscientific account of why novelty might lead to recollective confabulation. The basic idea is that signals produced in the temporal lobe are misinterpreted as signalling the retrieval of information from memory, rather than the usual encoding activity. This neuroscientific account is supported by hippocampal mechanisms based on theta activity, such that the phase of theta is switched through 180 degrees between encoding and retrieval in the hippocampus. Theta oscillation is an approximately 4–10 Hz oscillation, which is very prominent in the EEG recorded from the hippocampal formation. A strong determinant of whether information is subsequently remembered or forgotten is the phase of theta that the information arrives at. For more about the seemingly paradoxical role of the hippocampus in both novelty detection and remembering, see Barbeau, Chauvel, Moulin, Regis and Liégeois-Chauvel (2017).

Largely based on research from non-human animal subjects, it has been suggested that theta oscillation separates encoding and retrieval modes in the hippocampal memory system (Hasselmo, Bodelón, & Wyble, 2002). A simple explanation, but one that is very difficult to test, is that recollective confabulation arises because of a faulty interpretation of the theta signal by a second system or structure which is responsible for monitoring the firing of the hippocampus, either in response to a memory task, or novelty detection. This idea is intuitive and based on sound neuroscientific data, at least from rodents, but is unsupported in any subsequent work. O'Connor et al. sum up this theory as follows (2010, p. 139):

> Although our hypothesis is not testable using fMRI, it can be tested using electrophysiological recordings of both EEG and single neuron firing patterns. Using electrodes implanted in the hippocampus, evidence in support of our hypothesis would include the following:
>
> - When stimuli are presented that elicit false recollection, CA1 or the downstream neocortical region neurons fire with a similar mean theta phase of firing as that occurring during genuine recollection of past events.
> - However, when stimuli are presented that do not elicit false recollection, the CA1 or neocortical neurons fire with a different mean theta phase of firing to that occurring during genuine recollection.
> - A complementary approach is to show that the downstream neocortical neurons, which typically fire during recollection-elicited states of high theta coupling between the hippocampus and the neocortical region in question, can also fire in abnormal circumstances (seizures, pharmacological intervention), and when they do fire, subjective sensations of 'recollection' accompany such firing.

Recollective confabulation as reduplicative paramnesia

Recollective confabulation may also be described as reduplicative paramnesia. Reduplicative paramnesia has been described as a "rare memory disorder characterized by the subjective conviction that a place, person or event is duplicated" (Pisani, Marra, & Silveri, 2000, p. 324). Feinberg and Shapiro (1989, p. 40) describe a form of reduplication where "the patient maintains that his current experiences are a repeat of past experiences". They suggest that reduplicative syndromes occur where an unfamiliar environment or event appears in a 'pathologically familiar form', and they specify that reduplicative paramnesias may resemble déjà vu.

Reduplicative syndromes are classified within the category of delusional misidentification and are experienced in a wide range of neuropsychiatric aetiologies (for a review, see Feinberg & Roane, 2005). Delusions more generally are not uncommon in dementia, with estimates as high as 30–40 per cent of all Alzheimer's patients having had delusions (Sultzer et al., 2003). Lyketsos et al. (2002) surveyed 362 patients with dementia and 320 with Mild Cognitive Impairment (MCI) using the Neuropsychiatric Inventory (NPI; Kaufer et al., 1998). From the onset of cognitive symptoms, the cumulative prevalence of delusions in their dementia sample was 30 per cent. Of relevance here are delusional misidentification syndromes, which have been reported in dementia. Capgras' delusion, which is the delusion that a familiar person has been replaced by a double, is thought to occur in about 2–30 per cent of patients with Alzheimer's disease.

Mendez (1992) reports seven cases of dementia with delusional misidentification syndromes, where the focus is on misidentification of people (and Capgras' delusion). Of these seven cases, two present with reduplications which involve time. Case 4 was an 83-year-old who claimed that her nurse had been replaced by a substitute who intended to harm her. In addition, she "had episodes of déjà vu, e.g. saw a person on a bicycle and claimed that 'I have seen all this before'" (p. 415). Case 6, an 88-year-old woman, denied the identity of her daughter and claimed there was a good and a bad version of her. In addition, "She had episodes of unfamiliar events appearing familiar, e.g. driving on unfamiliar streets she said 'that car is always here every time we go by here'" (p. 415). She also had visual hallucinations of familiar persons.

These cases and the definition of reduplicative paramnesia show a clear overlap with the concept of recollective confabulation. The accounts above about observations of reduplication for seeing people whilst walking down the street resonate with AKP's observations that people must have very regular habits, always passing by the same place at the same time. Critically, reduplicative paramnesias, including Capgras, are usually described as deriving from inappropriate familiarity, whereby the core delusion is driven by a lack of subjective familiarity, which is then interpreted by intact long-term memory systems that apply justifications to the underlying sensation. For instance, a patient with Capgras will be able to recognise his wife (i.e. they are not prosopagnosic), but will nonetheless find her unfamiliar. To reconcile this clash in evaluations, the patient will justify this mismatch with the belief that the wife has been replaced by a double – such that it appears like her, but is not her – i.e. is simultaneously 'known' but unfamiliar. In the case of reduplication the underlying sensation is familiarity rather than unfamiliarity (as described by Pick, 1903). For instance, in the Frégoli delusion, one misidentifies an unfamiliar person as a more familiar one. Finally, according to Pisani et al. (2000), reduplicative paramnesia is caused by "difficulties in organizing, in the right space and time, memories that are similar and can be distinguished only by a correct contextual analysis and encoding" (p. 327). The delusion arises then because the patient attempts to resolve intact factual knowledge of the world with erroneous feelings or inappropriate affective signals. This resonates with the source monitoring account proposed by Turner et al. (2017) outlined above.

The role of the frontal lobes in recollective confabulation

Neuroanatomically, several different strands of evidence converge on the expectation that frontal structures (specifically in the right prefrontal cortex) are critical in the generation of recollective confabulation. Traditionally, in terms of memory function, frontal structures are thought of as controlling and monitoring the output from the temporal lobes (e.g. Moscovitch, 1994). The frontal lobes are also involved in source monitoring (see Mitchell & Johnson, 2009, for an overview). Also, frontal lobe damage is thought to be involved in reduplicative paramnesia. These strands of evidence are presented below.

Acquired brain damage in the right frontal lobe has been shown to give rise to false recognition. Schacter et al. (1996) present a case of false recognition following right frontal lobe infarction, BG. This case is different from those presented here in that he did not have false recognition that resulted in disturbances to daily life or spontaneous recollective confabulation. Nonetheless, he was prone to making very high rates of false positives on recognition memory tests, and was prone to report subjective remembering as the basis for his endorsement of non-studied items. In line with this view, Schacter et al. suggest that their patient had an over-reliance on memory for the general features of the study episode, possibly based on an initial fast familiarity-like assessment, but that this was re-experienced as remembering due to a failure of strategic monitoring of memory. In support, Hintzman and Curran (1994) have shown that initially, healthy participants assess items in a recognition memory test on familiarity, looking for a general similarity between study and test items. In this initial familiarity-based assessment, false positives to similar items are particularly prevalent. Ninety milliseconds later, when recollection can bring to bear on the recognition decision, false positives are less likely, when retrieval of specifics can correct the initial feeling of familiarity based on similarity.

Reduplicative paramnesias are also thought to arise due to a misconnection or disruption to fronto-temporal circuits, particularly following damage to right frontal areas (Feinberg & Roane, 2005). Feinberg and Shapiro (1989) specify that a right frontal disruption leads to a disturbance of familiarity, and that this leads to an illogical attempt – a confabulation – of why the "familiar is experienced as strange or vice versa" (p. 46). Feinberg and Shapiro reviewed 96 published cases of reduplicative syndrome patients, and found significantly more patients with right hemisphere damage.

Tabet and Sivaloganathan (2001) present a case that resembles those presented in this chapter; an 87-year-old woman who presented with an 8-week history of "subjective feelings of familiarity where new events were viewed as an exact repetition of previous ones" (p. 18). There was no feeling of precognition. However, the patient was unlike the recollective confabulation patients presented here because she was distressed by her episodes, and she showed insight into her problem. Her EEG was normal, but she showed a generalised atrophy and a well-defined high-density mass lesion in the right frontal lobe.

In the published cases of recollective confabulation given in Table 8.1, relatively little is known about the brains of the patients. In Moulin's large study of a group of patients, neuroimaging is weak if non-existent for many of the patients, although neuropsychological test scores do point to executive function deficits in a few of the patients, including AKP, which Moulin et al. (2005) cited as supporting the idea of frontal involvement in recollective confabulation. However, patient HF (Shanks et al., 2014) showed no such deficits on executive function tests, and an MRI scan showed mild generalised atrophy in temporal and parietal regions with more substantial neuronal loss in the right hippocampus. There are no functional imaging reports of patients with recollective confabulation.

Perhaps the clearest neuroanatomical evidence comes from Craik et al. (2014). VL showed low normal executive function test scores at worse, and as in Moulin et al. (2005) this was mainly due to poor semantic category fluency scores. The MRI investigation of VL's brain included statistical tests and a group of healthy, age-matched controls. In a whole-brain analysis, she showed significantly lower grey matter volume in both the right and left frontal lobes (particularly on the lateral surfaces). VL also showed significantly lower grey matter volume in the right temporal lobe. She also showed marginally reduced grey matter in the left temporal lobe, left and right occipital lobes and the left basal ganglia. A second analysis focused more specifically on the temporal lobe in detail, comparing the hippocampus, parahippocampal cortex and amygdala–entorhinal–perirhinal (AEP) complex. VL showed significantly reduced volume bilaterally in the hippocampus and parahippocampal cortex, whilst the AEP complex was reported to be within normal limits. This gives us the clearest picture of recollective confabulation arising from a fronto-temporal network. Craik et al. propose this neuropsychological account: "we suggest that owing to binding failures in MTL [medial temporal lobe] regions, VL's recognition processes were forced to rely on earlier than normal stages of analysis. Environmental features on a given recognition trial may have combined with fragments persisting from previous trials resulting in erroneous feelings of familiarity and of recollection that were not discounted or edited out, due to her impaired frontal processes" (Craik et al., 2014, p. 367).

Summary: groundhog days and déjà vu

What do these patients tell us about déjà vu?

These cases of recollective confabulation do not have a déjà vu, even though it may be described as being like permanent déjà vu by others (such as carers and medics). A critical feature of déjà vu is that it involves a *knowing* clash of evaluations. Where the experience is not recognised as false by the experient, as in the cases presented here, it is not déjà vu. By comparison, one can have fleeting feelings that a familiar face somehow looks different, such as an old friend looking older when you study their face closely, and this may briefly feel strange. But this mismatch between familiarity and unfamiliarity is not resolved in a pathological manner – fleeting (and normal) experiences like this are not Capgras' delusion, in the same way that these patients do not have déjà vu. It can be proposed that if these recollective confabulation patients did have intact metacognition, they may experience their false familiarity as constant déjà vu. However, it will remain necessary to use a variety of déjà experience terms (déjà vu, déjà vécu) with these patients simply because they are used by carers and clinicians to convey the unusualness of the experience.

Conceptually, understanding why recollective confabulation is not the same as déjà vu offers some insight into what causes healthy déjà vu. Recollective confabulation points to a metacognitive failure that results in erroneous familiarity being acted upon, and recollective details being confabulated in support of the erroneous recognition. Déjà vu, on the other hand, is produced when the experient is aware of the false nature of the déjà vu experience. These patients thus illustrate the importance of intact metacognition and appropriate evaluations in the generation of déjà vu (and also the suppression of false memories). The two-factor model is critical here. It is the double deficit in recollective confabulation that leads to the distinct character of the delusional false memories. When the second factor is intact, brief sensations of false familiarity can be generated but then corrected or rejected as false.

What does recollective confabulation tell us about recognition memory?

The recollective confabulation patients point to there being a relationship between familiarity and recollection which is of interest to how they are supposed to interact in the healthy memory system. Familiarity is presumed to operate as a trace strength mechanism. Stimuli generating high levels of familiarity should normally be able to be remembered – material can be generated which supports the high level of familiarity. (Although there are exceptions to this, such as the butcher on the bus phenomenon, whereby a familiar item which appears out of context does not generate successful retrieval – the frustrating experience of not being able to 'place' someone.) As outlined in Chapter 3, some researchers suggest that an initial assessment of familiarity is used to assess recognition memory and trigger other more strategic processes (e.g. Koriat, 1993; Mandler, 2008). For instance, Mandler (2008, p. 391) states that: "If a target is not immediately recognized (on the basis of perceptual familiarity), one searches memory for additional information, which may provide the identity of a familiar target." According to this approach, recollective confabulation arises not from a deficit in recollection itself, but from generating recollection-like justifications for intense (and erroneous) sensations of familiarity.

Previous researchers have previously theorised that familiarity and recollection work in the undamaged memory system in this way. Koriat and Levy-Sadot (2001), for example, suggest that they may act sequentially. The idea is that a fast familiarity response guides retrieval processes until recollection provides a subjective feeling of remembering, and delivers additional contextual information (e.g. Metcalfe, Schwartz, & Joaquim, 1993), or even perhaps a post-hoc 'confabulated' justification. The experient acts metacognitively upon these sensations of familiarity and recollection in order to reflect upon their mental operations and to make a recognition 'decision'. Thus, familiarity is used at a 'pre-retrieval stage' (Koriat & Levy-Sadot, 2001) to trigger a preliminary assessment of memory which helps in the selection of the retrieval strategy. At a subsequent stage, the process underlying memory predictions may become more analytic, influenced by explicit consideration of the content of the cues (or partial information, or contextual details) that came to mind during the search of the target. This two-stage process based on intuitive and quick feelings followed by the search for contextual specifics guided by strategic process has been proposed in models of how epistemic feelings guide cognitive processes (e.g. Arango-Muñoz, 2011).

In sum, recollective confabulation is in part a metacognitive error, an incorrect interpretation of a memory signal (probably familiarity) for a particular stimulus. It points to a divergence between objective and subjective familiarity, whereby presumably an underlying memory deficit or mismatch between memory traces results in false recognition. Due to a delusional-like process, this false recognition is not opposed by retrieval of specifics, but rather the level of familiarity leads to the confabulation of a prior study episode. The reason why the phenomenon is more often seen for novel events and experiences could merely be because this is when the mismatch between the objective and subjective familiarity is highest, and there is therefore the greatest need to confabulate a prior experience to justify the erroneous sensation of familiarity. This phenomenon has parallels in healthy memory, neatly encapsulated in Whittlesea and Williams' (1998) paradox of strangers and friends and familiarity. Feelings of familiarity are more likely to be invoked in surprising contexts. When feelings of fluency, ease of processing and pastness are encountered which are in concert with expectations and prior experience, there is no striking feeling of familiarity.

Note

1 In fact, in the earlier papers, this sensation was almost always referred to as déjà vécu, according to the idea that déjà vu could be split into familiarity- and recollection-based forms. This has been a source of major confusion, and some authors use 'déjà vécu' to describe this kind of delusional memory experience. In fact, because it is argued that healthy people and people with epilepsy can experience déjà vécu, it is unhelpful to think of déjà vécu as this more extreme pathological form of false memory (as argued in Chapter 4). Déjà vécu should not be used merely to refer to this pathological form of false recognition, and as such recollective confabulation is perhaps a better term.

9

THE COGNITIVE NEUROPSYCHIATRY OF DÉJÀ VU

To study the abnormal is the best way of understanding the normal.

William James

In describing recollective confabulation in Chapter 8, it was explained that the justified belief that life was repeating was comparable to other forms of delusion, and that recollective confabulation, described by clinicians and carers as being like constant déjà vu, could also be described as reduplicative paramnesia. In discussing the cognitive mechanisms involved in such a delusion, one powerful explanatory tool is to consider cognitive concepts, such as familiarity, metacognition and source monitoring. In short, this is the cognitive neuropsychiatry approach – applying the rationale of cognitive neuropsychology not to damaged and dysfunctional brains with deficits, but to consider the cognitive profile of psychiatric symptoms and disorders (e.g. Coltheart, 2007). In this chapter, the term cognitive neuropsychiatry is used loosely to group together the literature on déjà vu in a range of psychiatric conditions and also the influence of pharmacology on déjà vu. The emphasis here is not on delusional familiarity (as in the previous chapter), but rather on genuine déjà vu where the experient is aware of the erroneous nature of the experience. As such, the chapter will focus on déjà vu in anxiety, the possibility that there exists a particular form of chronic déjà vu without an organic basis, psychogenic déjà vu, and the relationship between dissociative experiences and déjà vu. First, the literature on déjà vu in schizophrenia is discussed.

Déjà vu and delusion in schizophrenia

Schizophrenia is a mental disorder featuring a breakdown in the relation between thought, emotion and behaviour. Its key characteristics are delusion and hallucination which lead to inappropriate actions and feelings. It is also known to have a complex profile of cognitive impairment and preservation. For instance, people with schizophrenia often have a subtle episodic memory deficit, although meta-cognition, as measured by the feeling-of-knowing (FOK) paradigm, appears to be intact (Souchay, Bacon, & Danion, 2006). Given the possible relationship between delusional beliefs and déjà vu, it is interesting to consider the status of déjà vu in schizophrenia, where delusions are common. Schizophrenia leads to a number of different disruptions which converge on déjà vu and recollective confabulation. For example, people with schizophrenia are known to experience distortions of time perception (for a review see Allman & Meck, 2012), delusions of misidentification (such as Capgras) and temporal reduplication (Förstl et al., 1991) and false memories (Kopelman, 1999). However, despite a historical debate about pathological and psychopathological déjà vu in mental disease and disorder (see Brown, 2004, for an overview), there has been relatively little work on déjà vu in schizophrenia, and a major problem is knowing how to categorise and diagnose case reports of patients that predate contemporary classifications of psychiatric and neurological disorders. Thus, here the literature is restricted to more recent evaluations of déjà vu in schizophrenia.

In an early influential article, Sno, Linszen and de Jonghe (1992) present the case of a 19-year-old woman with schizophrenia. On admission she presented with a range of delusions and distortions of reality, including the belief that she could see holes in her head, that she had had a son who had been kidnapped (she had not had children) and she had the mistaken belief that at some point in the past she had already seen the psychiatrist, who was in fact examining her for the first time. Her history was complex and disturbing, including childhood fears and anxiety, a brother with epilepsy, and being raped whilst on holiday. After initial treatment, a more stable pattern emerged (p. 567):

> It then became apparent that for years, the patient had been convinced she was the reincarnation of Marilyn Monroe. All the photographs and films she had seen of this famous film star had seemed very familiar to her. Thus, she must have experienced it all before. During one of the sessions with her psychiatrist, the patient claimed that several weeks before her admission, she had met one of her later fellow patients in a park. On that occasion she suddenly realised that she had already experienced the incident before. She also felt that she was already familiar with the ward and with the people who worked there, and thought she had experienced many of the daily situations in the hospital or with individual patients at some point in the past. By way of an explanation for what she alternately called her auras, flashbacks or déjà vu phenomena, she later stated that she was living in a later year than the one on the calendar.

Sno et al. do not go into any more detail about the déjà vu experiences, and the same case is reported again – almost verbatim – in Sno et al. (1994). In both Sno et al. (1992) and Sno et al. (1994) this single case is presented to support the idea that déjà vu lies on a continuum with reduplicative paramnesia. Sno et al. (1994) state (p. 146):

> Concerning Marilyn Monroe, she had probably initially had minor forms of déjà vu experiences. At a given moment, possibly concurrent with the traumatic experiences of her parents' divorce and her own rape, the subjective inappropriateness of these experiences disappeared and the subjectively inappropriate impressions of familiarity became a delusion of familiarity, interpreted as a reduplication of time and person. In other words the déjà vu experiences were transformed into reduplicative paramnesia.

It is easy to criticise this view, particularly because the key idea – that 'minor' forms of déjà vu 'transform' into reduplicative paramnesia – is based on the supposition that she 'probably' had experienced déjà vu before developing the delusional belief. However, there is much of Sno's classification which resonates with the use of recollective confabulation to better understand healthy déjà vu, and in schizophrenia it might be argued that where patients do not experience déjà vu, it is because they accept this false familiarity as a true sensation based on a repetition of a previous event and construct a delusional justification to support this view, which is no different from the account of recollective confabulation in the previous chapter. In this way, Sno was ahead of his time in proposing a familiarity-based mechanism that offers a cognitive neuropsychiatric account of a very strange delusion. However, it is unclear as to whether, as with Arnaud's (1896) patient Louis or with Moulin et al.'s AKP, this schizophrenic patient did also experience déjà vu in the same way as healthy groups. As noted by Shanks et al. (2014), several cases of recollective confabulation do, as with Sno's case, present with other types of delusion and misidentification.

The idea of a continuum between temporal reduplication and déjà vu is perhaps conceptually useful, but one must be careful to specify what mechanisms are involved in the continuum between the two extremes, and one presumes it is not merely a question of degree. One might present other continua like this – such as a continuum between healthy tip-of-the-tongue states on one hand, and anomia on the other (e.g. Kay & Ellis, 1987), but it is really only conceptually useful if one can pinpoint the cognitive and neurological differences between the two. In healthy déjà vu the experient is aware of the false familiarity and can act on it (even if it is chronic – see below), whereas in temporal reduplication, the delusion is complete, and rather than opposing the false familiarity, the patient accepts and endorses it with bizarre and implausible justifications. Thus, whereas descriptively this might be a continuum, in terms of mechanisms, one might talk of a one-factor cause (déjà vu) and a two-factor cause (temporal reduplication) according to Coltheart's view of delusion (Coltheart, 2007; presented in the previous chapter). Hereafter, this chapter will consider just 'healthy' déjà vu experiences in schizophrenia and other conditions, that is, déjà vu experiences that are declared as such and can be reported by the patient themselves. Of course, the range of familiarity deficits and delusions in schizophrenia and their relationship to déjà vu remains an area in need of much more research. As with epilepsy, déjà vu research in schizophrenia is a priority because it could be clinically meaningful. According to Sno's logic, for example, patients with déjà vu may be more resistant to developing delusions, or the development of déjà vu may precede more debilitating delusional states, but this theorising is dangerously short on empirical evidence.

The quality and quantity of déjà vu in schizophrenia

Two questions, as with research into epilepsy, present themselves in studying déjà vu in schizophrenia. Is déjà vu more or less frequent in schizophrenia (the quantity question), and (the quality question) is déjà vu any more or less intense/bizarre/disturbing in schizophrenia? Thus far, the idea that déjà vu 'transforms' into delusional beliefs leads one to believe that patients with schizophrenia might experience it less than healthy controls. On the other hand, the fact that metacognition appears intact in schizophrenia, combined with an episodic memory deficit, may generate the appropriate conditions to experience déjà vu. In addition, the characterisation of déjà vu as a minor dissociative event (see below; Sno et al., 1992) means that by some it can be seen as a core feature of psychiatric disturbance. In terms of quality, it seems that patients who have disturbances to core cognitive systems and perception may generate déjà vu experiences that are qualitatively different from those with relatively healthy cognitive systems.

The contemporary research into déjà vu in schizophrenia is dominated by two papers by Adachi and colleagues. First, Adachi et al. (2006) examined déjà vu in 113 people with schizophrenia and 386 controls. They used a Japanese translation of the IDEA (Adachi, Adachi, Kimura, Akanuma, & Kato, 2001). They found that people with schizophrenia actually experienced déjà vu less frequently than controls, with a mean rating of 1.8 compared to 2.1, where 1 = never, and 5 = at least weekly. Nearly half (53) of the 116 patients had never had déjà vu. In terms of déjà vu quantity, it appears that people with schizophrenia experience it less than the healthy population. However, whereas the standard correlations with age (younger = more déjà vu) and education (more education = more déjà vu) were found in the control group, the correlations were non-significant in the group with schizophrenia. Perhaps more interestingly, of all the different phenomena in the IDEA (see Table 6.4), there were very few significant differences between people with schizophrenia and controls – only the item on precognitive dreams was significant, and again this was because people with schizophrenia experienced them less, not more.

Additionally, the déjà vu characteristics as assessed by the qualitative aspect of the questionnaire (Part B, see Table 6.4) were in general described by Adachi et al. as being no different from controls, although they note that the 60 people with schizophrenia who had déjà vu reported being more distressed by the experience. The IDEA produces a long list of variables and characteristics, some of which, even after Bonferonni correction, were significantly different between the two groups. People with schizophrenia were more likely to associate the déjà vu with alarm, a feeling of 'oppression' and disturbance as 'effects' of the déjà vu. They were more likely to attribute the sensation to or associate it with anxiety, mental fatigue, depression, anger, fear, physical illness and confusion. Finally, it was more likely to be associated with headache and blackout, meaning that overall the pattern is like Warren-Gash and Zeman's (2014) study on epilepsy, also using the IDEA: déjà vu is different in these populations because of the 'company it keeps': there were non-significant differences in precognition, depersonalisation and duration, for instance. The authors note in a later study that the "patients tended to show more prolonged and repetitive experiences than did the control subjects and often felt them uncomfortable" (Adachi et al., 2007, p. 593). However, these uncorrected p values of .029 (duration) and .026 (repetition) would not be significant if corrected.

Adachi et al. (2006) conclude that the low level of déjà vu reported, and its similarity to healthy experiences of déjà vu, means that déjà vu is not an inherently pathological experience. A second study (Adachi et al., 2007), again on the same sample of 113 patients, aimed to identify why people with schizophrenia show a lower frequency of déjà vu experiences. They targeted anti-psychotic mediation and psychopathological variables as two factors which might shed light on this question. Psychopathological symptoms were assessed with the Brief Psychiatric Rating Scale (BPRS; Overall & Gorham, 1962) and an analysis was carried out which considered medication use. The analysis examined the differences between patients who did and did not report having déjà vu according to the first part of the IDEA.

The BPRS divided the psychiatric symptoms into four factors: negative symptoms (e.g. blunted affect, motor retardation, emotional withdrawal, conceptual disorganisation and mannerisms); neurotic and depressive symptoms (anxiety, depressive mood, tension, somatic concern and guilt feelings); positive symptoms (unusual thought, hallucination, suspiciousness and conceptual disorganisation); and hostile and aggressive symptoms (grandiosity, hostility, uncooperativeness, mannerisms and conceptual disorganisation). Of these, only the negative symptoms factor showed a significant difference with déjà vu experience, with people who had experienced déjà vu having a lower score. Moreover, the frequency of déjà vu experience was negatively correlated with scores on this factor: the fewer negative symptoms that were experienced, the higher the frequency of déjà vu. The other factors did not correlate significantly with déjà vu frequency. In terms of medication, the type of anti-psychotic medication, first-generation (butyrophenones, phenothiazines, benzamides, and thiepins) versus second-generation (serotonin-dopamine antagonists, dibenzothiazepines, and multi-acting receptor-targeted anti-psychotics) did not influence the frequency of déjà vu, nor did it differ between those patients who did and did not report having had a déjà vu experience. However, both the number of anti-psychotic medications and the dosage of the medications correlated positively with the frequency of déjà vu.

Adachi et al. (2007) point out that the negative symptoms are associated with a "wide range of cognitive dysfunctions", and that the brain-level dysfunction which leads to cognitive disturbance also interferes with the generation of the déjà vu experience. One must not compare people with schizophrenia with healthy older adults, but it should be noted that, just as with age-related changes, it seems that a more intact cognitive system is required to experience déjà vu. The finding that déjà vu is unrelated to positive symptoms gives no support to the idea that a déjà vu experience is like a 'minor' psychopathological episode, but neither does it support the idea that people who have delusional beliefs will be less likely to (or unable) to have déjà vu. A major problem in interpreting the results about anti-psychotic medication is that the IDEA probed déjà vu in any part of the lifespan, which includes experiences which could have occurred before the onset of schizophrenia. However, the data clearly show that the frequency of déjà vu experiences increased in patients who took a high dosage of medication compared with those who took a low dosage. Adachi et al. suggest that medication can improve 'subjective experience' in patients with schizophrenia and thus some patients who had improved subjective experiences after treatment might have experienced déjà vu more frequently. Certainly, if déjà vu is seen as a 'healthy' phenomenon, then a crude view is that a medicated reduction in symptoms and improved cognition should lead to more, not less, déjà vu.

Finally, another recent large study (100 patients and 422 controls) from China has considered déjà vu alongside superstition and 'psi belief' (Shiah et al., 2014). This study started with the premise that déjà vu is associated with paranormal 'psi' beliefs, and that equally, in the general population, inventories measuring schizophrenic symptoms correlate with belief in the paranormal (e.g. Thalbourne, 1994). In general, the study, again using a translation of the IDEA, replicated the findings of the previous study by Adachi: healthy participants had significantly higher scores than schizophrenic patients on déjà vu, derealisation, remembering dreams and travel frequency. Total scores on the IDEA did not significantly correlate with their scale measuring paranormal beliefs in the group of people with schizophrenia, although these two measures were correlated in healthy adults. They conclude that déjà vu experiences are positively related to paranormal beliefs in healthy adults but not in schizophrenic patients. However, the group with schizophrenia were significantly more likely than controls to believe in psi and have superstitious beliefs. The dissociation between paranormal beliefs and déjà vu in schizophrenia means that these two entities are not inextricably linked – whereas people with schizophrenia experience fewer déjà vu episodes, at least in this Chinese sample, they are more likely to have spiritual and paranormal beliefs.

In conclusion, on the basis of these two large samples of patients with schizophrenia using the IDEA, there is little evidence that people with schizophrenia experience more déjà vu, or déjà vu that is of a different quality. In fact, if anything, déjà vu is experienced less in schizophrenia, and this appears to be due to a reduction in cognitive resources (at least as measured by the presence of negative symptoms), and as yet the relationship with delusions (or positive symptoms) is unclear, if not absent. As with the research into epilepsy, there appears therefore to be nothing diagnostic about déjà vu, and although it may be experienced as distressing for people with schizophrenia, it appears to be related to fewer negative symptoms. Also, as with epilepsy research, one should not overlook the fact that people with schizo-phrenia are likely to have a different emotional response and interpretation of this unusual cognitive phenomenon.

Déjà vu and dissociation

Dissociation is a psychological concept that describes the separation of normally related mental processes. Early definitions of dissociative disorders emphasised extreme cases, such as multiple personality disorder, where one personality splits off from another (for a historical overview see Sierra and Berrios, 1998). Contemporary definitions emphasise the loss of our normal sense of contact with our "emo-tions, bodies, actions, thoughts or surroundings" (Warren-Gash & Zeman, 2003). According to this view, dissociative symptoms include subjective states of feeling outside of our bodies, or of having mental processes that are beyond our control. Feelings of unreality, such as those experienced in jamais vu (see Chapter 4), are common. Modern diagnostic schedules consider 'depersonalisation' and 'derealisa-tion', defined by Hunter, Sierra, and David (2004) as follows (p. 9):

> Depersonalisation is an experience in which the individual feels a sense of unreality and detachment from themselves. Symptoms often include a dream-like state, loss of empathy, and a sense of disconnection with bodily parts to the extent that sufferers feel as though they are observing the world from behind glass.
>
> Depersonalisation is often accompanied by the symptom of derealisation in which the external environment also appears unfamiliar, with other people appearing as though actors and the world appearing as if two-dimensional or like a stage set.

The literature on dissociation, derealisation and depersonalisation is long and extremely interesting, but a little outside the scope of this book. Déjà vu has long been considered a dissociative symptom (e.g. Harper, 1969), and strictly, in cog-nitive terms, if a split between the normal processing of the environment and the feeling of familiarity is considered, it is by definition a dissociative experience, even though it is more difficult to conceive of déjà vu as fitting into the two defini-tions of depersonalisation and derealisation above (because déjà vu appears to be the polar opposite). As a clinical entity, however, déjà vu has often been considered alongside other dissociative states (e.g. Warren-Gash & Zeman, 2003). Warren-Gash and Zeman suggest that epileptic déjà vu is more likely than healthy déjà vu to be accompanied by symptoms of 'dissociation' (see below), but there is relatively little empirical work on dissociative symptoms and déjà vu.

Dissociative experiences are routinely measured with the Dissociative Experience Scale (DES; Bernstein & Putnam, 1993), which includes items which clearly resonate with phenomena which are related to déjà vu, such as jamais vu ("Some people have the experience of being in a familiar place but finding it strange and unfamiliar"), or lapses of attention and memory which may provoke déjà vu (e.g. "Some people sometimes find that they cannot remember whether they have done something or have just thought about doing that thing (for example, not knowing whether they have just mailed a letter or have just thought about mailing it)").

Unsurprisingly, some researchers have used the dissociative experiences scale to measure déjà vu and to assess whether it could be described as a dissociative phenomena. In the development of the IDEA, Sno et al. (1994) reported a chi-squared analysis of those people who did and did not report having déjà vu and their scores on the DES: people who reported never having had déjà vu produced lower scores on the DES. They conclude: "The results of our study confirmed the theoretically assumed link between déjà vu experiences and dissociative phenomena" (p. 32).

More recently, Adachi et al. (2008) have reported contrasting results. Unlike Sno et al., who tested a range of different clinical and healthy participants, Adachi et al. examined 227 healthy participants. Again, they used the IDEA, and alongside it the DES. Of their sample, 71 per cent had experienced déjà vu. In this sample, dream recall, precognitive dreams and depersonalisation all correlated with the frequency of experiencing déjà vu. Although their sample was putatively healthy, 12 people had a score over the clinical threshold of 30. In a comparison of those people reporting déjà vu and those who did not, a significant difference in DES scores was found (replicating Sno et al.'s result above). However, given that age and other factors also significantly contribute to déjà vu experience, Adachi et al. carried out a multiple regression analysis seeking to explain the DES scores. Using stepwise procedures, a model with age, jamais vu, depersonalisation and precognitive dreams produced the best fit ($r = .43$), and déjà vu was not a significant predictor in this model. Perhaps more tellingly, of those 12 people who had abnormally high DES scores, three of them reported having no déjà vu, and nine of them reported having déjà vu (respectively, 4.6 per cent and 5.6 per cent of their samples).

Adachi et al.'s study perhaps sums up the complexity of research into this area. They did in fact find a simple correlation between frequency of déjà vu experiences and DES, such that people with more déjà vu had more dissociative symptomology. However, they point out that there is significant multiple colinearity in their data, and once controlling for a number of factors which correlate with déjà vu (including age and jamais vu), déjà vu is no longer a predictor of DES score. On face value, therefore, déjà vu experiences are related to dissociative phenomena, but Adachi et al. concluded that dissociation was not a major factor in the generation of déjà vu, and that "déjà vu experiences were not equivalent to core pathological dissociative experiences". This issue possibly warrants extra research, but the extent to which one concludes that déjà vu is or is not a dissociative experience probably rests upon one's faith in the statistical methods and psychological instruments used. A more promising approach, considered below, is to consider whether within anxiety, for instance, dissociative phenomena might be related to déjà vu.

Déjà vu and anxiety

There has been relatively little research on déjà vu in anxiety disorders, although there is a clear relation with dissociation: dissociative symptoms can often be found as part of the presentation of clinical anxiety. Most notably, there has been some exploration of the prevalence of déjà vu in what was once described as phobic–anxiety–depersonalisation syndrome (PADS; Roth & Harper, 1962). PADS was a diagnostic term introduced by Roth (1959) to describe people with high levels of anxiety, alongside chronic depersonalisation: "in which a combination of phobias for unfamiliar surroundings and depersonalization follow closely upon some calamitous circumstance such as a bereavement, an acute physical illness, or childbirth. Unlike the normal psychological reactions to stress, the illness, once initiated, often runs a protracted course with sustained emotional disturbance and considerable social disability" (Harper & Roth, 1962, p. 132).

In their work, Roth and Harper draw parallels between the phenomenology of the epileptic dreamy state, drawing heavily on Hughlings Jacksons' conceptualisations of consciousness and the epileptic aura (see Chapter 7), and the experience of people with PADS. They describe the depersonalisation as sometimes occurring in the form of acute attacks. They specify that in "40 per cent of cases, features reminiscent of temporal lobe dysfunction, other than depersonalization, are present; these include déjà vu experiences, perceptual disorders such as olfactory or visual hallucinations and micropsia. In 60 per cent of cases the state of chronic tension is punctuated by abrupt attacks of acute panic often with fears of impending death. As these attacks, as also the bouts of depersonalization, occur without provocation on many occasions, difficulties in diagnosis may arise" (p. 132). They emphasise that psychiatric (such as anxiety) or situational factors (such as trauma) can alter or diminish consciousness in much the same way as a neurological deficit, such as epilepsy.

Roth and Harper (1962) considered that anxiety disorders might be difficult to differentiate from epilepsy, and their empirical work was motivated by this concern. They conducted structured interviews with 30 people with TLE and 30 people with PADS, and looked at the prevalence of a range of phenomena, which they described as typical 'temporal lobe symptoms'. It is perhaps difficult to offer a contemporary analysis on this work because the diagnostic criteria and technologies for making a diagnosis have vastly improved since the study was corrected. That said, the study is very thorough, considering personality differences and EEG findings amongst a large range of measures (but sadly no neuropsychological testing, so we cannot consider memory function in these groups). Moreover, it is of interest to students of the déjà vu phenomenon that there is a clear overlap between the features of PADS and the group of patients with epilepsy. This even includes blackouts and loss of memory in the PADS group (see Table 9.1 for a list of phenomena). The authors do not provide a definition of déjà vu, but they do draw on Hughlings Jackson's conception of a dreamy state that included 'reminiscence'. In sum, déjà vu was reported by 12 PADS patients compared to seven TLE patients. This difference was not significant, and in fact, incidence of jamais vu was one of

TABLE 9.1 Selected 'temporal lobe' symptomology in 30 people with a phobic–anxiety–depersonalisation syndrome (PADS) and 30 cases with temporal lobe epilepsy (TLE) (adapted from Roth and Harper, 1962)

	PADS (anxiety)	TLE (epilepsy)
Déjà vu	12	7
Jamais vu	9	1
Depersonalisation	17	11
Derealisation	11	0
Hallucinations	11	4
Sensed presence	14	7

Note that only the incidence of derealisation and jamais vu differed significantly between groups.

the few differences between the two groups, with the anxious group having far more experiences of jamais vu. This is in line with Adachi et al.'s (2008) group study into dissociation reported above: perhaps jamais vu is more related to dissociation than is déjà vu.

Aside of this, it is difficult to draw too much out of these findings because the research considered the episodes of disturbed consciousness as a whole rather than focusing on déjà vu. The authors found that the episodes ('attacks') of temporal lobe symptoms were much longer and more frequent in the PADS group than in the TLE group, and suggest that "Déjà vu and depersonalization lasting for minutes or hours, on the other hand, did not occur in the epileptic group, although this is common in the phobic anxiety–depersonalization syndrome and this distinction may therefore be useful in diagnosis" (p. 140), but no further details are given. The study underlines that as well as TLE, people showing psychiatric symptoms including phobias and suicidal thoughts present with what they describe as 'temporal lobe symptoms'. They propose that the anxiety group also presented with some extra physiological symptoms, such as shaky legs, olfactory hallucinations and perceptual distortions (even incontinence in two cases). It is perhaps difficult to differentiate the role of dissociation and anxiety in the Roth and Harper study, and their sample is certainly a set of people with relatively unusual and severe forms of anxiety which are by definition linked to depersonalisation and derealisation. Moreover, it is difficult to ascertain whether people with anxiety disorders more generally experience more déjà vu than does the healthy population.

Wells et al. (in preparation) were motivated to study déjà vu more specifically in a large sample of people with anxiety and controls. In a questionnaire study, there were 153 participants who reported having a diagnosis of clinical anxiety (mean age = 26.8 years). There were 199 participants in the healthy control group (mean age = 25.4). Before answering questions about déjà vu, participants were provided with a definition: "Déjà vu is the name we give to a strange sensation, where we feel like we have encountered something before, but we know that we have not. It might be meeting a person for the first time, going to a new place, or just having a conversation." They were then asked a set of questions about their experience of déjà vu, including the frequency of déjà vu occurrence, the average duration of these episodes, possible triggers/circumstances related to the onset of déjà vu and whether participants felt their déjà vu episodes caused them undue distress. They also gave demographic characteristics (age, gender, handedness, and years of education) and completed a range of standardised measures of anxiety, depression, dissociation and stress.

This study again corroborates some of the classic patterns found in individual difference studies of déjà vu (see Chapter 6); for instance, the correlation between frequency of déjà vu and age, which was found in both the anxious and healthy group. Most importantly, déjà vu frequency positively correlated with all standardised measures of anxiety, dissociation, stress and depression in both the control and anxiety groups. The more anxious, depressed or stressed the participants were, the higher the frequency of experiencing déjà vu – this was the case in both groups. The anxiety group reported a significantly higher mean frequency of déjà vu over the past month (2.94 times per month) compared to controls (2.30 times per month). However, these differences are rather slight, and if we compare the reported frequency over 12 months, less than one déjà vu experience per year separates the two groups. This means that people with anxiety may only be slightly more likely to experience déjà vu than are healthy controls.

Unlike Roth and Harper's observation, there was no suggestion that the déjà vu experiences were any longer in the anxious group than in the control group – participants provided information about the duration of their déjà vu experiences

TABLE 9.2 Mean reported frequency of déjà vu in the last month and in the last year; correlations (Pearson's *r*) with the Dissociative Experiences Scale (DES; Bernstein & Putnam, 1986); and percentage of the sample reporting triggers for their déjà vu for people reporting clinical anxiety and healthy controls (taken from Wells et al., in preparation)

	Anxiety group	*Healthy controls*
Frequency		
In last month	2.94	2.30
In last year	7.30	6.43
Correlations with DES (*r*)		
In last month	.27	.27
In last year	.38	.25
Some triggers of déjà vu (percentage of cases reporting the trigger)		
Anxiety	24.8	10.6
Stress	20.9	14.1
Recreational drugs	3.9	5.0
Tiredness	24.2	26.6

Note that all correlations are significant at $p < .001$.

in terms of whether it lasted 'seconds', 'minutes' or 'hours'. In terms of the triggers for their déjà vu, anxiety was the only trigger more frequently reported by the anxiety group than the control group (both groups gave 'conversations' as the most likely trigger for having déjà vu). Additionally, the anxiety group reported déjà vu as causing them undue distress. This suggests that a 'feedback loop' may intensify the déjà vu experiences and add to their frequency and distress – déjà vu experiences may trigger anxiety which in turn may lead to more experiences of déjà vu.

In contrast to Adachi et al. (2008), both groups showed a significant relationship between the frequency of déjà vu and their scores on the DES, although in this case, only a simple correlation was carried out. Within the anxiety group, however, those participants who experienced déjà vu more than 15 times per year scored significantly higher on the DES than those in the anxiety group who reported never having experienced déjà vu.

Therefore, Wells et al. present a set of complex data that suggest that, on the whole, a group of people with a clinical diagnosis of anxiety do not experience a great deal more déjà vu than a healthy group (in terms of effect size, it is equivalent to one more experience per year). However, across all participants, it is clear that anxiety is related to déjà vu – there exist significant correlations between scores of anxiety and the reported frequency of déjà vu. Moreover, in the clinical group, anxiety is reported as a possible trigger of déjà vu in about 20 per cent of the participants, and this group also report that déjà vu causes them some distress. However, the data also repeat the idea that dissociative experiences are part of the déjà vu experience – the anxiety group has significantly more dissociative experiences than the control group, and both groups show the same relationship between dissociation and déjà vu. Thus, it remains possible that rather than anxiety per se leading to déjà vu experiences, it is the relationship between dissociative experiences and anxiety which is critical in the experience of déjà vu.

Psychogenic déjà vu

Whilst the complex relationship between anxiety, dissociation and déjà vu remains to be elucidated fully, it is clear that on an individual basis, people can experience intense déjà vu which is not of an organic origin and which is probably associated with an anxiety disorder. Wells et al. (2014) present a case of what has been termed psychogenic déjà vu. This terminology of psychogenic déjà vu was used to distinguish a non-organic, psychologically induced form from an organic, brain-based form, in much the same way that organic and psychogenic amnesias have been differentiated (although purely organic and non-organic distinctions are likely to be overly simplistic, e.g. Markowitsch, 2003). Psychogenic amnesia has been used to describe "episodes of retrograde and/or anterograde memory loss, which are precipitated by psychological stresses and occur in the absence of identifiable brain damage" (Staniloiu, Markowitsch, & Brand, 2010, p. 779). The term psychogenic amnesia is somewhat synonymous with dissociative or medically unexplained amnesia, and in modern diagnostic classifications would be identified as a dissociative disorder. Thus, it is a useful term for describing a pathological form of déjà vu experience which results from psychological stress and which is not related to identifiable brain damage or disorder.

Wells et al.'s patient with psychogenic déjà vu was a 23-year-old male. He reported having had frequent, if not constant, déjà vu symptoms since early 2007, shortly after starting university. He had a history of feeling anxious, particularly in relation to contamination, leading him to wash his hands very frequently and shower 2–3 times per day, and this anxiety worsened when he began university. Anxiety and low mood led him to take a break from university, at which point he began experiencing déjà vu. He complained that these early episodes lasted for minutes, and could also be extremely prolonged, in line with Roth and Harper's assertion above. As an example, whilst on holiday in a destination that he had previously visited, he reported feeling as though he had become 'trapped in a time loop'. He found these experiences extremely frightening.

He returned to university in 2007, when the déjà vu episodes were becoming more intense. He took LSD once, and then claimed that from then on the déjà vu was fairly continuous. In 2008 he was referred to specialists for EEG and MRI, both of which were both normal. He was given a diagnosis of depersonalisation and treated with a range of medications.

Wells et al. tested him in 2010, at which point he claimed that his déjà vu was almost constant, and very disturbing. In contrast with the recollective confabulation patients (Chapter 7), he was aware of the false nature of the familiarity, but he also reported feeling able to predict the future and that it was sometimes very difficult to know whether he had actually experienced an event before or not.

The patient was assessed by Adam Zeman in 2010, at which point his persistent déjà vu caused him to avoid watching television and listening to the radio, as well as reading papers and magazines, as he felt he had already encountered the content before. Neurological examination was normal. At the time of assessment he reported a chronically low mood and felt anxious much of the time, although his compulsive behaviours were not a problem.

At the time of testing, his DES score (35.36) was abnormal (cut off = 30). Wells et al. were interested to see whether he showed any deficits in memory function. The same recognition memory task as used in the recollective confabulation patients (Moulin et al., 2005) was used. This yielded unremarkable results in comparison to a control group of 11 undergraduates. Contrary to expectations, the patient made no false positives. His performance did not suggest he had a memory deficit, but his conservative performance (relatively low number of R hits compared to controls and no guess responses) suggests that he was less confident in his memory ability than were the controls.

The critical issue was that whereas the déjà vu was constant and for long periods of time, this patient was aware of the abnormal familiarity in his memory and was, in fact, greatly distressed by it. In this psychogenic case, the patient is aware of the unreality of his experiences and they are constantly accompanied and caused by pathological levels of anxiety. Wells et al. suggest that distress caused by the déjà experience may itself lead to increased levels of déjà vu – similar feedback loops in psychological symptoms are reported in other anxiety states, such as panic attacks. Interestingly, as with the large study on undergraduates using the recollective experience paradigm (O'Connor & Moulin, 2013) reported in Chapter 5, the memory test failed to capture any chronic changes in memory. Unlike the recollective confabulation patients, who might also be described as having chronic déjà vu by clinicians and carers, this patient made no false positives at all on a recognition memory test.

It is likely that psychogenic déjà vu is actually under-reported, and those who experience it, where it does not cause distress, are unlikely to seek medical attention, or if they do, are unlikely to find an explanation. Again, there is the critical issue that déjà vu is subjective and does not have a behavioural corollary, and more critically in this case, there will be no brain state or other symptom to support the idea of an organic cause for the déjà vu. It will be a priority for future research to better document and describe these rare – but not infrequent – cases of psychogenic déjà vu, especially where they cause so much distress for the person experiencing this problem.

Given that ultimately we should expect every psychological symptom to have some manifestation in the physical brain, the distinction between organic and psychogenic may prove simplistic. Moreover, one possibility is that these cases might not be psychogenic at all. It is possible that limitations in technology or knowledge mean that we cannot detect the brain changes responsible for the déjà vu. As such, researchers and clinicians need to exhaustively test the idea that the déjà vu does not stem from subtle epileptic changes, and this will almost always require hospitalisation and EEG video investigation over several days. Agkül et al. (2013) present a case of a 13-year-old girl with persistent déjà vu but with no clear symptoms of epilepsy. However, their detailed neurological examinations (longer-term EEG video monitoring) revealed the déjà vu feelings were auras associated with TLE seizures (this was not discovered until the second day). In her own words, the patient described her experiences as "this weird feeling that whatever happens to me in daily life, I feel that I have experienced it before" (Agkül et al., 2010, p. 552). This experience provoked anxiety and was followed by palpitations and a feeling of nausea. She reported no headaches, language or memory difficulties, or visual deficits associated with the déjà vu. There was no history of seizures or other complications. The authors point out that the reason the patient presented was that the feelings of déjà vu were difficult to explain and caused anxiety because of how unusual they were. Using a standardised measure they showed that there were no clinical levels of background anxiety in the patient; therefore, they concluded that the anxiety was a reaction to the déjà vu, rather than a cause of it.

Pharmacologically induced déjà vu

Some clinicians have also reported single cases of pharmacologically induced déjà vu. These are not directly related to the psychiatric disorders reported above, and it should be noted that there is a relative lack of research into prescription and non-prescription drugs and déjà vu. Brown (2004) reviews the existent research into drugs and déjà vu, reporting that only one large-scale survey (Palmer, 1979) has investigated drug use and déjà vu, giving no significant relationship between drug use and déjà vu. A clearer pattern has emerged with alcohol use and déjà vu, with Brown summarising the results of several large-scale questionnaires which point to people who have déjà vu reporting drinking more alcohol than those who have not experienced déjà vu. Whether this result is caused by a relationship between alcohol and déjà vu directly, or whether it reflects age or socio–cultural differences, stress, or fatigue is not clear. Because large-scale studies are so few, most of the pharmacological studies of déjà vu focus on case studies.

As an example, Taiminen and Jääskeläinen (2001) report a case of a 39-year-old man – himself a physician – who suffered from déjà vu as a result of disruptions to the dopaminergic brain system. Their brief report is of an otherwise healthy male taking amantadine and phenylpropanolamine together to relieve influenza symptoms. Neuroscientifically, they suggested that the déjà vu experiences were related to hyperdopaminergic dysfunction in the medial temporal lobe. The subject experiencing déjà vu completed the course of medicines and described it as a pleasant experience (p. 461):

> the subject started to experience several intense déjà vu experiences per hour, each lasting from a few seconds to minutes. Experiences were all-inclusive occurring in every sensory modality. The subject did not find déjà vu incidents unpleasant, rather amusing and puzzling. He suspected that amantadine might be causing déjà vu experiences, but, because he did not find them annoying, he decided to continue the medication. Few times he woke up during the night and had an intense feeling of déjà vu regarding the dream he had just had.

Kalra et al. (2007), on the other hand, report the case of a 42-year-old woman whose persistent déjà vu was so severe that she shut herself in a darkened room:

> Everything that had happened on Tuesday happened again. This time I went to my room switched off TV, turned off the phone and asked to be left alone. I had the same feeling of having seen and done all of this before … The funny thing with all of this was that if you asked me what was going to happen I didn't know, I just felt that as things were happening I had done it all before and it felt natural for me to know all of this.
>
> *Kalra et al. (2007, p. 312)*

Kalra et al. speculate a serotinergic mechanism: this otherwise healthy woman had received 5-hydroxytryptophan, in combination with carbidopa, as treatment for palatal tremor (distressing, repetitive and involuntary movements of the soft palate), on two separate occasions. Each time, she experienced intense, protracted déjà vu, lasting for several hours. Finally, Singh (2007) reports the case of a 15-year-old boy who was hospitalised with paranoia, déjà vu and mental slowing after taking salvia, a hallucinogen. He complained frequently of déjà vu without concurrent hallucinations, but became paranoid towards those who tried to reassure him that events or conversations had not occurred before. Singh suggests that this drug may be associated with long-term effects, one of which could be déjà vu. Certainly, anecdotally, and even in the case of psychogenic déjà vu above, there appears to be a contributory factor in déjà vu experiences in drug use, but this needs to be examined in more detail. The proposal that either dopaminergic or serotinergic mechanisms in the temporal lobe might be behind the déjà vu experience is something that warrants further examination. There is as yet no clear account of the neurochemical profile of familiarity disturbances in déjà vu, but taken with the medication-related effects reported in schizophrenia, this could be a promising line of research.

Summary: the psychopathology of déjà vu

This chapter converges on the idea, that as with déjà vu in epilepsy, there is nothing diagnostic about déjà vu per se. People with anxiety may be marginally more likely to experience déjà vu, and people with schizophrenia may be less likely to experience déjà vu, but it seems unlikely that déjà vu is anything particularly indicative of psychopathology. Although the relationship between déjà vu and delusion is of great interest theoretically in both recollective confabulation and schizophrenia, there is very little evidence that they lie on a continuum, but this is an idea that would be relatively easy to test. One theme which, again, has come to light in this chapter is the idea that déjà vu is actually a symptom that points to a healthy cognitive system. In schizophrenia, déjà vu is experienced less, not more, and it is related (negatively) to the negative symptoms related to cognitive dysfunction, and not the presence of delusions and hallucinations. Taken with the research into aging, and into epilepsy previously reviewed in this book, one might conclude that déjà vu is a fragile phenomenon, if not most likely to be experienced in healthy people, then more likely to be experienced by people with the requisite cognitive resources to detect or generate the conflict in mental evaluations at the core of the experience.

The status of déjà vu as a dissociative symptom, on the other hand, is less clearcut. Whereas several studies report simple correlations between déjà vu frequency and dissociation, this relationship appears to be influenced by other factors, such that, statistically, déjà vu and dissociation do not appear to be directly related. If anything, it appears that jamais vu and not déjà vu might be better described as a dissociative experience. For déjà vu, dissociation may be an important factor in extreme cases of psychogenic déjà vu. As yet, there is just one published case on psychogenic déjà vu, and as such it is a little difficult to know what to make of this presentation. Correspondence and anecdotal reports suggest that this is experienced only very rarely (an estimate would be about 4–5 people contacting the author per year with the same problem), but that other people identify with this published case and describe a very similar profile. These people tend to be young, with a history of anxiety problems and are mostly male. More research needs to be carried out into this condition, as this is one area where the déjà vu experience is very distressing, and people with this problem are usually unable to function normally in their daily life. It needs to be stressed that despite the chronic and intense nature of psychogenic déjà vu, it is not comparable to recollective confabulation or delusion: people with this problem are aware that they are experiencing déjà vu, and describe the constant fatigue of monitoring and managing their cognitive system, trying not to succumb to the idea that their whole life is a repeat. As yet, however, unfortunately, this research is little more than anecdotal.

This chapter cannot be concluded without noting the poor quality of evidence on the whole in this domain. There are several well-powered studies using standardised psychological instruments, but there is a real lack of 'strength in depth' of the studies reviewed here. Notably, there is an over-reliance on the IDEA in the large-scale studies, with each study using this questionnaire. Aside of these retrospective questionnaire studies, there are only a handful of single cases. As such, the field is underdeveloped, and there is a lack of the kind of neuropsychological and empirical approach based on cognitive experimentation that has been a feature of the other domains reviewed in this book. Although there has been a lot of research into episodic memory in schizophrenia (for a review see Heinrichs & Zakzanis, 1998), there has been (to the author's best knowledge) no examination of how recollection and familiarity processes relate to déjà vu. There is, however, a literature that is well-enough developed in schizophrenia that there has been a 'quantitative reanalysis' of 19 published studies examining recollection and familiarity (Libby, Yonelinas, Ranganath, & Ragland, 2013). This review found that both familiarity and recollection were impaired in schizophrenia (with larger and more consistent effects in recollection), leading to the conclusion of "multi-focal medial temporal lobe and/or prefrontal cortex dysfunction" in schizophrenia. Again, as with epilepsy, it might be expected that déjà vu is only experienced by people with schizophrenia who have intact recollection, and the relatively low levels of déjà vu in this population may be explained by a recollection deficit. These are interesting research leads, but it should be noted that the case study of psychogenic amnesia did use the standard remember/know task that was insightful in recollective confabulation, but it yielded very little in terms of new research leads or a cognitive explanation of the permanent déjà vu. A final criticism of most of this research is that it is rarely longitudinal, and does not differentiate between déjà vu frequency before and after receiving a diagnosis, nor does it track changes in déjà vu experience within people according to medication use or the severity of psychopathological episodes.

10

PRODUCING DÉJÀ VU IN THE LABORATORY

> There are three principal means of acquiring knowledge … observation of
> nature, reflection, and experimentation. Observation collects facts; reflection
> combines them; experimentation verifies the result of that combination.
>
> *Diderot (1713–1784)*

The rationale in this chapter is to document briefly the search for the paradigm or
paradigms that could bring the study of déjà vu into the laboratory. On the face of
it, we seem to have a working definition of déjà vu as erroneous familiarity combined with a feeling that this familiarity is false. In this regard, it seems that it should
be possible to produce déjà vu in experimental settings. Familiarity and fluency
of processing a stimulus have been successfully manipulated many times, even in
the context of déjà vu research, as covered in Chapters 3 and 4. In short, a number of procedures have been used which successfully produce déjà vu, or at least
something akin to it (summarised in Table 10.1). These experiments offer empirical
support for various cognitive theories of déjà vu. A critical issue in this chapter is
whether such 'laboratory' experiences truly are déjà vu, and what they might tell
us about déjà vu formation. Parallels with false memory research and tip-of-the-
tongue research are drawn. The problem of demand characteristics in laboratory
tasks, and the comparison with real-world déjà vu, is discussed.

An illusion of memory: comparisons with false memory research

Memory researchers have been somewhat slow to use déjà vu in their theoretical
work. This is probably due to the fact that there is no one agreed paradigm with
which we can reliably produce déjà vu. The search for a suitable paradigm draws
a comparison with false memory research, a domain that was greatly advanced by

TABLE 10.1 Published research that has successfully created déjà vu (or an analogue of déjà vu) in the laboratory

	Methods and theoretical proposal	Percentage of participants reporting (at least one) déjà vu experience on post-experimental questioning
Hypnosis		
O'Connor, Barnier, & Cox (2008)	Post-hypnotic suggestions of amnesia and familiarity. Déjà vu is produced by a conflict generated under hypnosis. After hypnosis, participants either encounter something they have already encountered but have been told to forget (generating conflict), or the opposite: finding something familiar that they have not encountered before	83 per cent experienced a 'strong sense of déjà vu' – in the familiarity condition
DRM-inspired task		
Urquhart & O'Connor (2014)	Conflict generated between familiarity of the stimulus (DRM-style 'gist') and the knowledge that this familiarity is false (provided by participant-generated information reproduced from the study phase). Conflict between gist and information from study phase generates déjà vu	60 per cent
Implicit memory/unattended processing		
Jacoby & Whitehouse (1989)	A recognition memory test for words, but where subliminal primes are presented in the test phase (covered in detail in Chapter 5). Déjà vu (described as 'paramnesia' in this article) arises because of a previous brief, unattended presentation of stimulus which unconsciously activates the sensation of familiarity. This study was the inspiration for Brown and Marsh (2009)	Not tested
Brown & Marsh (2008)	Two experiments on 'false beliefs about autobiographical experience'. Participants superficially process scenes from university campuses they have and have not visited. One week or three weeks later, they are asked to report how likely they were to have visited that location in real life. The results are pertinent to déjà vu because prior exposure to images inflates the ratings of how likely it was they had visited the location	Not tested

TABLE 10.1 *(cont.)*

	Methods and theoretical proposal	*Percentage of participants reporting (at least one) déjà vu experience on post-experimental questioning*
Brown & Marsh (2009)	A priming experiment, similar to Jacoby & Whitehouse (1989) but using symbols. Participants were asked if they had encountered symbols before having taken part in the study and symbols ranged from being very familiar to novel (the disabled 'wheelchair symbol', for instance, being familiar). There was no study phase. Déjà vu was operationalised as arising from subliminal presentation of the identical stimulus before being asked about its prior exposure	50 per cent
Brown & Marsh (2010)	This article neatly summarises the two articles above (2008, 2009) plus reports otherwise unpublished studies looking at déjà vu and false familiarity more generally	46 per cent

(Gestalt) similarity experiments

Cleary, Ryals, & Nomi (2009)	A recognition without identification paradigm in two experiments: participants study scenes with labels, which they learn. Then at test they see configurally similar scenes that are novel, for which they cannot name, since they were never studied. Conflict between configural similarity which generates familiarity, combined with the failure to produce a name generates déjà vu	Not tested
Cleary, Brown, Sawyer, Nomi, Ajoku, & Ryals (2012)	Similar to the above, but using virtual reality in two experiments in 'déjà ville'	Not tested
Sugimori & Kusumi (2014)	Aims to reconcile questionnaire findings and methods with a Cleary-style task with the aim of integrating findings from naturalistic 'real-world' studies and experimentally induced déjà vu	

the development of the DRM (Deese-Roediger and McDermott) task. In this paradigm, proposed by Roediger and McDermott (1985), participants study different categorised lists, e.g. 'thread', 'haystack', 'pin', and 'cotton'. In the recognition phase, participants are presented with studied items (*targets*; 'thread', 'pin') and non-studied items (*critical* or *related lures* such as 'needle'; and *non-related lures*, other categorised items such as 'red', 'blue'). At test, critical lures are likely to be falsely recognised because they match the *gist* information formed at study about related concepts. If a participant is able to consciously recollect the specifics of encoding with certainty, however, they will not make such an error. Thus, we might say that the DRM test measures the ability to overcome familiarity with a concept or activation of a word. Actually, we know that most people are very susceptible to creating 'false memories' on this task and these are most likely to be experienced as 'remembering'. This has been termed 'illusory recollection' and levels of remembering are as high as those for items that people have actually seen, and not usually lower than 25 per cent of all items (see Geraci & McCabe, 2006).

The DRM shows an interesting profile in memory impairment, because people apparently need a certain level of memory function to show the effect clearly. For instance, memory for both gist and detail information decreases in Alzheimer's disease (Hudon et al., 2006). This is presumably because Alzheimer's disease patients cannot create gist information. The DRM paradigm has also been used in many applications and neuropsychological groups. For example, people with 'memories' of having been abducted by aliens are more likely to generate false memories on a DRM task (Clancy, McNally, Schacter, Lenzenweger, & Pitman, 2002). For applications relevant to the populations of patients studied in this book, it has been shown that false memories are increased in temporal lobe epilepsy, and volumetric analysis showed that the volume of hippocampi and volume of the right hippocampus correlated with false memory function (Chiu et al., 2010). (This article sees false memory responses as positive, reflective of a healthy capacity to extract 'gist' from the original study list – and note that the correlation too is positive, the higher the volume of the hippocampal structures, the more false memories are formed.) In schizophrenia, there are several studies examining DRM performance, with equivocal findings, although it seems in summary that people with schizophrenia are not more likely to generate false memories on the DRM, but they may show more confidence in their false recognition than do controls (Moritz, Woodward, & Rodriguez-Raecke, 2006). Developing this idea, and in agreement with the theory of recollective confabulation presented in Chapter 8, Moritz and Woodward (2006) suggest that it is a failure of metacognitive monitoring of memory, and in particular overconfidence in memory, which leads to delusional thinking in schizophrenia.

The déjà vu experience, however, is not a false memory. Critically, for false memories of any description, the experient does not know that the memories are not true, even though in patient groups they can be fantastic and implausible. Déjà vu is clearly not merely the same as false memory, because it requires two opposing sensations or evaluations. We can quite readily produce memories based on the gist of 'remembering' 'needle', but this does not produce déjà vu. For déjà vu to occur, there needs to be the sensation of retrieving something from memory combined with the knowledge that you have, in fact, not encountered it before. To continue with this example, we would have to simultaneously produce the sensation of having encountered 'needle' before whilst somehow making the participant certain that they had not encountered the word before. This idea is captured in the DRM-inspired experiment carried out by Urquhart and O'Connor (2014), reviewed below.

Déjà vu and hypnosis

Banister and Zangwill (1941) observed that when people hypnotised to forget material re-encountered that material, it generated sensations similar to déjà vu: there was a clash between how the material felt (familiar) combined with the knowledge (imposed under hypnosis) that they had not encountered the material before. Following up on this work, O'Connor, Barnier and Cox (2008) added a reverse procedure, where instead of suggesting amnesia for studied items, they also suggested familiarity for non-studied items. Using the forgetting procedure with simple word lists, approximately 30 per cent of participants reported a déjà vu-like experience during a recognition memory test. One reported: "some words seemed a lot more familiar than others, even though I wasn't sure they had appeared in the main word list" (quoted in O'Connor et al., 2008, p. 429).

O'Connor et al. (2008) directly compared the post-hypnotic amnesia task with the post-hypnotic familiarity method. Their task involved moving pieces shaped like trains, wagons and carriages around a board. The post-hypnotic familiarity condition yielded significantly more reports of déjà vu than did the post-hypnotic amnesia condition. O'Connor et al. gave their participants this suggestion that they would find aspects of the task familiar:

> "After you wake up, I will give you a puzzle task to do. You will feel as though you have done the task before but you will not understand why you are having this feeling. As you lean forward to look at the task, you will have an overwhelming and surprising sense of familiarity – of having done this exact action before. When you notice the little red engine and the exit gate, you will believe that you have seen them before."
>
> O'Connor et al. (2008, p. 434)

This suggestion resulted in 67 per cent of participants having a strong sense of familiarity for the puzzle and 83 per cent of participants feeling a 'strong' sense of déjà vu (in comparison no participants reported a strong sense of déjà vu in the amnesia induction). Participants spontaneously likened this sensation to déjà vu, even though no reference of it was made in the suggestion (pp. 440–441):

Participant: I think I've done something like this before. I dunno … I was just looking at what had to go where and how it could be manipulated. Actually, when I first looked at it I thought I wouldn't expect to finish it but once I started doing it, it made sense. It was just a bit odd.

Hypnotist: So you told me that you felt as though you had done it before. Tell me a bit about that.

Participant: It was pretty déjà vu. It seems like a real childhood toy kind of thing. I think I've done something similar to it before.

Hypnotist: Can you tell me when you might have done that?

Participant: I'm not sure. Probably when I was a kid or something.

Hypnotist: Were there any particular aspects of the task that seemed familiar?

Participant: Like the engine … how it feels and how it slides on the board. It just seems familiar.

These results from hypnosis studies are easy to incorporate into contemporary theories of déjà vu formation. In the case of post-hypnotic amnesia, it is clear that the result is not unlike the source amnesia account presented in Chapter 5. The experient arrives at processing fluently an already seen stimulus, but is unable to account for its familiarity. The post-hypnotic familiarity suggestion is an analogue of the decoupled familiarity hypothesis: the participant finds a new item familiar according to the suggestion given under hypnosis, but is unable to pinpoint why. The fact that a familiarity rather than amnesic induction appears more likely to generate a feeling of déjà vu is perhaps evidence in favour of the decoupled familiarity hypothesis. This is possibly the only occasion where two theories of déjà vu formation have been tested and compared experimentally.

If there is a concern with hypnosis research, it is that the participants are, by definition, very suggestible. This may mean that their responses to questions may follow demand characteristics, or they may be likely to say that they have had déjà vu just because, like hypnosis, it is a difficult-to-describe subjective state that has clear links with consciousness.

Experiments using superficial or subliminal presentation of stimuli

The results of these following experiments, which Brown and Marsh describe as a 'perceptual explanation', are neatly summarised in their review article (Brown & Marsh, 2010). The experiments of Jacoby and Whitehouse (1989) and Brown and Marsh (2008) are explained in Chapter 5 and appear in Table 10.1. These two experiments both centre on the brief exposure to materials in recognition memory paradigms before participants have to report if they have encountered the information before. Jacoby and Whitehouse's (1989) two experiments are a fairly standard episodic memory word recognition experiment, except that during the test phase the subjects were primed by brief presentations of the word. This influenced the endorsement of the item as being old, but only when people were not aware of the prime – they attributed the fluent processing of the word to a prior occurrence of having seen the word. Again, reviewed in detail in Chapter 5, Brown and Marsh

Mundane Campus Photo   Unique Campus Photo

FIGURE 10.1 Example photographs of campus scenes used in Brown and Marsh (2008). Used with permission.

(2008) looked at a similar episodic memory recognition test design, but this time for pictures of scenes (taken from the university campus, see Figure 10.1). They did not use subliminal presentation, but in two experiments looked at the effects of prior exposure of the scenes in a task which required only superficial processing (finding a cross in one of the four corners of the screen) on later ratings of how likely it was that they had visited the places (either one week or three weeks later). These two articles are alike in that they do not explicitly test déjà vu formation, and it is not known whether participants experienced déjà vu or even strong levels of subjective familiarity, even though the mechanisms implicated are clearly pertinent to déjà vu.

In a follow-up to their 2008 article, Brown and Marsh (2009) examined the effect of superficial processing at encoding on familiarity for geometric designs, drawing heavily on the Jacoby and Whitehouse article, and borrowing the same quotes from Titchener. Their paradigm was very similar, except that there was no study phase, and the symbols were either previously known (e.g. the disabled person symbol, or the divide symbol ÷) or novel. (Previously known symbols were split into high and low familiarity.) Participants were primed with either the identical or a different symbol (35 ms). The test question assessed whether the participant had 'encountered' the symbol prior to the study. Critically, however, Brown and Marsh did also directly ask participants if they had experienced déjà vu at the end of the experiment. First, of their high-familiarity symbols, the probability of identifying them as having been seen before the experiment was .87. For the novel and low-familiarity symbols, when primed with the exact same symbol, the false positive rates were .15 and .28, respectively. When the prime was different or there was no prime, this rate of false positives dropped considerably. For the novel symbols, .03 of items in the different and no prime conditions were assessed as having been seen prior to the experiment. This replicates the effect of priming in the Jacoby and Whitehouse article. For the incidence of déjà vu, Brown and Marsh note:

> On the questionnaire, 19 subjects (79%) indicated that they were sometimes confused about whether they had seen a symbol before the experiment, and 12 (50%) said they had experienced déjà vu during the study. This later finding is impressive given that self-reports indicated déjà vu was infrequent in everyday life: Four subjects reported never having experienced it, 3 subjects reported it occurred less than once a year, 10 subjects said it happened about every 6 months, and 7 subjects said it occurred monthly.
>
> *Brown and Marsh (2009, p. 536)*

Brown and Marsh (2010) briefly run through a number of replications and extensions to their studies. In one, they used the same design and materials as their 2009 experiment but ask participants to rate their familiarity on a scale from 1 to 6, showing that brief exposure increased the subjective familiarity of symbols, but interestingly, they also asked about the source of the familiarity, whether it was induced in the experiment or came from before the experiment (recall that there is no study phase). For those trials where the symbol was primed with an identical symbol, the source was predominantly given as within the experiment on 81 per cent of trials, which tempers somewhat the conclusions from the first (2009) experiment. Importantly, the post-experiment questionnaire again revealed that about half (46 per cent) of the participants reported experiencing déjà vu during the procedure.

In another follow-up experiment with the same design and materials, the prime appeared to one side of the target symbol, in peripheral vision, in order to test the notion of a 'perceptual double take' in déjà vu. It used the same six-point rating scale as above, and replicated again the change in familiarity according to the brief exposure of the same symbol. They do not report how many participants reported déjà vu – or indeed whether they asked this question – at the end of the experiment. The change in familiarity ratings for novel symbols between central or peripheral presentation of the prime was comparable (mean ratings were 4.3 for central and 4.1 for peripheral, where 1 = definitely no, 6 = definitely yes). For low-familiarity symbols these respective values were 4.8 and 4.5. There is no evidence, then, that peripheral presentation is any more likely to generate déjà vu than a centrally viewed brief presentation of a stimulus.

The various results of Brown and Marsh, taken at face value, are very impressive. They suggest that "Our paradigm models the experience of seeing a Martian for the first time (preceded, of course, by a glance) and feeling that one has seen such a creature sometime in one's past" (p. 536). However, it is still not clear whether the déjà vu experience reported by their participants shares the phenomenological characteristics of the real, unprovoked experience. Brown and Marsh place a great emphasis on their paradigm being closer to real life than those previous, suggesting that the false familiarity in the novel symbols was like reporting that people had experienced the information before in 'some vaguely defined point' in the personal past. More critically, it is not possible to tie the déjà vu to a particular class of item, or experimental condition, if participants merely give a global evaluation of the experiment at the end. It should be that déjà vu is elicited on the trials whereby there is a manipulation of familiarity but not on the other trials, but this is not known. As has is developed below in experimentation by Jersakova et al. (2016), Brown and Marsh (2010) also noted concerns about creating expectations if they had asked about déjà vu after each trial.

Experiments testing the Gestalt similarity hypothesis

Another major class of experiments uses a similar methodology and rationale to generate déjà vu. However, the Gestalt similarity hypothesis proposes that familiarity is generated by the conceptual or configural similarity between a previous and current experience rather than a perceptual double-take or a superficial encoding of the very same stimulus. This again should be presumably easy to recreate in the laboratory, and it has been used as the focus of study by Cleary and her group. Cleary's research into déjà vu (for a brief theoretical statement, see Cleary, 2008) is embedded into an impactful programme of research which considers recognition without identification more generally, for example considering familiarity phenomena such as "when people cannot 'name that tune' but can recognize it as familiar" (e.g. Kostic & Cleary, 2009).

Cleary, et al. (2009) used a recognition with identification paradigm in which participants first study pictures of internal and external scenes, such as pictures of a room or a street, and later are presented with new scenes some of which are similar to the pictures they studied. The similarity between scenes is created by positioning different features of a scene in a common configuration, so that the features across different pictures are perceptually comparable in how they relate to each other (see Figure 10.2). An example in daily life might be driving down a country road for the first time and seeing a church by a fountain on the left. You may not have seen that church and that fountain before, but you may have been somewhere before with a similar configuration of a building with a spire and fountain. In Cleary's experiments, participants were asked to indicate whether a presented new scene was similar in its configuration to one of the studied scenes, rate its familiarity and recall the studied scene. On the occasions when participants indicated a scene was similar and yet were unable to recall the original, they were asked whether they had experienced déjà vu. In these instances, participants reported déjà vu significantly more often when they identified a similar new scene as familiar (17 per cent) compared to when they identified an unrelated new scene as familiar (13 per cent). The strength of this approach is that it allows the researchers to capture and isolate instances where subjective awareness of familiarity occurs in the absence of recall – something that undoubtedly does occur when déjà vu is experienced.

This approach has been extended by Cleary et al. (2012) to 3D virtual reality environments. Once again, the configural similarity of objects was compared, this

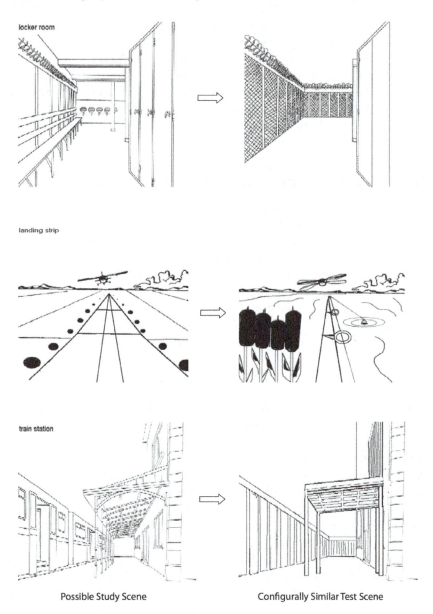

Possible Study Scene   Configurally Similar Test Scene

FIGURE 10.2 Example study and configurally similar test scenes used by Cleary et al. (2009).

time across a number of virtual 'rooms' (paired up to configurally similar locations). Cleary et al. (2012) assessed the experience of familiarity but also the experience of newness. They asked participants to rate the familiarity of scenes that they said were new (not part of a configural pair) and whether they experienced déjà vu whilst viewing them. This is different to the above paradigm where familiarity and déjà vu were assessed for scenes that were said to be similar rather than new. Cleary et al. (2012) also included actually studied scenes in the recognition phase. They found that the probability of déjà vu being reported was highest for old scenes incorrectly identified as new (51 per cent), followed by configurally similar scenes correctly identified as new (33 per cent) and new scenes identified as new (18 per cent). Crucially, familiarity ratings followed the same pattern. This correspondence between déjà vu reports and familiarity ratings is consistent with bottom-up theories of déjà vu: we find something familiar, but cannot retrieve why, so the result is a conflict in evaluations. The conclusion Cleary draws from this empirical work is that déjà vu results from situations similar to previous experiences. This creates a feeling of familiarity that can nevertheless sit alongside an explicit assessment of novelty, creating a clash between the subjective experience and the objective evaluation of the situation:

> Ours is the first study to empirically support the idea that the configuration of objects in 3-dimensional space can produce familiarity in the absence of recall, and to suggest that this may be related to déjà vu.
>
> *Cleary et al. (2012, p. 975)*

On the face of it, these studies are the closest scientists have come in over 100 years of research to producing déjà vu in the lab on a trial-by-trial basis and therefore understanding its formation. However, as pointed out by O'Connor and Moulin (2010), Cleary et al. have to explain how this recognition without identification is different from a simple experience of familiarity without recollection, something which happens often in daily life and which does not cause déjà vu. As discussed in Chapter 3, memory researchers typically recall Mandler's (1980) description of the butcher on the bus to illustrate a strong sensation of familiarity ("I know that person on the bus from somewhere") in the absence of recollection ("but I don't know who it is"). This experience can be a result of mismatched context (recollection failed because the butcher we are used to seeing in the supermarket was seen on the bus).

Producing a 'clash' in evaluations

As Cleary notes, very few researchers have focused on perhaps what is more important in the déjà vu experience, the impression that the familiarity is indeed false:

> Perhaps most importantly, déjà vu is specifically defined as a sense of oldness alongside the realization that the situation is new (Brown, 2004), yet no published studies have modelled this in the laboratory
>
> *Cleary et al. (2012, p. 974)*

The idea of a certainty in something being new, based on the retrieval of contextual specifics – "this feels familiar but I know I have never been to New York before!" – was explicitly tested in a recent experiment by Urquhart and O'Connor (2014). They used a DRM-like procedure to generate a sense of familiarity in non-studied words in 30 undergraduate participants. There was a standard study phase with lists which converge on critical non-presented lures, as described above, but Urquhart and O'Connor also asked the participants to monitor the to-be-encoded materials for certain letter strings. In their example, participants study lists such as *blanket, awake, snooze, nap, dream, rest, doze, snore, peace, wake, tired, bed*. The critical lure '*sleep*' is not presented. While studying the items, participants have to monitor for strings such as 'SLE', described as a 'novel' string which never appears on the study list and 'B' which occurs twice – the initial letter of bed and blanket. Participants report the number of times they have seen each string. Urquhart and O'Connor predicted that in the high-novelty conditions, there should be a high likelihood to report déjà vu: 'sleep' will normally be likely to be endorsed as old, because it is related to the studied list, but at the same time, if the participant can remember that no words contained the string SLE, there will be a clash in evaluations. To emphasise this decision-making process, the number of words beginning with each letter string was re-presented to the participants at the test phase: therefore, they should be clear that they endorsed no words beginning with SLE for the critical lure. Naturally, the test phase included intermixed targets, distracters and critical lures for novel and control items.

They found that using this procedure, déjà vu was reported at least once by 60 per cent of their participants. On a trial-by-trial basis, they found higher reports of déjà vu for the novel items in general than for the low-novelty words, plus déjà vu reports were highest for critical lures rather than other distracters (or indeed previously studied words):

> Crucially, critical lures in the low novelty condition remained comparable to other word conditions in their likelihood of yielding déjà vu reports, in the region of 10%, whereas those in the high novelty condition elicited déjà vu responding around 25% of the time.
>
> *Urquhart & O'Connor (2014, p. 9)*

Urquhart and O'Connor's experiment is the first to set objective characteristics and a certainty that a stimulus has not been studied before with induced familiarity. It is a promising approach for future studies, although it might be more natural to run these kinds of experiments with episodic and implicit memory materials and scenes, rather than relying on the semantic relatedness and gist in the case of the DRM paradigm. The results suggest that familiarity alone is not enough to generate reports of déjà vu – as argued above, false memories on such paradigms are not usually experienced as déjà vu. What may be problematic for such paradigms, however, is the use of trial-by-trial questioning of whether participants have déjà vu. Even in Urquhart and O'Connor's control conditions there was a baseline of 10 per cent experiences of déjà vu.

Concerns about demand characteristics and social desirability

Orne (1962) introduced the idea of demand characteristics, conceptualised as cues in the experiment that convey the experimental hypothesis to the participant without the experimenter intending them to. Research has shown that participants tailor their responses to what they perceive to be the expectations of the experimenter in an attempt to be relevant (Norenzayan and Schwarz, 1999). In the context of déjà vu research, this may mean that when participants are asked repeatedly about experiencing déjà vu, they might simply assume they ought to be experiencing it and they might even want to respond affirmatively so as to give what they suspect is the expected result.

Jersakova et al. (2016) considered the possibility that reports of déjà vu were influenced by demand characteristics. To return to Cleary and colleagues' work as an example, across two experiments they found that participants report experiencing déjà vu in 17 per cent and 26 per cent of their critical trials. However, participants in the same experiments reported déjà vu in 13 per cent and 23 per cent of control trials. Thus, the difference between déjà vu reports on critical and control trials, while significant, is surprisingly small. One must ask what else about the experimental paradigm might have led to reports of déjà vu on the control trials and how this might have influenced déjà vu reports on the critical trials. It is of course possible that the familiarity manipulation and source amnesia leads to general confusion and dissociation across all trials within the experiment, and that the reports of déjà vu on control trials are genuine. However, Jersakova et al. considered whether reports of déjà vu on a trial-by-trial basis might be biased or exaggerated.

Two possibilities present themselves as to why this might be the case. First, participants might interpret being asked about whether they are experiencing déjà vu as indicative that they *should* be experiencing it. This would be especially the case with a participant who is unsure of what exactly he or she is experiencing: they might conclude that their current state is that which the experimenter is interested in, and respond positively when asked whether they are experiencing déjà vu. The fact that participants are asked whether they have experienced déjà vu repeatedly, on almost trial-by-trial basis, adds to this possibility. This is analogous to an acquiescence effect or positive responding regardless of question content (Winkler, Kanouse, & Ware, 1982).

Alternatively, it could be that the communication between the experimenter and participants about the exact nature of the studied experience is not clear. In the Cleary et al. (2009) study, the researchers observed an increase in déjà vu reports when participants were *not* given a definition of déjà vu as compared to when they were. Further, when they asked an independent group to define déjà vu, the majority defined it merely as familiarity, while only six of the 92 participants gave the operational definition used by the researchers (a sense of familiarity combined with the awareness that it is false).

To address these issues, Jersakova et al. carried out four online experiments with a continuous recognition paradigm (ns = 224, 273, 123 and 154). They explored the effect of questioning method on reported occurrence of déjà vu, using the tip of the tongue (TOT) as a comparison experience. In all experiments, participants carried out a long recognition task, with 120 items (40 items presented once and 40 items presented twice). The ongoing task was just to report whether a given item was old or new. Note that this task was *not* expected to induce déjà vu or TOT. Interspersed within the ongoing recognition task were questions about other experiences, which were manipulated between subject. For instance, in the first experiment, one group of participants had to report every 12 trials whether they had seen any words presented in yellow (words were presented in a variety of colours but never in yellow); another group had to report if they had experienced déjà vu in the last 12 trials; another had the same for TOT; and there was also a final control condition with no questions asked during the recognition phase. All participants had a common final post-experimental questionnaire similar to that used by Brown and Marsh (2009) that asked about the incidence of déjà vu, TOT and yellow words during the experiment. The hypothesis was that asking frequently about déjà vu would lead to an elevated level of déjà vu reporting in the déjà vu condition.

First, Jersakova et al. were surprised to find that in each condition and experiment, between 33 per cent and 58 per cent of participants nonetheless reported experiencing déjà vu or TOT – even if they had been in a condition where they had not been asked repeatedly about déjà vu. For instance, in the control condition in Experiment 1, 37.3 per cent of the sample reported having déjà vu during the preceding continuous recognition task (in the same condition, 33.3 per cent of people reported having a TOT). By comparison, 8.9 per cent of the sample reported having seen a yellow word (even though there were none) – this might be a baseline measure of suggestibility. In their subsequent experiments, changing the definition of déjà vu or asking participants to bring to mind a real-life instance of déjà vu or TOT before completing the recognition task had no impact on reporting rates in the post-experimental questionnaire.

For the report of subjective experiences during the task, there was an indication that changing the method of requesting subjective reports impacted reporting of déjà vu and TOT. More specifically, Jersakova et al. compared the commonly used retrospective questioning (e.g. "Have you experienced déjà vu?") to free report instructions (e.g. "Indicate whenever you experience déjà vu"). This led to a reduction in the total number of reported déjà vu (and TOT) occurrences. Jersakova et al. were also able to compare this 'laboratory' déjà vu (and TOT) to the real-world experience of déjà vu, because participants rated the salience, intensity and emotionality of the experience during the task in comparison to the naturally occurring variety. Real-life déjà vu and TOT experiences were rated higher on all measures as compared to their experimentally generated analogues.

Thus, there may be some bias towards reporting déjà vu according to questioning, but the interpretation of the results is largely swayed by whether your belief is that a common-or-garden continuous recognition task should produce TOT or déjà vu experiences. At the least, there is some evidence of a bias to report having had a déjà vu experience when prompted, even though that experience is far less intense than those experienced in the real world. It was found that the rate of participants reporting seeing words presented in yellow never exceeded 18 per cent across all experiments, whereas the lowest proportion of déjà vu and TOT reporters was 33 per cent. Jersakova et al. concluded that the remaining difference between these two values reflects the degree of uncertainty attached to interpreting subjective experiences that is not present when evaluating more objectively veri-fiable phenomena. The study does advocate the move to free reporting of déjà vu (and other subjective phenomena) to reduce the number of false positives in the experience.

Comparisons of déjà vu in the laboratory and in the real world

As with Jersakova et al., most researchers who seek to produce déjà vu in the lab-oratory have acknowledged that there may exist differences between the qualities and intensity of experiences in the real world and those in the laboratory, and this in some way might parallel the similar debate about déjà vu experienced in healthy participants and those with epilepsy or schizophrenia. However, in experimental conditions, it is at least possible to ask people to compare their own experiences of déjà vu in the laboratory and in the real world.

Urquhart and O'Connor asked their 30 participants to complete a pre-experimental questionnaire that gave a definition of the déjà vu experience and asked them to provide a short description of a typical déjà vu experience they had had. They were specifically asked to give "some detail concerning the following points: Emotional intensity of a typical déjà vu experience; Duration of a typical déjà vu experience; How a déjà vu experience might typically make you feel about the reliability of your memory" (p. 5). At the end of the experiment the same ques-tions were given, but this time participants were invited to write about an expe-rience from within the experiment. Urquhart and O'Connor report the results of the 15 participants who had experienced déjà vu both prior to and during the experiment. Their analysis concerned a textual analysis of the statements generated by participants using n-grams. n-grams are sequences of n words found within a passage/sentence of prose. Urquhart and O'Connor's analysis concerned unigrams (n-grams with n = 1 and n = 2) that had significantly different frequencies in the real world and laboratory descriptions.

Some of the outcomes were not very insightful. One common theme, unsur-prisingly, was the presence of words describing the specificity of the experience. Laboratory descriptions were characterised by descriptions relating to the stimuli ("word[s]", "the word[s]"), modality of presentation ("seen", "had seen") or the context ("experiment", "the experiment"), e.g. "Sometimes, I had a very slight feeling that I had seen a particular word before." Real-world experiences were more or less specific, frequently including the words ("situation", "experience"), e.g. "Typically a scenario or situation I am in just seems familiar." More interestingly, the analysis pointed to differences in duration: 'Minutes' was used more frequently to describe naturalistic experiences, e.g. "A typical déjà vu experience for me lasts a couple of minutes." Urquhart and O'Connor report that some people who had experienced déjà vu in the experiment were more cautious about describing their experience after the experiment, e.g. "I am unsure whether it was exactly déjà vu but in some cases I saw words usually words I was expecting to see in the groups but did not, and it felt as if I had seen them" and "I am not really sure I had the two déjà vu I reported, or if I think I had them only because it was the task of the experiment". These comments, as the authors point out, echo the concerns of social desirability and conformity in responding discussed above.

Sugimori and Kusumi (2014) more directly address the relationship between real-world and laboratory déjà vu. Their experiment used a recognition without identification design and 120 black and white line drawing scenes (as used in Cleary et al., 2009), but they added a remember–know judgement in the test phase, and measured performance on a scale of familiarity, rather than asking about déjà vu on a trial-by-trial basis. Participants also underwent a task in which they explicitly evaluated the similarity of two scenes. They also took some questionnaire measures in their 44 participants. Most importantly, they surveyed previous experiences of déjà vu and other phenomena using questions adapted from the IDEA (Sno et al., 1994), and questionnaires of nostalgia and regret. Seven questions considered the extent to which participants experienced subjective familiarity, similarity and memory in daily life (p. 50):

(1) You go to a new place and feel as if you have been there before (déjà vu).
(2) You meet someone for the first time and feel as if you have met that person before (déjà vu).
(3) You recollect past experiences and feel nostalgic (feeling of nostalgia).
(4) You wish you could return to the past and make a fresh start in life (feeling of regret).
(5) Music and/or photographs from the past evoke nostalgic feelings in you (feeling of nostalgia).
(6) When you read a story or watch a TV show or a movie for the first time, you recollect a similar story you have previously read or watched (sensitivity to similarity).
(7) When you listen to a piece of music for the first time, you recollect similar music you have listened to previously (sensitivity to similarity).

The elegance of Sugimori and Kusumi's experiment is that it directly measures the sensitivity to configural similarity and uses exactly the paradigm which Cleary and colleagues have used to provoke déjà vu in laboratory situations, except that no explicit question about déjà vu was asked in Sugimori and Kusumi's laboratory task. However, it might be assumed that this task provoked déjà vu: indeed, the familiarity ratings replicated the effect that similar but novel scenes were rated as subjectively more familiar than novel–dissimilar scenes, even though the remember/know procedure indicated that most novel scenes at test were identified as new. Most importantly, Sugimori and Kusumi report that the correlation between the frequency of déjà vu experiences in daily life and the familiarity ratings for novel similar scenes was 'high' ($r = 0.66$). There was likewise a strong correlation between déjà vu frequency and the questions about configural or conceptual similarity ($r = .57$), but the correlation between their task which measured sensitivity to configural similarity in the laboratory and the frequency of experiencing déjà vu in real life was weaker ($r = .38$).

Sugimori and Kusumi's experiment would be equally at home on the chapter on individual differences approaches (Chapter 6) because it uses a correlational approach of measuring real-world experiences to corroborate the results of an experimental induction of déjà vu. A priority now might be to more explicitly test the relationship between the two forms of déjà vu considering the strength and amount of déjà vu generated in experimental tasks and in the real world using individual differences. It would also be helpful to see if the various means of producing déjà vu in the laboratory converge on the same construct: would those people who experience déjà vu using recognition without identification also be more likely to generate it using the DRM-like procedure? In sum, whereas it might be concluded that the experimental tasks capture a subjective experience which is comparable to déjà vu, more research is needed to address whether it might ever be spontaneously described as déjà vu, and how it differs in terms of intensity, duration and other qualities. If one follows the logic of 'surprising' fluency and the attributional nature of recognition memory advanced by Whittlesea (1997), it will necessarily be the case that déjà vu experienced in the context of a memory experiment (especially one where you have been told (or have guessed) that the aim is to generate déjà vu), is always likely to be less striking and less surprising.

Summary: synthetic déjà vu

In summary, following Brown's (2003) influential review, there has been an increase in experiments with the aim of inducing déjà vu-like sensations and memory illusions in laboratory settings. This approach is the main empirical underpinning of the source amnesia and Gestalt similarity accounts of déjà vu, and warrants much further examination. The results of the various experiments here are mostly well-powered and have mostly been replicated, although there is a tendency for each research group to continue using their own preferred task. It is, however, safe to conclude that our careful observation and theorising has lead us to a point where there are now established paradigms which pertain to theories of déjà vu formation. The methods all converge on the experience of familiarity, either induced by the repetition of a previously seen stimulus which is forgotten or superficially encoded or by similarity. In Cleary and colleagues' work the similarity is configural, or perceptual, whereas in Urquhart and O'Connor the similarity is conceptual, based on pre-existing semantic concepts in list of words. In Sugimori and Kusumi's work, there is the suggestion that the sensitivity to similarity in the real world is an important predictor of the frequency of déjà vu. All the experiments also involve some form of conflict or dissociation. In the early priming experiments, the illusion of déjà vu is not generated if people are consciously aware that the same information is being presented twice: conflict is not generated if one knows that the feeling of familiarity derives from the double presentation of the stimulus. In the recognition without identification paradigm there is a mismatch between identification and the feeling of familiarity, and in the Urquhart and O'Connor task, there is a direct manipulation of conflict using information provided by the participants themselves which contradicts the feeling of familiarity.

As a cautionary note, there is concern that the report of déjà vu is grossly exaggerated in experimental tasks, especially when participants are asked about it on a trial-by-trial basis. The fact that people are happy to report TOT and déjà vu for a continuous recognition task where we would not normally predict the occurrence of either suggests that the labels that people use to describe their experiences – in the laboratory and beyond – are very malleable, and this points to the need to discover more objective and concrete measures of the experience. It is clear, however, that research into déjà vu will challenge existing means of measuring subjective experience, and in that regard what is learned from provoking and measuring déjà vu in the laboratory will be of critical importance in cognitive psychology more generally.

One issue is addressing what *does not* produce déjà vu in the laboratory. The 'file drawer problem' was a term coined by Rosenthal (1979) to explain the publication bias in psychology: one cannot tell how many studies have been conducted but never reported. It is not known whether people have tried and failed to generate déjà vu in experimental settings. In a similar fashion, it remains an outside possibility, as suggested in the Jersakova et al. task, that memory researchers are routinely generating déjà vu-like experiences, but because they are not asked about it, participants do not report having it.

Future experimental work should fuse the various approaches reported in this book. It would be of interest to examine how neuropsychological populations (and even older adults) respond to the various paradigms reported above. Neuropsychological research could help triangulate on the causes of déjà vu and verify that these tasks measure something that relates to observations in clinical groups. In older adults, one should predict fewer reports of déjà vu, for example. In patients with epilepsy without the requisite recollection processes, we should see fewer reports of déjà vu on tasks reported above. Moreover, taking these déjà vu paradigms into groups of psychiatric patients with and without déjà vu in their daily life or with and without delusions would be equally interesting.

One way of producing déjà vu experimentally is with the direct stimulation of the cortex in people waiting for neurosurgery. However, this is far from being a reliable means of generating déjà vu because not all patients have electrodes in the correct areas, and moreover, not all stimulations lead to the generation of déjà vu. In fact, the generation of déjà vu by experimental means is more reliable. A conservative estimate would be 50 per cent of participants experiencing déjà vu in the paradigms reviewed here. In comparison, Penfield and Perot (1963) report that only 7.7 per cent of all their 520 temporal lobe patients had any kind of 'experiential response' (including, but not limited to, déjà vu). Nonetheless, an interesting possibility for future research is the stimulation of healthy brains, by less invasive means. Saroka and Persinger (2013) report the attempts to stimulate 'Hughlings Jackson's 'parasitic consciousness' in healthy patients using the application of "weak, physiologically-patterned magnetic fields", noting that about 30 per cent of their sample reported having 'sensed presence' and out-of-body experiences, which relate broadly to the dreamy states discussed in Chapter 7, although there is no explicit mention of déjà vu.

A clear priority, however, is to use déjà vu-producing paradigms in neuroimaging settings. At the time of going to press, O'Connor's team was preparing for publication a report of a neuroimaging version of their DRM-inspired task (described above; Urquhart & O'Connor, 2014). This work was presented at the International Conference of Memory (2016) and reported extensively in the media (e.g. Hamzelou, 2016). The results of the study appear to converge on the idea of conflict being at the centre of the déjà vu experience: prefrontal cortex activation (rather than temporal lobe activation) separated those trials on which people reported déjà vu and did not report déjà vu, and this area has been previously proposed to monitor cognitive processes for conflict. The déjà vu experience was therefore linked to the detection of a conflict in the memory system, which the journalist elegantly wrote up as "a sign of our brain checking its memory". O'Connor's work seems to suggest a larger network of regions is at play in déjà vu than just the temporal lobe, and thus using an experimental approach, his data need to be reconciled with the differences in recollection and familiarity reported by Martin et al. (2012) in their study of people with epilepsy with and without déjà vu. It can be proposed that intact recollection may be required to deliver information to oppose the feeling of familiarity, but that, in addition, the resultant signals from the familiarity and recollection networks need to be brought together in a final higher-level integration in the frontal lobe.

11

DÉJÀ VU

Where have we been and where are we going?

the accumulating body of intriguing research on déjà vu will hopefully encourage us to spend more effort delving into memory illusions as a means of understanding normal memory function ... These obtuse messages from the brain are potentially packed with fascinating secrets about cognitive function.

Brown & Marsh (2010, p. 60)

A scientific account of déjà vu

There are now sufficient scientific studies to make a concrete proposal about what déjà vu is and its basis in the brain (a schematic representation is given in Figure 11.1). It is a rare occurrence because usually the feeling of familiarity and the retrieval of information work in concert. However, at times, this association between familiarity and prior occurrence breaks down. A cognitive explanation of this breakdown would be that conceptual or perceptual similarity or unattended processing generate a feeling of familiarity (probably through enhanced fluency), whereas a neurological account would be that the familiarity circuit becomes temporally and erroneously activated in the human memory network, for some physiological reason. The two accounts are not mutually exclusive, and déjà vu should be thought of as having multiple causality, and different levels of explanation converging on one core symptom.

In the brain, déjà vu has long been associated with the temporal lobes. Here, it is proposed that no 'zone' for déjà vu exists. Instead, the memory network must act on and interpret lower-level familiarity signals and the integration of top-down reasoning and the detection of this conflict seem to involve frontal processes. The neuroimaging and patient evidence for this frontal involvement is currently weak, but neuropsychologically and conceptually it seems reasonable to posit a 'higher-order'

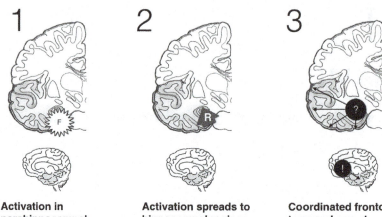

Activation in parahippocampal regions due to overstimulation (decoupled familiarity) or conceptual or perceptual similarity between stimulus and stored representation

Activation spreads to hippocampal regions where usually conceptual specifics and episodic information are retrieved

Coordinated fronto-temporal search rapidly returns information which contradicts initial familiarity, **frontal areas signal conflict** between temporal zones

FIGURE 11.1 A schematic representation of the déjà vu experience, from initial feelings of familiarity (1), activation of recollective circuits (2) and the detection of conflict between the two (3).

structure that is responsible for detecting conflict and essentially overcoming or correcting the false feeling of familiarity. The research on epilepsy suggests that this mechanism will also rely on the relationship between the hippocampal (recollection) and parahippocampal (familiarity) circuits, but again, it can be proposed that a third region may be needed to evaluate the mismatch of activity between the two. If recollective confabulation can indeed be conceptualised as an ungated form of hyperfamiliarity, then the finding that this arises due to frontal lobe deficits would be of major relevance to the déjà vu literature: déjà vu can only arise when frontal systems are intact. More research into déjà vu in healthy older populations (often conceptualised as having a very mild frontal lobe dysfunction) would shed light on this matter.

Déjà vu, therefore, may remain an unusual and unpredictable mental event, but it is no longer an unexplained phenomenon. It would be wrong for parapsychologists to claim that mainstream cognitive neuropsychologists have no idea what causes it. Parapsychologists would do as well to use the TOT experience in their reasoning as déjà vu. TOT events are, after all, as subjective and as unpredictable as déjà vu, even if they are experienced more frequently. Déjà vu is not a paranormal event, and it appears not to be a pathological one either. Across a number of different pathologies, déjà vu does not appear to be an inherently pathological symptom, nor is it more frequent in several groups, in general. Few studies can identify key differences between déjà vu experienced in the context of health and psychological distress or impairment. If anything, déjà vu is associated with youth and a better functioning memory system (as operationalised as recollection, and as seen in epilepsy). It possibly requires an active and well-organised 'fact-checking' system to generate the experience, and déjà vu may point to people who have a healthy relationship with their memory, less prone to false memories, and delusions.

Déjà vu and metacognition

A major theme in this book is that déjà vu is metacognitive. It is only because we are able to metacognitively reflect on the error at the heart of the illusion of familiarity that we are aware of it at all. In this way, the déjà vu state suggests that there are two levels of attribution at play in recognition memory: a fast and obligatorily sensed feeling that something is familiar, and an evaluation arriving moments later that this feeling is false.

It should be noted that this is not the first account of déjà vu describing it as metacognitive (see Kusumi, 2006). Kusumi's Typicality and Analogical Reminding model (reproduced in Figure 11.2) proposes that part of the percept-memory system is constantly active, looking for overlaps between the current environment and stored representations (the numbers in the figure are the proposed percentage of

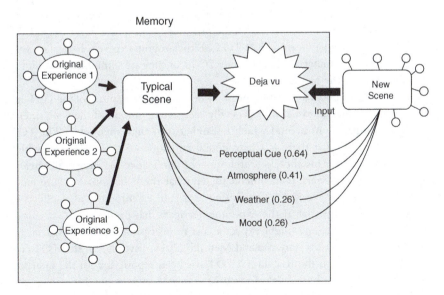

FIGURE 11.2 Kusumi's (2006) Typicality and Analogical Reminding model (reprinted with permission of the author), showing how the similarity between a typical and a new scene creates a metacognitive conflict. Note that the déjà vu mechanism is proposed to arise in the memory system, with stored representations in memory, and the novel scene or experience lying outside the memory system.

times the trigger is an effective cue for retrieval. (This model is broadly consistent with the Gestalt similarity account.) Kusumi proposes several different forms of metacognitive component: 'feelings of a strong familiarity', 'judgements of similarity and dissimilarity' and reality monitoring. As such, there are clear overlaps between a source (or reality) monitoring account of déjà vu and the idea that there are two levels of metacognition, fast obligatory feelings of familiarity in a constantly active system, and more contemplative, top-down judgements of similarity and novelty which map onto recollective sources and the pinpointing of prior occurrence and contextual specifics.

One strand of evidence that helps put déjà vu in a metacognitive context is the relationship between déjà vu and the TOT experience (see also Cleary, 2014). In older adults, there is even a relationship between déjà vu and TOT: people who experienced a TOT more recently had also experienced déjà vu more frequently. This correlation may point to the fact that some people are more aware of their cognitive failings and epistemic feelings than others. More than just conceptually, the relationship between TOT and déjà vu may help guide further research, just because the field of TOT research is much more advanced than that of déjà vu.

In TOT research there is an accepted laboratory analogue, and as with déjà vu, the TOT seems somewhat easier to produce in the laboratory, where it is experienced multiple times on one test, whereas diary studies indicate that it is experienced only about once a week in real life. Heine, Ober and Shenaut (1999), for instance, examined diary TOT and laboratory TOT rates in the same groups of participants. In the laboratory, their group of young adults (mean age 21 years) generated 23 TOTs on a 112-item test. In the real world, over a four-week period, the same group repeated a mean of 5.21 TOTs. Either cognitive psychologists are very good at producing materials that generate TOTs, or they are something different in the laboratory to the real world.

In general, the déjà vu literature needs to develop in the manner of the TOT literature, which does at least share a generally accepted definition of the phenomena, and a central paradigm behind which researchers can align themselves. The TOT has the advantage that there is a behavioural consequence to the feeling (which can be measured, for instance, as 'search time' or confidence that they will retrieve later the correct answer). It is difficult to see what the behavioural consequence of a déjà vu experience is. One promising idea is to examine the after-effects of the déjà vu-eliciting trial. If the experimenter really has produced an attention-grabbing experience, one might expect a cost to processing on the next trial (or possibly on a dual task). Schwartz and Metcalfe (2011) have shown that TOTs are less likely to occur in the trial after a TOT has been reported, with the interpretation being that the high level of resources required to generate a metacognitive evaluation have been depleted and take a while to recover. This occurs even though recall is not affected for the subsequent trial. Such a design is needed in déjà vu research. Schwartz has also shown the effects of carrying out a concurrent task on rates of TOT generation, and this approach has proved very useful in metacognition more generally (e.g. Sacher, Taconnat, Souchay, & Isingrini, 2009). Thus, we should anticipate a reduction in déjà vu with a concurrent task, for instance, because there will be a lack of the necessary mental control to oppose the false familiarity (in line with Sacher et al., 2009). Likewise, we should see after-effects on subsequent trials if déjà vu is resource-demanding.

Turning to the brain, one of the ways of thinking about metacognition is to consider it as reflecting the relationship between our memory system and our experience of it. In the déjà vu experience, one must consciously reflect on the signals being generated by the memory system, and we assume that this requires a rich network of brain regions and a complex interaction of cognitive processes; in this way, the metacognitive component of déjà vu is captured in the relationship with the frontal lobe. Neuroimaging studies of feelings such as the TOT or the feeling of knowing (FOK), although rare, have suggested the involvement of common neural substrates. Such studies (e.g. Maril, Simons, Mitchell, Schwartz, & Schacter, 2003; Reggev, Zuckerman, & Maril, 2011) have revealed a set of fronto-temporal and anterior cingulate brain regions activated during making metacognitive judgements in recognition memory. Similarly, fMRI studies exploring TOT states have revealed the crucial role of the frontal lobes. Maril, Wagner and Schacter (2001) showed that compared to Know or Don't know responses, TOT responses were associated with a greater activation of the right prefrontal cortex.

Priorities for future research

Better measuring déjà vu

The greatest challenge facing déjà vu is the necessary reliance on subjective self-reports. Unlike memory impairments where researchers can objectively assess memory performance, the experience of déjà vu is entirely subjective. This means the only way to assess whether the experience has been replicated in the lab is to ask participants a question like "Have you experienced déjà vu?" This may lead to a high level of déjà vu responses on baseline conditions and in tasks where we would not theoretically expect déjà vu to be generated.

As is the case with the remember/know distinction (Gardiner & Java, 1993), many studies explain the difference carefully before asking participants to make judgements on which one they experienced. A similar kind of dialogue between participants and experimenters should be established in the study of déjà vu, and many déjà vu researchers have now adopted this protocol. Studies need to continue to ask participants to bring to mind specific instances of their previous déjà vu experiences to make them fully appreciate the nature of the experience before they are asked whether they have experienced it during an experiment. As such, the next important step for further déjà vu research is to establish better methodologies that allow the study of the experience whilst simultaneously eliminating (or at least minimising) demand characteristics. The results of Jersakova et al. (2016) also suggest that having an open format where participants can press a button any time they experience déjà vu rather than being asked on every trial will reduce the number of false positive déjà vu experiences. Chapter 10 emphasised the need to consider the differences between real-world and laboratory déjà vu (as discussed in TOT research, above) and in doing this, the concerns about whether we are accurately measuring déjà vu will also be addressed.

As well as having a number of experimental analogues, the field has converged on one questionnaire measure of déjà vu – Sno et al.'s (1994) IDEA. This common use of the same tool, translated into different languages, should be seen as a strength of the field. There is, however, a worry that this measure overlooks some of the more recent theoretical advances and links to memory and metacognition that are clearer in experimental tasks. In particular, it is this measure on which we are over-reliant when concluding that there is no difference in déjà vu experiences between people with and without epilepsy and schizophrenia. Our ability to look at differences in the experience may be limited by the tool that we use to measure these differences. Thus, for the part of the questionnaire which looks at déjà vu experience more generally (Part A), it would be interesting to look at other metacognitive phenomena, prescience, involuntary memories, the sensitivity to similarity and the differences between recollection and familiarity. For Part B, looking at a specific experience of déjà vu, nowadays, it is easier to measure infrequent mental experiences more rapidly and in more detail using smart phones and online technologies, and this is a priority for future research, to reduce the retrospective bias.

Relationship between déjà vu and other phenomena

The relationship between déjà vu and TOT (and other metacognitive phenomena) is something that could be further examined to help triangulate on the metacognitive nature of déjà vu. Likewise, the consideration of whether people who experience less déjà vu are more likely to have false memories is a hypothesis which has been untested, and this should consider longitudinal changes in the aging process and déjà vu in schizophrenia, for instance. Given the idea of a constantly active 'reminding system' based on a familiarity system geared up to find similarity in the environment (Kusumi, 2006), the relationship between déjà vu and the reproduction of material from memory, especially in the form of involuntary memory, needs to be explored.

In the experiences of TLE patients undergoing stimulation of the temporal lobe, production of fragmentary images from 'complete' memories is common alongside reports of déjà vu. Just as with déjà vu, their status in healthy aging may point to the underlying memory mechanisms responsible for their formation. So far, there is only weak evidence for déjà vu existing on a continuum with involuntary memory, in the form of a correlation between the two mental experiences in older adults. There is mixed evidence about involuntary memories in older adults according to differing methodology. Questionnaires by Berntsen and Rubin (2002) and diary studies by Schlagman, Kliegel, Schulz and Kvavilashvili (2009) found that older adults report fewer involuntary memories than younger people during their day-to-day lives, but a later study by Rubin and Berntsen (2009) with participants aged 15 to over 90 concluded that involuntary memories had similar frequencies. There are laboratory analogues of involuntary memories, which show that older adults are less likely to spontaneously generate such memories (e.g. Schlagman & Kvavilashvili, 2008).

A link between déjà vu and involuntary memories would suggest that uncontrolled, random neural and cognitive events influenced by fatigue, boredom or mind-wandering may be responsible for both phenomena, and the TLE data suggest that both might be due to temporary disruptions to processing in the temporal lobe (Bradley, Moulin, & Kvavilashvili, 2013). Recent neuroimaging and experimental work has considered the medial temporal lobe in traumatic flashbacks, where it seems the defining neural basis of these uncontrolled memories is decreased activation in the temporal lobe combined with increased activation in the visual and motor cortices (Whalley et al., 2013).

Neuroimaging, neuroimaging, neuroimaging

The neuropsychological literature examining special populations has converged on the combined frontal/temporal hypothesis of déjà vu formation outlined above. Undoubtedly, the examination of déjà vu in healthy groups needs now to consider the use of the experimental protocols reviewed in Chapter 10 in neuroimaging designs where the functional activation of the memory systems involved in déjà vu can be examined. This could take the form of EEG/MEG or fMRI investigations, but what would be most insightful would be the use of event-related methodologies such that trials eliciting déjà vu can be compared to trials which do not elicit déjà vu, thus allowing a precise examination of the specific mechanism involved in déjà vu production.

Clinical issues

Whilst déjà vu might not be a diagnostically important symptom in and of itself in epilepsy or in schizophrenia, it is of clinical relevance for many people. Numerous case studies have shown that in a minority of cases, the déjà vu experience is debilitating and intensely traumatic. Wells et al. have proposed that there exists a form of chronic déjà vu which is psychogenic, and more research into this distressing and probably anxiety-related dysfunction needs to be carried out. People experiencing déjà vu need to be taken seriously; whilst it is not experienced more frequently on the whole in epilepsy, it is diagnostically relevant for some people in that it can herald an upcoming seizure. Temporal lobe epilepsy remains the most likely cause of frequent experiences of déjà vu, but the diagnosis of epilepsy, naturally, will not be based on the experience of déjà vu alone. In schizophrenia and in dementia, there are clear differences between déjà vu and delusion or recollective confabulation, and clinicians possibly need to think more of déjà vu as a healthy symptom, indicating that the patient is able to contradict and resist episodic bouts of extreme familiarity. Now that there is a scientific consensus on what causes déjà vu, more needs to be done with patients using cognitive behavioural therapy methods to introduce symptom education. This will enable sensible metacognitive evaluations of déjà vu, reduce the stressful and unsettling nature of déjà vu and reduce anxiety associated with déjà vu. This may even, in turn, reduce the intensity or frequency of déjà vu, given that there is some evidence that it is triggered by stress and acute anxiety. Certainly, with what is known about déjà vu, it would be unfortunate if patients felt the only means of explaining their déjà vu is through parapsychological and 'anomalous' interpretations.

ACKNOWLEDGEMENTS

The French system still necessitates passing a further higher degree, a 'Habilitation à diriger des recherches' (HDR), which requires the production of a long thesis-like document. Although the HDR should be considered as a waste of time for the modern academic researcher, being an unwelcome extra pressure in the busy researcher's life, it is undoubtedly a good thing to be forced to reflect on one's output. I was always keen that what I produced for my HDR should not be wasted, and that it should be ultimately published as a monograph. I could not have been more delighted and honoured that Psychology Press, thanks to the responsive and enthusiastic work of Ceri Griffiths, agreed to publish this work. Ceri remained patient and supportive whilst the project mutated. Nearly everything got rewritten.

Another bonus of the HDR is it allows the assembling of a panel of experts to publicly examine the thesis. My work on déjà vu has thus been greatly shaped by those who came to Dijon in June 2015 for my *soutenance*: Martin Conway, Tim Hollins, Robert French, Emmanuel Barbeau, Laurence Tacconat, Marie Izaute and Denis Perrin. This panel has been at various points a major support and inspiration for my work. I should also like to acknowledge here that the peculiar professional misery and isolation that I felt whilst in Dijon was a major motivator for throwing myself into this project.

I gratefully acknowledge the following collaborators and students who have shared with me their student projects, early drafts, dissertations and project data on déjà vu and related topics: Narimène Alouani, Julie Bertrand, Rosemary Bradley, Sarah Buchanan, Alison Dref, Mathilde Drouot, Jonathan Fortier, Radka Jersakova, Nathan Illman, Léa Martinon, Akira O'Connor, Belinda Savage and Christine Wells. The following people enthusiastically commented on earlier drafts of parts of this book (for the HDR) and I am grateful for their help (although any mistakes, are, of course, my own): Nathan Illman, Radka Jersakova, Akira O'Connor, Kata

Pauly-Takacs, Clare Rathbone and Helen Williams. A special thanks goes to Akira O'Connor, who was always on call to talk about déjà vu.

Finally, I am indebted to the work of Alan Brown. His earlier Psychology Press book, *The Déjà vu Experience*, has been a source of inspiration and know-how. But it is not just as a scientific work this book has been important. Scholars' efforts shape the lives and careers of those who follow in their footsteps; without the credibility and cognitive theory Alan Brown has brought to déjà vu, it would have been impossible for researchers at an earlier stage in their career, such as myself, to investigate this fascinating topic.

The cover image was conceived and photographed by Cindy Bannani.

REFERENCES

Adachi, N., Adachi, T., Akanuma, N., Matsubara, R., Ito, M., Takekawa, Y., ... Arai, H. (2007). Déjà vu experiences in schizophrenia: Relations with psychopathology and antipsychotic medication. Comprehensive Psychiatry, 48, 592–596.

Adachi, N., Adachi, T., Kimura, M., Akanuma, N., & Kato, M. (2001). Development of the Japanese version of the Inventory of Déjà vu Experiences Assessment (IDEA). Seishin Igaku, 43, 1223–1231.

Adachi, T., Adachi, N., Takekawa, Y., Akanuma, N., Ito, M., Matsubara, R., ... Arai, H. (2006). Déjà vu experiences in patients with schizophrenia. Comprehensive Psychiatry, 47, 389–393.

Adachi, N., Akanu, N., Adachi, T., Takekawa, Y., Adachi, Y., Ito, M., & Ikeda, H. (2008). Déjà vu experiences are rarely associated with pathological dissociation. Journal of Nervous and Mental Disorders, 196, 417–419.

Adachi, N., Akanuma, N., Ito, M., Adachi, T., Takekawa, Y., Adachi, Y., ... Kato, M. (2010). Two forms of déjà vu experiences in patients with epilepsy. Epilepsy & Behavior: E&B, 18, 218–222.

Adachi, N., Koutroumanidis, M., Elwes, R. D. C., Polkey, C. E., Binnie, C. D., Reynolds, E. H., ... Panayiotopoulos, C. P. (1999). Interictal 18FDG PET findings in temporal lobe epilepsy with déja vu. Journal of Neuropsychiatry and Clinical Neurosciences, 11, 380–386.

Aggleton, J. P., & Brown, M. W. (1999). Episodic memory, amnesia and the hippocampal-anterior thalamic axis. Behavioral and Brain Sciences, 22, 425–498.

Akgül, S., Öksüz-Kanbur, N., & Turan, G. (2013). Persistent déjà vu associated with temporal lobe epilepsy in an adolescent. Turkish Journal of Pediatrics, 55, 552–554.

Allman, M. J., & Meck, W. H. (2012). Pathophysiological distortions in time perception and timed performance. Brain, 135, 656–677.

Andrews, T. J., Schluppeck, D., Homfray, D., Matthews, P., & Blakemore, C. (2002). Activity in the fusiform gyrus predicts conscious perception of Rubin's vase–face illusion. NeuroImage, 17, 890–901.

Arango-Muñoz, S. (2011). Two levels of metacognition. Philosophia, 39, 71–82.

Arnaud, F. L. (1896). Un cas d'illusion du 'déjà vu' ou de 'fausse mémoire'. Annales Médico-Psychologiques, 3, 455–471.

Arnold, K. (2002). Anti-epiphany and the Jungian manikin: Toward a theory of prepsychotic perceptual alterations. Journal of Phenomenological Psychology, 33, 245–275.

Attali, E., De Anna, F., Dubois, B., & Dalla Barba, G. (2009). Confabulation in Alzheimer's disease: Poor encoding and retrieval of over-learned information. Brain, 132, 204–212.

Aydemir, N., Tekcan, A. İ., & Özkara, Ç. (2009). Remembering the first seizure and the diagnosis of epilepsy: How much impact do they have in our lives? Epilepsy & Behavior, 16, 156–160.

Back, K. W., & Bourque, L. B. (1970). Life graphs: Aging and cohort effect. Journal of Gerontology, 25, 249–255.

Balota, D. A., & Black, S. (1997). Semantic satiation in healthy young and older adults. Memory & Cognition, 25, 190–202.

Balota, D. A., Cortese, M. J., Duchek, J. M., Adams, D., Roediger III, H. L., McDermott, K. B., & Yerys, B.E. (1999). Veridical and false memories in healthy older adults and in dementia of the Alzheimer's type. Cognitive Neuropsychology, 16, 361–384.

Bancaud, J., Brunet-Bourgin, F., Chauvel, P., & Halgren, E. (1994). Anatomical origin of déjà vu and vivid "memories" in human temporal lobe epilepsy. Brain, 117, 71–90.

Banister, H., & Zangwill, O.L. (1941). Experimentally induced visual paramnesias. British Journal of Psychology, 32, 30–51.

Barba, G. D. (1997). Recognition memory and recollective experience in Alzheimer's disease. Memory, 5, 657–672.

Barbeau, E., Chauvel, P., Moulin, C. J.A., Regis, J., & Liégeois-Chauvel, C. (2017). Hippocampus duality: Memory and novelty detection are subserved by distinct mechanisms. Hippocampus, 27, 405–416.

Barbeau, E., Wendling, F., Regis, J., Duncan, R., Poncet, M., Chauvel, P., & Bartolomei, F. (2005). Recollection of vivid memories after perirhinal region stimulations: Synchronization in the theta range of spatially distributed brain areas. Neuropsychologia, 43, 1329–1337.

Bartolomei, F., Barbeau, E., Gavaret, M., Guye, M., McGonigal, A., Regis, J., & Chauvel, P. (2004). Cortical stimulation study of the role of rhinal cortex in déja vu and reminiscence of memories. Neurology, 63, 858–864.

Bastin, C., & Van der Linden, M. (2003). The contribution of recollection and familiarity to recognition memory: A study of the effects of test format and aging. Neuropsychology, 17, 14–24.

Bering, J.M. (2006). The folk psychology of souls. Behavioral and Brain Sciences, 29, 453–462.

Bernstein, E., & Putnam, F. W. (1986). Development, reliability, and validity of a dissociation scale. The Journal of Nervous and Mental Disease, 174, 727–735.

Bernstein, E., & Putnam, F.W. (1993). An update on the Dissociative Experiences Scale. Dissociation: Progress in the Dissociative Disorders, 6, 16–27.

Berntsen, D., & Rubin, D. C. (2002). Emotionally charged autobiographical memories across the life span: The recall of happy, sad, traumatic and involuntary memories. Psychology and Aging, 17, 636.

Berrios, G. E. (1995). Déjà vu in France during the 19th century: A conceptual history. Comprehensive Psychiatry, 36, 123–129. Retrieved from www.ncbi.nlm.nih.gov/pubmed/7758298.

Berrios, G. E. (2012). Memory disorders and epilepsy during the nineteenth century. In A. Zeman, N. Kapur & M. Jones-Gotman (Eds.), Epilepsy and memory (pp. 51–62). Oxford, UK: Oxford University Press.

Berry, C. J., Shanks, D. R., Speekenbrink, M., & Henson, R. N. A. (2012). Models of recognition, repetition priming, and fluency: Exploring a new framework. Psychological Review, 119: 40–79.

Bertrand, J. M., Martinon, L. M., Souchay, C., & Moulin, C. J. (2017). History repeating itself: Arnaud's case of pathological déjà vu. Cortex, 87, 129–141.

Biéder, J. (2005). Un de Vanves, François-Léon Arnaud (1858–1927). Annales Médico-Psychologiques, Revue Psychiatrique, 163, 909–911.

Bigal, M. E., Lipton, R. B., Cohen, J., & Silberstein, S. D. (2003). Epilepsy and migraine. Epilepsy & Behavior, 4, 13–24.

Boirac, E. (1876/2014). http://thirdnews.wordpress.com/2013/12/19/emile-boiracs-1876-deja-vu-open-letter-a-christening/.

Boirac, E. (1902). Leçons de Psychologie Appliqué a L'Education. Paris, France: F. Alcan.

Boirac, E. (1917). Our hidden forces. New York, NY: Frederick A. Stokes Co.

Boirac, E. (1918). The psychology of the future. London, UK: Kegan Paul, Trench, Trubner & Co.

Bortolotti, L. (2010). Delusions and other irrational beliefs. Oxford, UK: Oxford University Press.

Bowles, B., Crupi, C., Pigott, S., Parrent, A., Wiebe, S., Janzen, L., & Köhler, S. (2010). Double dissociation of selective recollection and familiarity impairments following two different surgical treatments for temporal-lobe epilepsy. Neuropsychologia, 48, 2640–2647.

Bradley, R. J., Moulin, C. J. A., & Kvavilashvili, L. (2013). Involuntary autobiographical memories. Psychologist, 26, 190–193.

Brandt, K. R., Eysenck, M. W., Nielsen, M. K., & von Oertzen, T. J. (2016). Selective lesion to the entorhinal cortex leads to an impairment in familiarity but not recollection. Brain and Cognition, 104, 82–92.

Brázdil, M., Mareček, R., Urbanek, T., Kašparek, T., Mikl, M., Rektor, I., & Zeman, A. (2012). Unveiling the mystery of déjà vu: The structural anatomy of déjà vu. Cortex, 48, 1240–1243.

Brown, A. S. (2003). A review of the déjà vu experience. Psychological Bulletin, 129, 394–413.

Brown, A. S. (2004). The déjà vu experience. New York, NY: Psychology Press.

Brown, A. S., & Marsh, E. J. (2008). Evoking false beliefs about autobiographical experience. Psychonomic Bulletin and Review, 15, 186–190.

Brown, A. S., & Marsh, E. J. (2009). Creating illusions of past encounter through brief exposure. Psychological Science, 20, 534–538.

Brown, A. S., & Marsh, E. J. (2010). Digging into déjà vu: Recent research on possible mechanisms. In B. H. Ross (Ed.), The psychology of learning and motivation, 53 (pp. 33–62). Burlington, MA: Academic Press.

Brun, G., Doğuoğlu, U., & Kuenzle, D. (Eds.). (2008). Epistemology and emotions. Aldershot: Ashgate.

Burgess, P. W., & Shallice, T. (1996). Bizarre responses, rule detection and frontal lobe lesions. Cortex, 32(2), 241–259.

Chapman, A. H., & Mensh, I. N. (1951). Déjà vu experience and conscious fantasy in adults. Psychiatric Quarterly Supplement, 25, 163–175.

Chiu, M. J., Lin, C. W., Chen, C. C., Chen, T. F., Chen, Y. F., Liu, H. M., & Hua, M. S. (2010). Impaired gist memory in patients with temporal lobe epilepsy and hippocampal sclerosis. Epilepsia, 51, 1036–1042.

Clancy, S. A., McNally, R. J., Schacter, D. L., Lenzenweger, M. F., & Pitman, R. K. (2002). Memory distortion in people reporting abduction by aliens. Journal of Abnormal Psychology, 111, 455–461.

Claparède, E. (1907). Expériences sur la mémoire dans un cas de psychose de Korsakoff. Revue Médicale de la Suisse Romande, 27, 301–303.

Cleary, A. M. (2008). Recognition memory, familiarity, and deja vu experiences. Current Directions in Psychological Science, 17, 353–357.

Cleary, A. M. (2014). On the empirical study of déjà vu: Borrowing methodology from the study of the tip-of-the-tongue phenomenon. In B. L. Schwartz & A. S. Brown's

Tip-of-the-tongue States and Related Phenomena (pp. 264–280). Cambridge, UK: Cambridge University Press.

Cleary, A. M., Brown, A. S., Sawyer, B. D., Nomi, J. S., Ajoku, A. C., & Ryals, A. J. (2012). Familiarity from the configuration of objects in 3-dimensional space and its relation to déjà vu: A virtual reality investigation. Consciousness and Cognition, 21, 969–975.

Cleary, A. M., & Reyes, N. L. (2009). Scene recognition without identification. Acta Psychologica, 131, 53–62.

Cleary, A. M., Ryals, A. J., & Nomi, J. S. (2009). Can déjà vu result from similarity to a prior experience? Support for the similarity hypothesis of déjà vu. Psychonomic Bulletin & Review, 16, 1082–1088.

Cohen, M. R., & Maunsell, J. H. R. (2009). Attention improves performance primarily by reducing interneuronal correlations. Nature Neuroscience, 12, 1594–1600.

Coltheart, M. (2007). The 33rd Sir Frederick Bartlett Lecture: Cognitive neuropsychiatry and delusional belief. The Quarterly Journal of Experimental Psychology, 60, 1041–1062.

Coltheart, M. (2017). Confabulation and conversation. Cortex, 87, 62–68.

Conway, M. A. (2005). Memory and the self. Journal of Memory and Language, 53, 594–628.

Conway, M. A. (2009). Episodic memories. Neuropsychologia, 47, 2305–2313.

Conway, M. A., Collins, A. F., Gathercole, S. E., & Anderson, S. J. (1996). Recollections of true and false autobiographical memories. Journal of Experimental Psychology: General, 125, 69–95.

Conway, M. A., Gardiner, J. M., Perfect, T. J., Anderson, S. J., & Cohen, G. M. (1997). Changes in memory awareness during learning: The acquisition of knowledge by psychology undergraduates. Journal of Experimental Psychology: General, 126, 393–413.

Craik, F. I., Barense, M. D., Rathbone, C. J., Grusec, J. E., Stuss, D. T., Gao, F., … Black, S. E. (2014). VL: A further case of erroneous recollection. Neuropsychologia, 56, 367–380.

Crichton-Browne, J. (1895). Dreamy Mental States. Reprinted in Stray Leaves from a Physician's Portfolio (1927) (pp. 1–42). London, UK: Hodder and Stoughton.

Curran, T., Schacter, D. L., Norman, K. A., & Galluccio, L. (1997). False recognition after a right frontal lobe infarction: Memory for general and specific information. Neuropsychologia, 35, 1035–1049.

Darwin, C. (1887). The life and letters of Charles Darwin, including an autobiographical chapter. London, UK: John Murray.

Dashiell, J. F. (1937). Fundamentals of objective psychology. Boston, MA: Houghton Mifflin Company.

de Camp Wilson, T., & Nisbett, R. E. (1978). The accuracy of verbal reports about the effects of stimuli on evaluations and behavior. Social Psychology, 118–131.

de Sousa, R. (2009). Epistemic feelings. Mind & Matter, 7, 139–161.

della Rocchetta, A. I., & Milner, B. (1993). Strategic search and retrieval inhibition: The role of the frontal lobes. Neuropsychologia, 31, 503–524.

Dennett, D. (1991). Consciousness explained. London: Penguin Books.

Dewhurst, S. A., & Anderson, S. J. (1999). Effects of exact and category repetition in true and false recognition memory. Memory & Cognition, 27, 665–673.

Diana, R. A., Reder, L. M., Arndt, A., & Park, H. (2006). Models of recognition: A review of arguments in favor of a dual-process account. Psychonomic Bulletin & Review, 13, 1–21.

Diana, R. A., Yonelinas, A. P., & Ranganath, C. (2007). Imaging recollection and familiarity in the medial temporal lobe: A three-component model. Trends in Cognitive Sciences, 11, 379–386.

Donaldson, W. (1996). The role of decision processes in remembering and knowing. Memory & Cognition, 24, 523–533.

Dunn, J. C. (2004). Remember–know: A matter of confidence. Psychological Review, 111, 524–542.

Eichenbaum, H., Yonelinas, A. P., & Ranganath, C. (2007). The medial temporal lobe and recognition memory. Annual Review of Neuroscience, 30, 123–152.

Ellis, H. D., Luauté, J. P., & Retterstøl, N. (1994). Delusional misidentification syndromes. Psychopathology, 27, 117–120.

Evans, J. (2008). Dual-processing accounts of reasoning, judgement and social cognition. Annual Review of Psychology, 59, 255–278.

Eysenck, H. J. (1953). Uses and abuses of psychology. London, UK: Penguin Books.

Fair, D. A., Cohen, A. L., Power, J. D., Dosenbach, N. U., Church, J. A., Miezin, F. M., … Petersen, S. E. (2009). Functional brain networks develop from a "local to distributed" organization. PLoS Computational Biology, 5(5): e1000381.

Feinberg, T. E. (2011). Neuropathologies of the self: Clinical and anatomical features. Consciousness and Cognition, 20, 75–81.

Feinberg, T. E., & Roane, D. M. (2005). Delusion misidentification. Psychiatric Clinics of North America, 28, 665–683.

Feinberg, T. E., & Shapiro, R. M. (1989). Misidentification-reduplication and the right hemisphere. Neuropsychiatry, Neuropsychology and Behavioural Neurology, 2, 39–48.

Flavell, J. H. (2004). Theory-of-mind development: Retrospect and prospect. Merrill-Palmer Quarterly, 50, 274–290.

Fletcher, P. C., & Henson, R. N. A. (2001). Frontal lobes and human memory. Brain, 124, 849–881.

Förstl, H., Almeida, O. P., Owen, A. M., Burns, A., & Howard, R. (1991). Psychiatric, neurological and medical aspects of misidentification syndromes: A review of 260 cases. Psychological Medicine, 21, 905–910.

Fortier, J., & Moulin, C. J. A. (2015). What's French for déjà vu? Descriptions of déjà vu in native French and English speakers. Consciousness and Cognition, 36, 12–18.

Fox, J. W. (1992). The structure, stability, and social antecedents of reported paranormal experiences. Sociological Analysis, 53, 417–431.

Freud, S. (1939). The psychopathology of everyday life. Hounslow, UK: Penguin Books.

Fukao, K., Murai, T., Yamada, M., Sengoku, A., & Kusumi, T. (2005). Déja vu and jamais vu as ictal symptoms: Qualitative comparison with those occurring in normal subjects using a questionnaire. Epilepsia, 46(3), 26.

Funkhouser, A. (1995). Three types of déjà vu. Mental Science Network, 57, 20–22.

Funkhouser, A., & Schredl, M. (2010). The frequency of déjà vu (déjà rêve) and the effects of age, dream recall frequency and personality factors. International Journal of Dream Research, 3, 60–64.

Gallo, D. A. (2010). False memories and fantastic beliefs: 15 years of the DRM illusion. Memory & Cognition, 38, 833–848.

Gallo, D. A., Bell, D. M., Beier, J. S., & Schacter, D. L. (2006). Two types of recollection-based monitoring in younger and older adults: Recall-to-reject and the distinctiveness heuristic. Memory, 14, 730–741.

Gallup, G. H., & Newport, F. (1991). Belief in paranormal phenomena among adult Americans. Skeptical Inquirer, 15, 137–146.

Gardiner, J. M., & Java, R. I. (1990). Recollective experience in word and nonword recognition. Memory & Cognition, 18, 23–30.

Gardiner, J. M., & Java, R. I. (1993). Recognition memory and awareness: An experiential approach. European Journal of Cognitive Psychology, 5, 337–346.

Gardiner, J. M., Java, R. I., & Richardson-Klavehn, A. (1996). How level of processing really influences awareness in recognition memory. Canadian Journal of Experimental Psychology, 50, 114–122.

Gardiner, J. M., & Richardson-Klavehn, A. (2000). Remembering and knowing. In E. Tulving & F. I. M. Craik (Eds.), Handbook of memory (pp. 229–244). New York, NY: Oxford University Press.

Geraci, L., & McCabe, D. P. (2006). Examining the basis for illusory recollection: The role of remember/know instructions. Psychonomic Bulletin & Review, 13, 466–473.

Gerrans, P. (2014). Pathologies of hyperfamiliarity in dreams, delusions and déjà vu. Frontiers in Psychology, 5, 97.

Giele, C. L., van den Hout, M. A., Engelhard, I. M., Dek, E. C., Hoogers, E. E., & de Wit, K. (2013). Ironic effects of compulsive perseveration. Memory, 21, 417–422.

Gloor, P. (1990). Experiential phenomena of temporal lobe epilepsy. Brain, 113, 1673–1694.

Gloor, P., Olivier, A., Quesney, L. F., Andermann, F., & Horowitz, S. (1982). The role of the limbic system in experiential phenomena of temporal lobe epilepsy. Annals of Neurology, 12, 129–144.

Goldinger, S. (2017). Recognition memory. Retrieved from www.public.asu.edu/~sgolding/research.html.

Goldinger, S. D., & Hansen, W. A. (2005). Remembering by the seat of your pants. Psychological Science, 16, 525–529.

Gopnik, A. (2000). Explanation as orgasm and the drive for causal knowledge: The function, evolution, and phenomenology of the theory formation system. In F. Keil & R. Wilson (Eds.), Cognition and explanation (pp. 299–323). Cambridge, MA: MIT Press.

Gregory, R. L. (1968). Perceptual illusions and brain models. Proceedings of the Royal Society of London Series B. Biological Sciences, 171, 279–296.

Guedj, E., Aubert, S., McGonigal, A., Mundler, O., & Bartolomei, F. (2010). Déjà-vu in temporal lobe epilepsy: Metabolic pattern of cortical involvement in patients with normal brain MRI. Neuropsychologia, 48, 2174–2181.

Halgren, E., Walter, R. D., Cherlow, D. G., & Crandall, P. H. (1978). Mental phenomena evoked by electrical stimulation of the human hippocampal formation and amygdala. Brain, 101, 83–117.

Hamani, C., McAndrews, M. P., Cohn, M., Oh, M., Zumsteg, D., Shapiro, C. M., … Lozano, A. M. (2008). Memory enhancement induced by hypothalamic/fornix deep brain stimulation. Annals of Neurology, 63, 119–123.

Hamzelou, J. (2016). Mystery of déjà vu explained – It's how we check our memories. The New Scientist, www.newscientist.com/article/2101089-mystery-of-deja-vu-explained-its-how-we-check-our-memories/

Harper, M. A. (1969). Déjà vu and depersonalisation in normal subjects. Australian and New Zealand Journal of Psychiatry, 3, 67–74.

Harper, M., & Roth, M. (1962). Temporal lobe epilepsy and the phobic anxiety–depersonalization syndrome. I. A comparative study. Comprehensive Psychiatry, 3, 129–151.

Hart, J. T. (1965). Memory and the feeling-of-knowing experiments. Journal of Educational Psychology, 56, 208–216.

Hartmann, E. (1991). Boundaries in the mind: A new psychology of personality. New York, NY: Basic Books.

Hasselmo, M. E., Bodelón, C., & Wyble, B. P. (2002). A proposed function for hippocampal theta rhythm: Separate phases of encoding and retrieval enhance reversal of prior learning. Neural Computation, 14, 793–817.

Hawthorne, N. (1863). Our old home: A series of English sketches. Boston, MA.

Heine, M. K., Ober, B. A., & Shenaut, G. K. (1999). Naturally occurring and experimentally induced tip-of-the-tongue experiences in three adult age groups. Psychology and Aging, 14, 445–457.

Heinrichs, R. W., & Zakzanis, K. K. (1998). Neurocognitive deficit in schizophrenia: A quantitative review of the evidence. Neuropsychology, 12, 426–445.

Henson, R. N., Rugg, M. D., Shallice, T., Josephs, O., & Dolan, R. J. (1999). Recollection and familiarity in recognition memory: An event-related functional magnetic resonance imaging study. Journal of Neuroscience, 19, 3962–3972.

Hintzman, D. L., & Curran, T. (1994). Retrieval dynamics of recognition and frequency judgments: Evidence of separate processes of familiarity and recall. Journal of Memory and Language, 33, 1–18.

Hogan, R. E., & Kaiboriboon, K. (2003). The "Dreamy State": John Hughlings-Jackson's ideas of epilepsy and consciousness. American Journal of Psychiatry, 160, 1740–1747.

Holland, H. (1840). On the brain as a double organ. In Chapters on Mental Physiology. London, UK: Longman, Green, Brown and Longmans (published 1852).

Hout, M. van den, & Kindt, M. (2003). Repeated checking causes memory distrust. Behaviour Research and Therapy, 41, 301–316.

Howard, C. E., Andrés, P., Broks, P., Noad, R., Sadler, M., Coker, D., & Mazzoni, G. (2010). Memory, metamemory and their dissociation in temporal lobe epilepsy. Neuropsychologia, 48, 921–932.

Hudon, C., Belleville, S., Souchay, C., Gély-Nargeot, M. C., Chertkow, H., & Gauthier, S. (2006). Memory for gist and detail information in Alzheimer's disease and mild cognitive impairment. Neuropsychology, 20, 566.

Hughlings Jackson, J. (1888). On a particular variety of epileptic intellectual aura: One case with symptoms of organic brain disease. Brain, 11, 179–207.

Hunter, E. C., Sierra, M., & David, A. S. (2004). The epidemiology of depersonalisation and derealisation. Social Psychiatry and Psychiatric Epidemiology, 39, 9–18.

Idro, R., Jenkins, N. E., & Newton, C. R. (2005). Pathogenesis, clinical features, and neurological outcome of cerebral malaria. The Lancet Neurology, 4, 827–840.

Illman, N. A., Butler, C. R., Souchay, C., & Moulin, C. J. A. (2012). Déjà experiences in temporal lobe epilepsy. Epilepsy Research and Treatment, 2012, Article ID 539567, 15 pages.

Illman, N. A., Rathbone, C. J., Kemp, S., & Moulin, C. J. A. (2011) Autobiographical memory and the self in a case of transient epileptic amnesia. Epilepsy & Behaviour, 21, 36–41.

Jacobs, J., Lega, B., & Anderson, C. (2012). Explaining how brain stimulation can evoke memories. Journal of Cognitive Neuroscience, 24, 553–563.

Jacoby, L. L., & Whitehouse, K. (1989). An illusion of memory: False recognition influenced by unconscious perception. Journal of Experimental Psychology: General, 118, 126.

James, W. (1882). On some hegelisms. Mind, 7(26), 186–208.

James, W. (1890). The principles of psychology. New York, NY: Holt.

James, W. (1902). The varieties of religious experience, a study in human nature. Retrieved from www.gutenberg.org/ebooks/621.

Jastrow, J. (1914). The Fanny Emden prize of the Paris Academy. Science, XXXIX(13), 786–787.

Jeewajee, A., Lever, C., Burton, S., O'Keefe, J., & Burgess, N. (2008). Environmental novelty is signaled by reduction of the hippocampal theta frequency. Hippocampus, 18, 340–348.

Jennings, J. M., & Jacoby, L. L. (2003). Improving memory in older adults: Training recollection. Neuropsychological Rehabilitation, 13, 417–440.

Jersakova, R., Moulin, C. J. A., & O'Connor, A. R. (2016). Investigating the role of assessment method on reports of déjà vu and tip-of-the-tongue states during standard recognition tests. PLoS ONE, 11(4): e0154334.

Johanson, M., Valli, K., Revonsuo, A., & Wedlund, J. E. (2008). Content analysis of subjective experience in partial epileptic seizures. Epilepsy and Behaviour, 12, 170–182.

Johnson, M. K., & Raye, C. L. (1981). Reality monitoring. Psychological Review, 88, 67.

Jung, C. (1961/1989). Memories, dreams, reflections. New York, NY: Vintage.

Kahneman, D. (2011). Thinking, fast and slow. London, UK: Macmillan.

Kalra, S., Chancellor, A., & Zeman, A. (2007). Recurring déjà vu associated with 5-hydroxytryptophan. Acta Neuropsychiatrica, 19, 311–313.

Kasper, B. S., Kasper, E. M., Pauli, E., & Stefan, H. (2010). Phenomenology of hallucinations, illusions, and delusions as part of seizure semiology. Epilepsy & Behavior, 18, 13–23.

Kaufer, D. I., Cummings, J. L., Christine, D., Bray, T., Castellon, S., Masterman, D., ... DeKosky, S. T. (1998). Assessing the impact of neuropsychiatric symptoms in Alzheimer's disease: The Neuropsychiatric Inventory Caregiver Distress Scale. Journal of the American Geriatrics Society, 46, 210–215.

Kay, J., & Ellis, A. (1987). A cognitive neuropsychological case study of anomia. Brain, 110, 613–629.

Kelley, C. M., & Jacoby, L. L. (1998). Subjective reports and process dissociation: Fluency, knowing, and feeling. Acta Psychologica, 98, 127–140.

Kemp, S., Illman, N. A., Moulin, C. J. A., & Baddeley, A. D. (2012). Accelerated long-term forgetting (ALF) and transient epileptic amnesia (TEA): Two cases of epilepsy related memory disorder. Epilepsy & Behaviour, 24, 382–388.

Klein, S. B., Robertson, T. E., & Delton, A. W. (2010). Facing the future: Memory as an evolved system for planning future acts. Memory & Cognition, 38, 13–22.

Knight, E. F. (1895). Where three empires meet: A narrative of recent travel in Kashmir, Western Tibet, Gilgit and the adjoining countries. London, UK: Longmans, Green & Co.

Kolers, P. A., & Palef, S. R. (1976). Knowing not. Memory & Cognition, 4, 553–558.

Kopelman, M. D. (1999). Varieties of false memory. Cognitive Neuropsychology, 16, 197–214.

Kopelman, M. D., Thomson, A. D., Guerrini, I., & Marshall, E. J. (2009). The Korsakoff syndrome: Clinical aspects, psychology and treatment. Alcohol and Alcoholism, 44, 148–154.

Koriat, A. (1993). How do we know that we know? The accessibility model of the feeling of knowing. Psychological Review, 100, 609.

Koriat, A. (2007). Metacognition and consciousness. In P. D. Zelazo, M. Moscovitch, & E. Thompson (Eds.), The Cambridge handbook of consciousness. Cambridge, UK: Cambridge University Press.

Koriat, A., & Levy-Sadot, R. (2001). The combined contributions of the cue-familiarity and accessibility heuristics to feelings-of-knowing. Journal of Experimental Psychology: Learning, Memory and Cognition, 27, 34–53.

Kostic, B., Booth, S. E., & Cleary, A. M. (2015). The role of analogy in reports of presque vu: Does reporting the presque vu state signal the near retrieval of a source analogy? Journal of Cognitive Psychology, 27, 739–754.

Kostic, B., & Cleary, A. M. (2009). Song recognition without identification: When people cannot "name that tune" but can recognize it as familiar. Journal of Experimental Psychology: General, 138, 146–159.

Kounios, J., & Beeman, M. (2014). The cognitive neuroscience of insight. Annual Review of Psychology, 65, 71–93.

Kovacs, N., Auer, T., Balas, I., Karadi, K., Zambo, K., Schwarcz, A., ... Janszky, J. (2009). Neuroimaging and cognitive changes during déjà vu. Epilepsy & Behavior, 14, 190–196.

Kusumi, T. (2006). Human metacognition and the déjà vu phenomenon. In K. Fujita & S. Itakura (Eds.), Diversity of cognition: Evolution, development, domestication, and pathology (pp. 302–314). Kyoto, Japan: Kyoto University Press.

Kvavilashvili, L., & Mandler, G. (2004). Out of one's mind: A study of involuntary semantic memories. Cognitive Psychology, 48, 47–94.

Labate, A., Cerasa, A., Mumoli, L., Ferlazzo, E., Aguglia, U., Quattrone, A., & Gambardella, A. (2015). Neuro-anatomical differences among epileptic and non-epileptic déjà-vu. Cortex, 64, 1–7.

Labate, A., & Gambardella, A. (2013). Comment on Brázdil (2012) "Unveiling the mystery of dèjà-vù: the structural anatomy of dèjà-vù". Cortex, 49, 1162.

Labate, A., Gambardella, A., Andermann, E., Aguglia, U., Cendes, F., Berkovic, S. F., & Andermann, F. (2011). Benign mesial temporal lobe epilepsy. Nature Reviews Neurology, 7, 237–240.

Lacinová, L., Michalcáková, R. N., Širucek, J., Ježek, S., Chromec, J., Masopustová, Z., ... Brázdil, M. (2016). Déjà vu experiences in healthy Czech adults. The Journal of Nervous and Mental Disease, 204, 925–930.

Laird, A. R., Eickhoff, S. B., Li, K., Robin, D. A., Glahn, D. C., & Fox, P. T. (2009). Investigating the functional heterogeneity of the default mode network using coordinate-based meta-analytic modeling. The Journal of Neuroscience, 29, 14496–14505.

Langdon, R., & Coltheart, M. (2000). The cognitive neuropsychology of delusions. Mind & Language, 15, 184–218.

Lazerson, B. H. (1994). Deja vu. American Speech, 69, 285–293.

Lee, D. J., Owen, C. M., Khanifar, E., Kim, R. C., & Binder, D. K. (2009). Isolated amygdala neurocysticercosis in a patient presenting with déjà vu and olfactory auras: Case report. Journal of Neurosurgery: Pediatrics, 3, 538–541.

Lee, H., Fell, J., & Axmacher, N. (2013). Electrical engram: How deep brain stimulation affects memory. Trends in Cognitive Sciences, 17, 574–584.

Lewis, M. B., & Ellis, H. D. (2000). Satiation in name and face recognition. Memory & Cognition, 28, 783–788.

Libby, L. A., Yonelinas, A. P., Ranganath, C., & Ragland, J. R. (2013). Recollection and familiarity in schizophrenia: A quantitative review. Biological Psychiatry, 73, 944–950.

Lin, Y., Michel, J., Aiden, E. L., Orwant, J., Brockman, W., & Petrov, S. (2012). Syntactic annotations for the Google Books Ngram corpus. Proceedings of the Annual Meeting of the Association for Computational Linguistics, July (pp. 169–174). Retrieved from http://aclweb.org/anthology/P/P12/P12-3029.pdf.

Loftus, E. F., & Loftus, G. R. (1980). On the permanence of stored information in the human brain. American Psychologist, 35, 116–129.

Lyketsos, C. G., Lopez, O., Jones, B., Fitzpatrick, A. L., Breitner, J., & DeKosky, S. (2002). Prevalence of neuropsychiatric symptoms in dementia and mild cognitive impairment: Results from the cardiovascular health study. Journal of the American Medical Association, 288, 1475–1483.

MacLaverty, S. N., & Hertzog, C. (2009). Do age-related differences in episodic feeling of knowing accuracy depend on the timing of the judgment? Memory, 17, 860–873.

Magiorkinis, E., Sidiropoulou, K., & Diamantis, A. (2010). Hallmarks in the history of epilepsy: Epilepsy in antiquity. Epilepsy & Behavior, 17, 103–108.

Mandler, G. (1980). Recognizing: The judgment of previous occurrence. Psychological Review, 87, 252–271.

Mandler, G. (2008). Familiarity breeds attempts. Perspectives on Psychological Science, 3, 390–399.

Maril, A., Simons, J. S., Mitchell, J. P., Schwartz, B. L., & Schacter, D. L. (2003). Feeling-of-knowing in episodic memory: An event-related fMRI study. NeuroImage, 18, 827–836.

Maril, A., Wagner, A. D., & Schacter, D. L. (2001). On the tip of the tongue: An event-related fMRI study of semantic retrieval failure and cognitive conflict. Neuron, 31, 653–660.

Markowitsch, H. J. (2003). Psychogenic amnesia. NeuroImage, 20, S132–S138.

Marmin, N. (2001). Métapsychique et psychologie en France (1880–1940). Revue d'Histoire Des Sciences Humaines, 4(4), 145–171.

Martin, C. B., Fiacconi, C. M., & Köhler, S. (2015). Déjà vu: A window into understanding the cognitive neuroscience of familiarity. In D. R. Addis, M. Barense, & A. Duarte (Eds.), The Wiley handbook on the cognitive neuroscience of memory (pp. 172–189). Chichester, UK: Wiley-Blackwell.

Martin, C. B., Mirsattari, S. M., Pruessner, J. C., Pietrantonio, S., Burneo, J. G., Hayman-Abello, B., & Köhler, S. (2012). Déjà vu in unilateral temporal-lobe epilepsy is associated with selective familiarity impairments on experimental tasks of recognition memory. Neuropsychologia, 50, 2981–2991.

McHugh, T. J., Jones, M. W., Quinn, J. J., Balthasar, N., Coppari, R., Elmquist, J. K., … Tonegawa, S. (2007). Dentate gyrus NMDA receptors mediate rapid pattern separation in the hippocampal network. Science, 317, 50–51.

Meares, R. (1999). The contribution of Hughlings Jackson to an understanding of dissociation. The American Journal of Psychiatry, 156, 1850–1855. Retrieved from www.ncbi.nlm.nih.gov/pubmed/10588396.

Mendez, M. (1992). Delusion misidentification of persons in dementia. British Journal of Psychiatry, 160, 414–446.

Metcalfe, J., Schwartz, B. L., & Joaquim, S. G. (1993). The cue-familiarity heuristic in metacognition. Journal of Experimental Psychology: Learning, Memory, and Cognition, 19, 851–861.

Metcalfe, J., & Wiebe, D. (1987). Intuition in insight and noninsight problem solving. Memory & Cognition, 15, 238–246.

Milton, F., Butler, C. R., & Zeman, A. Z. (2011). Transient epileptic amnesia: Déjà vu heralding recovery of lost memories. Journal of Neurology, Neurosurgery & Psychiatry, 82, 1178–1179.

Mitchell, K. J., & Johnson, M. K. (2009). Source monitoring 15 years later: What have we learned from fMRI about the neural mechanisms of source memory? Psychological Bulletin, 135, 638.

Montaldi, D., & Mayes, A. R. (2010). The role of recollection and familiarity in the functional differentiation of the medial temporal lobes. Hippocampus, 20, 1291–1314.

Moritz, S., & Woodward, T. S. (2006). Metacognitive control over false memories: A key determinant of delusional thinking. Current Psychiatry Reports, 8, 184–190.

Moritz, S., Woodward, T. S., & Rodriguez-Raecke, R. (2006). Patients with schizophrenia do not produce more false memories than controls but are more confident in them. Psychological Medicine, 36, 659.

Moscovitch, M. (1994). Cognitive resources and dual-task interference effects at retrieval in normal people: The role of the frontal lobes and medial temporal cortex. Neuropsychology, 8, 524–534.

Mosher, D. (2007). Origin of déjà vu pinpointed. www.livescience.com/1589-origin-deja-vu-pinpointed.html.

Moulin, C. J. A. (2013). Disordered recognition memory: Recollective confabulation. Cortex, 49, 1541–1552.

Moulin, C. J. A., & Chauvel, P. (2010). Déjà vu. In G. M. Davies, & D. B. Wright (Eds.), Current issues in applied memory research (pp. 206–235). Hove, UK: Psychology Press.

Moulin, C. J. A., Conway, M. A., Thompson, R. G., James, N., & Jones, R. W. (2005). Disordered memory awareness: Recollective confabulation in two cases of persistent déjà vécu. Neuropsychologia, 43, 1362–1378.

Moulin, C. J. A., James, N., Perfect, T. J., & Jones, R. W. (2003). Knowing what you cannot recognise: Further evidence for intact metacognition in Alzheimer's disease. Aging, Neuropsychology & Cognition, 10, 74–82.

Moulin, C. J. A., & Souchay, C. (2014). Epistemic feelings and memory. In T. Perfect, & S. Lindsay (Eds.), Sage handbook of applied memory (pp. 520–539). London, UK: Sage Publications.

Moulin, C. J. A., Souchay, C., Bradley, R., Buchanan, S., Karadoller, D. Z., & Akan, M. (2014). Déjà vu in older adults. In B. Schwartz, & A. Brown (Eds.), The tip of the tongue states and related phenomena (pp. 281–304). Cambridge, UK: Cambridge University Press.

Moulin, C. J. A., Souchay, C., & Morris, R. G. (2013). The cognitive neuropsychology of recollection. Cortex, 9, 1445–1451.

Mullan, S., & Penfield, W. (1959). Illusions of comparative interpretation and emotion: production by epileptic discharge and by electrical stimulation in the temporal cortex. Archives of Neurology and Psychiatry, 81, 269–284.

Murai, T., & Fukao, K. (2003). Paramnesic multiplication of autobiographical memory as a manifestation of interictal psychosis. Psychopathology, 36, 49–51.

Myers, F. H. W. (1903). Human personality and its survival of death. London, UK: Longmans.

Najjar, S., Pearlman, D. M., Alper, K., Najjar, A., & Devinsky, O. (2013). Neuroinflammation and psychiatric illness. Journal of Neuroinflammation, 10, 43.

Naveh-Benjamin, M., Moulin, C. J. A., & Souchay, C. (2009). Episodic memory and healthy ageing. Editorial of the Special Issue. Memory, 17.

Negro, E., D'Agata, F., Caroppo, P., Coriasco, M., Ferrio, F., Celeghin, A., & Pinessi, L. (2015). Neurofunctional signature of hyperfamiliarity for unknown faces. PLoS ONE, 10(7): e0129970.

Neisser, U. (1967). Cognitive psychology. Englewood Cliffs, NJ: Prentice-Hall.

Nelson, T. O. (1984). A comparison of current measures of feeling-of-knowing predictions. Psychological Bulletin, 95, 109–133.

Neppe, V. M. (1983). The psychology of déjà vu: have I been here before? Johannesburg, South Africa: Witwatersrand University Press.

Neppe, V. M. (2014). Déjà vu. Retrieved from www.pni.org/research/anomalous/deja/.

Neppe, V. M. (2015). Déjà vu. Retrieved from www.scholarpedia.org/article/Deja_Vu.

Nicolas, S. (1996). Experiments on implicit memory in a Korsakoff patient by Claparède (1907). Cognitive Neuropsychology, 13, 1193–1199.

Norenzayan, A., & Schwarz, N. (1999). Telling what they want to know: Participants tailor causal attributions to researchers' interests. European Journal of Social Psychology, 29, 1011–1020.

O'Connor, A. R. (2007). States of awareness and recognition: Insights from déjà vu. Leeds, UK: University of Leeds.

O'Connor, A. R., Barnier, A. J., & Cox, R. E. (2008). Deja vu in the laboratory: A behavioral and experiential comparison of posthypnotic amnesia and posthypnotic familiarity. International Journal of Clinical and Experimental Hypnosis, 56, 425–450.

O'Connor, A. R., Han, S., & Dobbins, I. G. (2010b). The inferior parietal lobule and recognition memory: Expectancy violation or successful retrieval? The Journal of Neuroscience, 30, 2924–2934.

O'Connor, A. R., Lever, C., & Moulin, C. J. A. (2010). Novel insights into false recollection: A model of déjà vécu. Cognitive Neuropsychiatry, 15, 118–144.

O'Connor, A. R., & Moulin, C. J. A. (2006). Normal patterns of déjà experience in a healthy, blind male: Challenging optical pathway delay theory. Brain and Cognition, 62, 246–249.

O'Connor, A. R., & Moulin, C. J. A. (2008). The persistence of erroneous familiarity in an epileptic male: Challenging perceptual theories of déjà vu activation. Brain and Cognition, 68, 144–147.

O'Connor, A. R., & Moulin, C. J. (2010). Recognition without identification, erroneous familiarity, and déjà vu. Current Psychiatry Reports, 12, 165–173.

O'Connor, A. R., & Moulin, C. J. (2013). Déjà vu experiences in healthy subjects are unrelated to laboratory tests of recollection and familiarity for word stimuli. Frontiers in Psychology, 4.

Orne, M. T. (1962). On the social psychology of the psychological experiment: With particular reference to demand characteristics and their implications. American Psychologist, 17, 776.

Osborn, H. F. (1884). Illusions of memory. North American Review, 138, 476–486.

Overall, J. E., & Gorham, D. R. (1962). The brief psychiatric rating scale. Psychological Reports, 10, 799–812.

Parapsychological Association (2014). www.parapsych.org/users/psyche/profile.aspx

Palmer, J. (1979). A community mail survey of psychic experiences. The Journal of the American Society for Psychical Research, 73, 221–251.

Peake, A. (2006). Is there life after death? The extraordinary science of what happens when we die. London, UK: Arcturus Publishing.

Penfield, W. (1955). The twenty-ninth Maudsley lecture: The role of the temporal cortex in certain psychical phenomena. Journal of Mental Science, 101, 451–465.

Penfield, W., & Perot, P. (1963). The brain's record of auditory and visual experience: A final summary and discussion. Brain, 86, 595–696.

Perfect, T. J., & Dasgupta, Z. R. (1997). What underlies the deficit in reported recollective experience in old age? Memory & Cognition, 25, 849–858.

Perfect, T. J., Mayes, A. R., Downes, J. J., & Van Eijk, R. (1996). Does context discriminate recollection from familiarity in recognition memory? Quarterly Journal of Experimental Psychology Section A: Human Experimental Psychology, 49, 797–813.

Perrin, D., & Rousset, S. (2014). The episodicity of memory. Review of Philosophy and Psychology, 5, 291–312.

Pick, A. (1903). On reduplicative paramnesia. Brain, 26, 260–267.

Pierce, B. H., Simons, J. S., & Schacter, D. L. (2003). Aging and the seven sins of memory. Advances in Cell Aging and Gerontology, 15, 1–40.

Pisani, A., Marra, C., & Silveri, M.C. (2000). Anatomical and psychological mechanism of reduplicative misidentification syndromes. Neurological Sciences, 21, 234–328.

Podoll, K. (2007). Déjà vu. Article at the Migraine Aura Foundation. Retrieved from www.migraine-aura.com/content/e27891/e27265/e26585/e48650/e48660/index_en.html.

Proust, J. (2007). Metacognition and metarepresentation: Is a self-directed theory of mind a precondition for metacognition? Synthese, 159, 271–295.

Reggev, N., Zuckerman, M., & Maril, A. (2011). Are all judgments created equal? An fMRI study of semantic and episodic metamemory predictions. Neuropsychologia, 49, 1332–1342.

Richardson, T. F., & Winokur, G. (1967). Déjà vu in psychiatric and neurosurgical patients. Archives of General Psychiatry, 17, 622–625.

Roediger, H. L., III. (1996). Memory illusions. Journal of Memory and Language, 35, 76–100.

Roediger, H. L., III, & McDermott, K. B. (1995). Creating false memories: Remembering words not presented on lists. Journal of Experimental Psychology: Learning, Memory, and Cognition, 21, 803–814.

Rosenbaum, R. S., Gilboa, A., & Moscovitch, M. (2014). Case studies continue to illuminate the cognitive neuroscience of memory. Annals of the New York Academy of Sciences, 1316, 105–133.

Rosenbloom, M. H., Smith, S., Akdal, G., & Geschwind, M. D. (2009). Immunologically mediated dementias. Current Neurology and Neuroscience Reports, 9, 359–367.

Rosenthal, R. (1979). The file drawer problem and tolerance for null results. Psychological Bulletin, 86, 638.

Roth, M. (1959). The phobic anxiety–depersonalization syndrome. Proceedings of the Royal Society of Medicine, 52, 587–595.

Roth, M., & Harper, M. (1962). Temporal lobe epilepsy and the phobic anxiety-depersonalization syndrome. II. Practical and theoretical considerations. Comprehensive Psychiatry, 3, 215–226.

Rouse, D. J. (2013). The Misoprostol vaginal insert. Obstetrics & Gynecology, 122, 193–194.

Rubin, D. C., & Berntsen, D. (2009). The frequency of voluntary and involuntary autobiographical memories across the life span. Memory & Cognition, 37, 679–688.

Sacher, M., Taconnat, L., Souchay, C., & Isingrini, M. (2009). Divided attention at encoding: Effect on feeling-of-knowing. Consciousness and Cognition, 18, 754–761.

Sadler, R. M., & Rahey, S. (2004). Prescience as an aura of temporal lobe epilepsy. Epilepsia, 45, 982–984.

Saroka, K. S., & Persinger, M. A. (2013). Potential production of Hughlings Jackson's "parasitic consciousness" by physiologically-patterned weak transcerebral magnetic fields: QEEG and source localization. Epilepsy & Behavior, 28, 395–407.

Saver, J. L., & Rabin, J. (1997). The neural substrates of religious experience. Journal of Neuropsychiatry and Clinical Neuroscience, 9, 498–510.

Schacter, D. L. (1999). The seven sins of memory: Insights from psychology and cognitive neuroscience. American Psychologist, 54, 182.

Schacter, D. L. (2001). The seven sins of memory: How the mind forgets and remembers. New York, NY: Houghton Mifflin.

Schacter, D.L., Addis, D. R., & Buckner, R. L. (2007). Remembering the past to imagine the future: The prospective brain. Nature Reviews Neuroscience, 8, 657–661.

Schacter, D. L., Curran, T., Galluccio, L., Milberg, W. P., & Bates, J. F. (1996). False recognition and the right frontal lobe: A case study. Neuropsychologia, 34, 793–808.

Schacter, D. L., Harbluk, J. L., & McLachlan, D. R. (1984). Retrieval without recollection: An experimental analysis of source amnesia. Journal of Verbal Learning and Verbal Behavior, 23, 593–611.

Schlagman, S., Kliegel, M., Schulz, J., & Kvavilashvili, L. (2009). Differential effects of age on involuntary and voluntary autobiographical memory. Psychology and Aging, 24, 397–411.

Schlagman, S., & Kvavilashvili, L. (2008). Involuntary autobiographical memories in and outside the laboratory: How different are they from voluntary autobiographical memories? Memory & Cognition, 36, 920–932.

Schredl, M., Kleinferchner, P., & Gell, T. (1996). Dreaming and personality: Thick vs. thin boundaries. Dreaming, 6, 219.

Schwartz, B. L., & Metcalfe, J. (2011). Tip-of-the-tongue (TOT) states: Retrieval, behavior, and experience. Memory & Cognition, 39, 737–749.

Severance, E., & Washburn, M. F. (1907). The loss of associative power in words after long fixation. The American Journal of Psychology, 182–186.

Shanks, M. F., McGeown, W. J., Guerrini, C., & Venneri, A. (2014). Awareness and confabulation. Neuropsychology, 28, 406.

Shaw, D. J., Mareček, R., & Brázdil, M. (2016). Structural covariance mapping delineates medial and medio-lateral temporal networks in déjà vu. Brain Imaging and Behavior, 10, 1068–1079.

Shiah, Y. J., Wu, Y. Z., Chen, Y. H., & Chiang, S. K. (2014). Schizophrenia and the paranormal: More psi belief and superstition, and less déjà vu in medicated schizophrenic patients. Comprehensive Psychiatry, 55, 688–692.

Shimamura, A. P., Janowsky, J. S., & Squire, L. R. (1990). Memory for the temporal order of events in patients with frontal lobe lesions and amnesic patients. Neuropsychologia, 28, 803–813.

Sierra, M., & Berrios, G. E. (1998). Depersonalization: Neurobiological perspectives. Biological Psychiatry, 44, 898–908.

Singh, S. (2007). Adolescent salvia substance abuse. Addiction, 102, 823–824.

Skinner, B. F. (1971). Beyond freedom and dignity. Harmondsworth, UK: Penguin Books.

Smith, L., & Klein, R. (1990). Evidence for semantic satiation: Repeating a category slows subsequent semantic processing. Journal of Experimental Psychology: Learning, Memory, and Cognition, 16, 852–861.

Sno, H. N., Linszen, D. H., & de Jonghe, F. (1992). Déjà vu experiences and reduplicative paramnesia. The British Journal of Psychiatry, 161, 565–568.

Sno, H. N., Schalken, H. F. A., de Jonghe, F., & Koeter, M. W. J. (1994). The inventory for déjà vu experiences assessment. The Journal of Nervous and Mental Disease, 182, 27–33.

Souchay, C. (2007). Metamemory in Alzheimer's disease. Cortex, 43, 987–1003.

Souchay, C., Bacon, E., & Danion, J. M. (2006). Metamemory in schizophrenia: An exploration of the feeling-of-knowing state. Journal of Clinical and Experimental Neuropsychology, 28, 828–840.

Souchay, C., Isingrini, M., & Espagnet, L. (2000). Aging, episodic memory feeling-of-knowing, and frontal functioning. Neuropsychology, 14, 299–309.

Souchay, C., & Moulin, C. J. A. (2009). Memory and consciousness in Alzheimer's disease. Current Alzheimer Research, 6, 186–195.

Souchay, C., Moulin, C. J. A., Clarys, D., Taconnat, L., & Isingrini, M. (2007). Diminished episodic memory awareness in older adults: Evidence from feeling of knowing and recollection. Consciousness and Cognition, 16, 769–784.

Spatt, J. (2002). Déja vu: Possible parahippocampal mechanisms. Journal of Neuropsychiatry and Clinical Neurosciences, 14, 6–10.

Squire, L. R. (1981). Two forms of human amnesia: An analysis of forgetting. Journal of Neuroscience, 1, 635–640.

Squire, L. R., Wixted, J. T., & Clark, R. E. (2007). Recognition memory and the medial temporal lobe: A new perspective. Nature Reviews Neuroscience, 8, 872–883.

Staniloiu, A., Markowitsch, H. J., & Brand, M. (2010). Psychogenic amnesia – A malady of the constricted self. Consciousness and Cognition, 19, 778–801.

Stuss, D. T., & Levine, B. (2002). Adult clinical neuropsychology: Lessons from studies of the frontal lobes. Annual Review of Psychology, 53, 401–433.

Sugimori, E., & Kusumi, T. (2014). The similarity hypothesis of déjà vu: On the relationship between frequency of real-life déjà vu experiences and sensitivity to configural resemblance. Journal of Cognitive Psychology, 26, 48–57.

Sultzer, D. L., Brown, C. V., Mandelkern, M. A., Mahler, M. E., Mendez, M. F., Chen, S. T., & Cummings, J. L. (2003). Delusional thoughts and regional frontal/temporal cortex metabolism in Alzheimer's disease. American Journal of Psychiatry, 160, 341–349.

Tabet, N., & Sivaloganathan, S. (2001). A case of persistent déjà vu in an elderly patient. Progress in Neurology and Psychiatry, 5, 18–19.

Taiminen, T., & Jääskeläinen, S. K. (2001). Intense and recurrent déjà vu experiences related to amantadine and phenylpropanolamine in a healthy male. Journal of Clinical Neuroscience, 8, 460–462.

Takeda, Y., Kurita, T., Sakurai, K., Shiga, T., Tamaki, N., & Koyama, T. (2011). Persistent déjà vu associated with hyperperfusion in the entorhinal cortex. Epilepsy & Behavior, 21, 196–199.

Taylor, D. C., & Marsh, S. M. (1980). Hughlings Jackson's Dr Z: The paradigm of temporal lobe epilepsy revealed. Journal of Neurology, Neurosurgery & Psychiatry, 43, 758–767.

Taylor, J. B., & Shuttleworth, S. (1998) Embodied selves: An anthology of psychological texts, 1830–1890. Oxford, UK: Clarendon Press.

Thalbourne, M. A. (1994). Belief in the paranormal and its relationship to schizophrenia-relevant measures: A confirmatory study. British Journal of Clinical Psychology, 33, 78–80.

The International League Against Epilepsy (2017). 2017 revised classification of seizures. Retrieved from www.epilepsy.com/article/2016/12/2017-revised-classification-seizures.

Titchener, E. B. (1919/1928). A textbook of psychology. New York, NY: Macmillan.

Tulving, E. (1985). Memory and consciousness. Canadian Psychologist, 26, 1–12.

Tulving, E. (1989). Remembering and knowing the past. American Scientist, 77, 361–367.

Tulving, E., Markowitsch, H. J., Craik, F. I., Habib, R., & Houle, S. (1996). Novelty and familiarity activations in PET studies of memory encoding and retrieval. Cerebral Cortex, 6, 71–79.

Turner, M. S., Shores, E. A., Breen, N., & Coltheart, M. (2017). Déjà vecu for news events but not personal events: A dissociation between autobiographical and non-autobiographical episodic memory processing. Cortex, 87, 142–155.

Urquhart, J., & O'Connor, A. R. (2014). The awareness of novelty for strangely familiar words: A laboratory analogue of the déjà vu expérience. PeerJ, 2, e666.

van den Hout, M. A., Engelhard, I. M., de Boer, C., du Bois, A., & Dek, E. (2008). Perseverative and compulsive-like staring causes uncertainty about perception. Behaviour Research and Therapy, 46, 1300–1304.

Van Paesschen, W., King, M. D., Duncan, J. S., & Connelly, A. (2001). The amygdala and temporal lobe simple partial seizures: A prospective and quantitative MRI study. Epilepsia, 42, 857–862.

Vignal, J. P., Maillard, L., McGonigal, A., & Chauvel, P. (2007). The dreamy state: Hallucinations of autobiographic memory evoked by temporal lobe stimulations and seizures. Brain, 130, 88–99.

Wagner, A. D., Shannon, B. J., Kahn, I., & Buckner, R. L. (2005). Parietal lobe contributions to episodic memory retrieval. Trends in Cognitive Sciences, 9, 445–453.

Wais, P. E., Squire, L. R., & Wixted, J. T. (2010). In search of recollection and familiarity in the hippocampus. Journal of Cognitive Neuroscience, 22, 109–123.

Walsh, V. (2004). Here we go again … (review of the Deja vu Experience by Alan S Brown). Trends in Cognitive Sciences, 8, 483–484.

Ward, J., Parkin, A. J., Powell, G., Squires, E. J., Townshend, J., & Bradley, V. (1999). False recognition of unfamiliar people: "Seeing film stars everywhere". Cognitive Neuropsychology, 16, 293–315.

Warren-Gash, C., & Zeman, A. (2003). Déjà vu. Practical Neurology, 3, 106–109.

Warren-Gash, C., & Zeman, A. (2014). Is there anything distinctive about epileptic déjà vu? Journal of Neurology, Neurosurgery & Psychiatry, 85, 143–147.

Weinand, M. E., Carter, L. P., Patton, D. D., Oommen, K. J., Labiner, D. M., & Talwar, D. (1994). Long-term surface cortical cerebral blood flow monitoring in temporal lobe epilepsy. Neurosurgery, 35, 657–664.

Wells, C. E., Moulin, C. J. A., Ethridge, P., Illman, N. A., Davies, E., & Zeman, A. (2014). Persistent psychogenic déjà vu: A case report. Journal of Medical Case Reports, 8, 414.

Wells, C. E., O'Connor, A. R., & Moulin, C. J. A. (in preparation). Déjà vu experiences in anxiety.

West, R. L. (1996). An application of prefrontal cortex function theory to cognitive aging. Psychological Bulletin, 120, 272.

Whalley, M. G., Kroes, M. C., Huntley, Z., Rugg, M. D., Davis, S. W., & Brewin, C. R. (2013). An fMRI investigation of posttraumatic flashbacks. Brain and Cognition, 81, 151–159.

Wheeler, M. A., Stuss, D. T., & Tulving, E. (1997). Toward a theory of episodic memory: The frontal lobes and autonoetic consciousness. Psychological Bulletin, 121, 331–354.

Whittlesea, B. W. A. (1997). Production, evaluation, and preservation of experiences: Constructive processing in remembering and performance tasks. In D. L. Medlin (Ed.), Psychology of learning and motivation (Vol. 37, pp. 211–264). New York, NY: Academic Press.

Whittlesea, B. W. A., & Williams, L. D. (1998). Why do strangers feel familiar, but friends don't? A discrepancy-attribution account of feelings of familiarity. Acta Psychologica, 98, 141–165.

Whittlesea, B. W., & Williams, L. D. (2001). The discrepancy-attribution hypothesis: I. The heuristic basis of feelings and familiarity. Journal of Experimental Psychology: Learning, Memory, and Cognition, 27, 14–33.

Williams, H. L., & Moulin, C. J. (2015). Know versus familiar: Differentiating states of awareness in others' subjective reports of recognition. Memory, 23, 981–990.

Wigan, A. L. (1844). A new view of insanity: The duality of the mind. London, UK: Longman.

Winkler, J. D., Kanouse, D. E., & Ware, J. E. (1982). Controlling for acquiescence response set in scale development. Journal of Applied Psychology, 67, 555–561.

Wixted, J. T. (2007). Dual-process theory and signal-detection theory of recognition memory. Psychological Review, 114, 152–176.

Wixted, J. T., & Squire, L. R. (2011). The medial temporal lobe and the attributes of memory. Trends in Cognitive Sciences, 15, 210–217.

Wixted, J. T., & Stretch, V. (2004). In defense of the signal detection interpretation of remember/know judgments. Psychonomic Bulletin & Review, 11, 616–641.

Wojcik, D. Z., Moulin, C. J., & Souchay, C. (2013). Metamemory in children with autism: Exploring "feeling-of-knowing" in episodic and semantic memory. Neuropsychology, 27, 19–27.

Yonelinas, A. P. (2002). The nature of recollection and familiarity: A review of 30 years of research. Journal of Memory and Language, 46, 441–517.

INDEX

Made in United States
North Haven, CT
25 October 2023

43171408R00117